# EFFICIENT PARALLEL ALGORITHMS

# EFFICIENT PARALLEL ALGORITHMS

## ALAN GIBBONS

*Department of Computer Science, Warwick University*

## WOJCIECH RYTTER

*Institute of Informatics, Warsaw University*

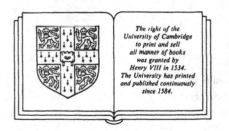

The right of the
University of Cambridge
to print and sell
all manner of books
was granted by
Henry VIII in 1534.
The University has printed
and published continuously
since 1584.

## CAMBRIDGE UNIVERSITY PRESS
*Cambridge*
*New York   Port Chester   Melbourne   Sydney*

CAMBRIDGE UNIVERSITY PRESS

Cambridge, New York, Melbourne, Madrid, Cape Town,
Singapore, São Paulo, Delhi, Tokyo, Mexico City

Cambridge University Press
The Edinburgh Building, Cambridge CB2 8RU, UK

Published in the United States of America by
Cambridge University Press, New York

www.cambridge.org
Information on this title: www.cambridge.org/9780521388412

First published 1988
First paperback edition 1989
Reprinted 1990

*A catalogue record for this publication is available from the British Library*

*Library of Congress Cataloguing in Publication data*
Gibbons, Alan (Alan M.)
Efficient parallel algorithms/Alan Gibbons, Wojciech Rytter.
259 pp.  cm.
Includes bibliographies and index.
ISBN 0–521–34585–5
1. Parallel programming (Computer science)   2. Algorithms.
I. Rytter, Wojciech.   II. Title.
QA76.6.G53   1988
005.1′1–dc19   87-31185-CIP

ISBN 978-0-521-34585-9 Hardback
ISBN 978-0-521-38841-2 Paperback

# CONTENTS

# PREFACE

In very recent years Computer Science has seen an explosion of interest in the field of parallel computations. From the theoretician's point of view, this has provided a challenging range of problems with new ground rules for the design and analysis of algorithms.

This text is intended to be an introduction to the field of efficient parallel algorithms and to techniques for efficient parallelisation. The emphasis is upon designing algorithms within the timeless and abstracted context of a high-level programming language rather than depending upon highly detailed machine architectures. This approach concentrates upon the essence of algorithmic theory and captures what coherence exists at present within a range of research activities. We therefore omit consideration of specific architectures such as cube-connected or perfect-shuffle computers and any particular pursuits in VLSI design. One view in an ideal situation might be to match the architecture to the problem. However, many low-level algorithms are refinements of high-level algorithms designed for a general model of parallel computation. Moreover, it is not clear at present what models of parallel computation are reasonable.

We have therefore selected that important stream of interest in the area of parallel computations which concentrates on determining and taking advantage of the inherently parallel nature of the problem in hand. Literature pertaining to this approach is of rapidly growing richness. The time therefore seems to be auspicious to collect together, and to present in elementary fashion, regularly used techniques and a range of algorithms which includes some of the more celebrated. In this regard we essentially and largely concentrate on problems which are known to have efficient parallel solutions. By this we mean that any such problem is in the (so-called) class $NC$. This merely means that the problem is solvable in polylogarithmic time using a polynomial number of processors. The problem, in other words, is highly parallelisable. On the other hand, some problems which are known to have polynomial sequential-time solutions do not seem to admit parallelisation readily. These form the class of so-called *P*-complete problems. In a short concluding chapter, and for the sake of a proper theoretical perspective, we also include a selection of some of these.

The text is largely self-contained, presuming no special knowledge of parallel computers or particular mathematics. However, the reader familiar with elementary ideas from the areas for which algorithms are described (for example, formal language theory and graph theory) will be at an advantage. This particular material will be commonplace for the computer scientist, as will elementary notions from complexity theory as applied to sequential computations. Hence the text is targeted at non-specialists who might wish to enter the field of parallel algorithms. From this point of view, it should prove useful for courses aimed either at advanced undergraduates or at new postgraduate students.

This book was written whilst one of us (W.R.) was on leave from the Institute of Informatics of Warsaw University. He wishes to record his thanks to the Department of Computer Science of Warwick University for their hospitality and for making their facilities available to him during the course of this work.

*Department of Computer Science,*                                  Alan Gibbons
*Warwick University,*                                                      Wojciech Rytter
*England*

                                                                                        *May, 1987.*

# CHAPTER 1

# INTRODUCTION

This book is essentially about techniques for efficient parallelisation. Moreover the techniques are exemplified through a collection of efficient parallel algorithms. Each chapter, in the main, concentrates on one area of interest. By an efficient parallel algorithm we mean one that takes polylogarithmic time using a polynomial number of processors. In practical terms, at most a polynomial number of processors is reckoned to be feasible. A polylogarithmic time algorithm takes $O(\log^k n)$ parallel time for some constant integer $k$, where $n$ is the problem size. Problems which can be solved within these constraints are universally regarded as having efficient parallel solutions and are said to belong to the class $NC$. This class name is an abbreviation for Nick (Pippenger)'s Class.

A subclass of problems of particular interest are those which have optimal parallel algorithms. An optimal parallel algorithm is an algorithm for which the product of the parallel time $t$ with the number of processors $p$ used is linear in the problem size $n$. That is, $pt = O(n)$. Optimality may also mean that the product $pt$ is equal to the computation time of the fastest known sequential-time algorithm for the problem. Here we specifically refer to the problem as having optimal speed-up.

For any problem for which there is no known polynomial-time sequential solution (for example, any $NP$-complete problem) we cannot expect to find an efficient parallel solution using a polynomial number of processors. However, we might wish to find such a parallel solution for a problem with a polynomial-time sequential algorithm (that is, a problem in the class $P$). There are, however, many such problems which do not seem to admit parallelisation readily. These problems, which we refer to as being hardly parallelisable, form the class of so-called $P$-complete problems. If an efficient parallel solution for any *P*-complete problem could be found then a similar solution would exist for any other. There is no proof, but a great deal of circumstantial evidence, that $P \neq NC$. The final chapter of the book concentrates on some members of this class of *P*-complete problems.

Let *F* be any function of the problem size *n*. The *parallel computation thesis* is that the class of problems that can be solved with unbounded parallelism in $F(n)^{O(1)}$ time is equal to the class of problems that can be solved by a sequential computation in $F(n)^{O(1)}$ space. Provided *F* is a polynomial in the problem size, this thesis is a theorem (see [10] for example) for the P-RAM model of computation. As we describe in the next section, the P-RAM is the central model of parallel computation used within this book. We note in passing here that, because of the parallel computation thesis, a pointer to the existence of an efficient parallel algorithm for a problem is that the problem is solvable in sequential polylog space.

## 1.1 The model of parallel computation

Many formal models of parallel computation appear in the literature. There is no general consensus as to which of these is best. In this book we make use of an idealised parallel computer known as the P-RAM (parallel random-access machine). This model essentially neglects any hardware constraints which a highly specified architecture would impose. In this respect the model gives free rein in the presentation of algorithms by not admitting limitations on parallelism which might be imposed by specific hardware. This implies that in any realisation of a P-RAM there will be all possible links between processors and memory locations. This complexity of linkages is not physically realisable in present-day hardware. On the other hand there are methods of simulating such an idealised computer on more reasonable parallel computers (usually fixed networks of processors with the number of linkages from any processor being bounded). Moreover, this simulation only costs polylogarithmic time (see [4]). An important preoccupation of this text is to present a collection of efficient parallel algorithms, specifically algorithms from the class *NC*. Since the cost of simulating a P-RAM on more reasonable models is polylogarithmic, the class *NC* does not change if we pass from the idealised computer to the more realistic. However, the degree of intricacy of algorithmic specification can grow considerably. From this point of view, the P-RAM suits our needs perfectly both for specifying algorithms and for justifying the inclusion of problems in *NC*. In due course new technologies will no doubt change our perceptions of what is physically realisable. However, because of its simplicity and universality, we believe that the P-RAM model will survive as a theoretically convenient model of parallel computation and as a starting point for a methodology.

The P-RAM is a shared memory model. There are a number of processors working synchronously and communicating through the common random-access memory. Each processor is a uniform-cost random-access machine (RAM) with usual operations and instructions. The cost of arithmetical operations (addition, subtraction, equality predicate and so on) is constant. We presume that the reader is familiar with the detailed definition of the RAM (see [1] for example).

The processors are indexed by the natural numbers $P_1, P_2, P_3, \ldots$, and they synchronously execute the same program (through the central main control). Although performing the same instructions, the processors can be working on different data (located in different storage locations). Hence such a model is also called a single-instruction, multiple-data-stream (SIMD) model.

In one step each processor can access (either reading from it or writing to it) one memory location. Models differ in regard to simultaneous access of the same memory location by more than one processor. We use the following natural convention for the P-RAM:

(a)  Any number of processors may simultaneously *read* from the same memory location;

(b)  No two processors may *write* simultaneously into the same memory location.

Throughout the text we shall be concentrating on algorithms which are realisable on the P-RAM. To this end algorithms will be described in a general style which will need no formal definition for the reader experienced in

*Figure 1.1.* The scheme of the P-RAM

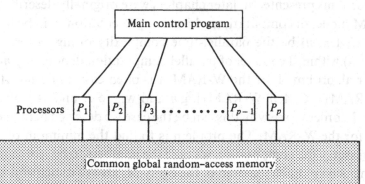

sequential programming. The admission of parallelism into our algorithmic descriptions will be only through the use of the following type of statement:

**for** all $x \in X$ **in parallel do** *instruction*$(x)$

Here $x$ is an element of the set $X$ and execution of the statement consists of
(a) assigning a processor to each element $x \in X$,
(b) executing, in parallel and by the assigned processors, all those operations specified by *instruction*$(x)$.

The execution stops when all the processors involved complete their (individual) computations. Two points need to be clarified, namely how the processors are assigned and how the processors are activated.

(i) Assigning processors. We require that the elements of $X$ are distinct integers or can be encoded by distinct integers. Then with every $x$ we associate the processor $P_{\text{code}(x)}$ where code$(x)$ is the integer corresponding to $x$. We assume that the finite control directs processor $i$ to work for $x = \text{code}^{-1}(i)$ in constant time.

(ii) Activating processors. We presume that there is an initial threshold time of $\log p$ to activate $p$ processors at the beginning of any computation. Here $p$ is the maximum number of processors required during the computation. This is consistent with one processor being active at first, then the number of active processors can be doubled in each time step as each active processor activates another.

Although throughout this text we shall be largely concerned with the P-RAM there is a stronger model sometimes used in parallel-algorithm design in which many processors are allowed to write to the same location. For this model, called a W-RAM, there is (amongst several different variations) one convention which allows the simultaneous writes to be to selected memory locations only. Moreover, these locations can only contain the numbers 0 or 1. Processors writing simultaneously into the same location must write the value 1. Some of the algorithms presented in later chapters were originally described within the W-RAM model of computation whilst our presentations will be for the P-RAM. Let $C(A, n, m)$ be the parallel-time complexity of algorithm $A$ (with problem size $n$) within the model of parallel computation denoted by $m$. Given a particular algorithm $A$ for the W-RAM it is often easy to design $A'$ where $C(A', n, \text{P-RAM}) = C(A, n, \text{W-RAM}) \log n$ and where $A$ and $A'$ solve the same problem. In order to see why this can be the case we describe here one simple algorithm for the W-RAM. The problem is to find the minimum of $n$ numbers. At the outset of the computation we take the numbers to be stored in the array $C$ of dimension $n$. Each location of the array $M$, also of dimension $n$, may be written simultaneously by many processors within the constraints of the convention just described. The algorithm is then as follows:

1. **for** all $i$, $1 \leqslant i \leqslant n$, **in parallel do** $M(i) \leftarrow 0$
2. **for** all (ordered) pairs $(i, j)$, $1 \leqslant i, j \leqslant n$, **in parallel do**
   **if** $C(i) < C(j)$ **then** $M(j) \leftarrow 1$
3. **for** all (ordered) pairs $(i, j)$, $1 \leqslant i, j \leqslant n$, **in parallel do**
   **if** $M(i) = 0$ **and** $i < j$ **then** $M(j) \leftarrow 1$
4. **for** all $i$, $1 \leqslant i \leqslant n$, **in parallel do if** $M(i) = 0$ **then** *minimum* $\leftarrow C(i)$

After execution of statement 2 it is obvious that $M(i) = 0$ if and only if $C(i)$ is a smallest element in the array $C$. The effect of statement 3 is to ensure that the array $M$ contains only one element with the value 0. Specifically this is the one with smallest index of those containing zero after the execution of statement 2. In this way only one processor attempts to write to the location called *minimum* in statement 4. Both statements 2 and 3 contain examples of possibly many processors attempting to write simultaneously to the same location.

Using $n^2$ processors, the algorithm just described finds the minimum of $n$ numbers in constant time. A constant time complexity for such a task is perhaps more pathological than realistic. Within the P-RAM model the same computation (as we shall shortly see) takes O($\log n$) time. The reader will have no difficulty in describing similar algorithms within the W-RAM model for the computation of the maximum of $n$ numbers, the computation of the logical **and** of $n$ Boolean variables and the similar computation for logical **or**. All these problems, whilst taking constant time on a W-RAM, require O($\log n$) time on a P-RAM. Each commonly occurs as a nested subtask in larger algorithms. This can then lead to a factor of $\log n$ between the complexities of implementations of the same algorithm within the two models of computation.

Within the literature there are a variety of acronyms to describe variations on the model of computation. The main ones are the EREW P-RAM (exclusive read exclusive write parallel random-access machine which allows no concurrent reads and no concurrent writes), the CREW P-RAM (concurrent reads allowed but only exclusive writes) and the CRCW P-RAM (in which both concurrent writes and concurrent reads are allowed). Throughout this book, unless otherwise specified, P-RAM specifically means the CREW P-RAM model.

## 1.2  Some general algorithmic techniques

We describe here a number of general techniques and principles of common use in the design of parallel algorithms. These appear many times as subtasks within algorithms presented in later chapters of this text.

We claim that the tree is a basic structure in parallel computations. In efficient parallel computations this structure commonly appears in many guises, for example in the structure of the computation, as a data structure or as a structure of processors. Such a claim will be supported by many example algorithms. In one sense this book is a story about various aspects of the tree as a major tool in the design of efficient parallel algorithms.

Throughout this section (as throughout the rest of the text unless otherwise specified) we presume the P-RAM model of computation. Here we shall be primarily concerned with justifying a (tight) polylogarithmic parallel time complexity for each of the techniques described. We shall be concerned with the number of processors only in passing at this stage. In the next section we consider this parameter in more detail.

*The balanced binary tree method*

The method makes use of a balanced binary tree. Each internal node corresponds to the computation of a subproblem with the root corresponding to the overall problem. The problems are solved in bottom-up order, with those at the same depth in the tree being computed in parallel. A typical computation is that of finding the maximum of $n$ elements. Such a computation is illustrated in figure 1.2. Here the $n$ elements are placed at the leaves of the tree and the computation proceeds in the obvious manner. There is a presumption in such a computation that $n$ is a power of two. If this is not the case, then a (minimum) number of dummy elements can always be added to ensure that this is the case. The depth of the tree will be bound by $\lceil \log n \rceil$ and so the

Figure 1.2

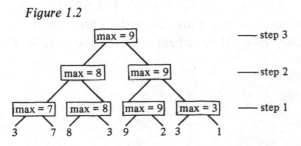

complexity of such an algorithm will be O(log $n$). The maximum number of processors employed in this description is $n/2$.

Let $n = 2^m$ and $A$ be an array of dimension $2n$. If at the outset we store the $n$ numbers whose maximum is to be found in the locations $A(n), A(n+1), \ldots, A(2n-1)$ then, in coded form, the algorithm for determining the maximum has the following description. At the end of the computation $A(1)$ stores the result.

> **for** $k \leftarrow m - 1$ **step** $-1$ **to** 0 **do**
> **for** all $j$, $2^k \leqslant j \leqslant 2^{k+1} - 1$, **in parallel do** $A(j) \leftarrow \max\{A(2j), A(2j+1)\}$

*The doubling technique*

This technique is normally applied to an array or to a list of elements. The computation proceeds by a recursive application of the calculation in hand to all elements over a certain distance (in the data structure) from each individual element. This distance doubles in successive steps. Thus after $k$ stages the computation has been performed (for each element) over all elements within a distance of $2^k$. The method is perhaps best described by the use of examples.

Let $L$ denote a list of $n$ elements and let us associate a processor with each element. The purpose of the following computation is to rank the elements of the list, that is, to associate a number $rank(k)$ with each element $k$ where $rank(k)$ is the order number of $k$ on the list. We can take this to be the distance of element $k$ from the end of the list. This list is supplied as a set of elements, each with a pointer to the next element of the list. The pointer for element $k$ is $next(k)$. If $k$ is the final element in the list then $next(k) = k$. The algorithm is then described as follows.

> **Algorithm** {rank list elements}
> **begin**
> **for** all $k \in L$ **in parallel do**
> > **begin**
> > $P(k) \leftarrow next(k)$
> > **if** $P(k) \neq k$ **then** $distance(k) \leftarrow 1$ **else** $distance(k) \leftarrow 0$
> > **end**
> **repeat** log $n$ **times**
> > **for** all $k \in L$ **in parallel do**
> > > **if** $P(k) \neq P(P(k))$ **then**
> > > > **begin**
> > > > $distance(k) \leftarrow distance(k) + distance(P(k))$

$$P(k) \leftarrow P(P(k))$$
**end**
**for** all $k \in L$ **in parallel do** $rank(k) \leftarrow distance(k)$
**end** of the algorithm

As is easily seen the algorithm computes the rank of each element of the list in O(log $n$) time using $n$ processors. The complexity arises from the number of re-assignments required to the $P(k)$ before, for all $k$, $P(k)$ is the final element of the list. Since $P(k)$ is recursively 'doubled' by the statement $P(k) \leftarrow P(P(k))$, we have that $P(k)(\neq$ last element) is a distance $2^i$ from $k$ after $i$ such doublings. Thus a logarithmic number of re-assignments is sufficient.

*Remark*
Notice that the repeat statement calls for 'log $n$' repetitions. Here and elsewhere in similar contexts we understand log $n$ to mean $\lceil \log n \rceil$.

Figure 1.3 illustrates the algorithm for a list of seven elements. Each pointer $P(k)$ is shown as an arc from one element to another and the arc from an element $k$ is labelled with the current value of distance($k$). The top of the figure

*Figure 1.3*

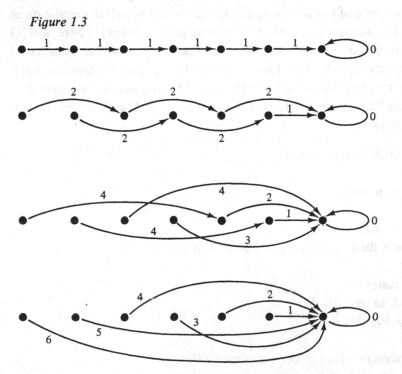

shows the initialisation of the $P(k)$ and the values of distance($k$) as induced by that part of the algorithm before the **repeat** statement. Then the figure shows successive situations after each iteration of the **repeat** statement.

We can use the principle of recursive doubling to underpin many different calculations over a set of elements stored in a list or an array. We shall return to the method again later in this chapter for further simple exemplification. We finish this section however by noting that the fast computation of $x^n$, where $n$ is a power of 2, by squaring $x$ successively $\log n$ times is another example of the doubling technique. If $x$ is an integer then only one processor is required. However, if $x$ is (say) a Boolean matrix then many processors can be employed in each squaring operation.

### The divide-and-conquer technique

Within this technique, a given problem is divided into a number of independent subproblems which are recursively dealt with. The parallel computation time for the overall problem is proportional to the depth of the recursion. The solution for a problem at one level of the recursion has to be composable from the solutions of its subproblems. If at each level of the recursion the subproblems have a size no larger than a fixed proportion of the size of their father problem, then the depth of the recursion will be logarithmic. The method of divide and conquer is widely applicable in sequential computation. In a parallel setting the method requires that the subproblems at the same level of recursion should be independently computed.

The binary tree method can be seen as a special case of divide-and-conquer. However, from the point of view of the computation tree, divide-and-conquer starts in top-down mode whilst the binary tree method is essentially a bottom-up process. However, we can contrive greater similarity. For example (taking the same example as was used to illustrate the binary tree method) we can find the maximum of $n$ numbers stored in an array. This problem can be divided into two problems. The first is that of finding the maximum of the first $n/2$ elements and the second is to find the maximum of the last $n/2$ elements. The solution to the original problem is simply the maximum of the results of the two subproblems.

There are several other examples of the divide-and-conquer technique applied in a parallel setting towards the end of the chapter on graph algorithms. These are of a less trivial nature. Although the field of algebraic and numerical computations is rather neglected in this text, we complete this description of the divide-and-conquer technique with an application to an algebraic problem. Suppose that we want to evaluate the polynomial $p(x)$ of degree $n$ at $x = x_0$. For convenience we assume here that $n = 2^k - 1$ for some integer $k$. We express $p(x)$ in the form $r(x) + x^{(n+1)/2}q(x)$, where $q(x)$ and $r(x)$ are polynomials of degree $2^{k-1} - 1$. Recursively we compute $q(x_0)$, $r(x_0)$ and $p(x_0)$ in parallel and combine the results in constant time to get $p(x_0)$. The algorithm has $O(\log n)$ depth. Figure 1.4 shows the recursion tree for the computation of a general polynomial of degree 7.

### Compression (collapsing) technique

We illustrate the method by once again considering the problem of finding the maximum of $n$ elements stored in an array $X$. For convenience we assume that $n$ is a power of 2 (if necessary we can always add, in constant parallel time, a minimum number of dummy elements to ensure that this is the case). Recursively, for each odd value of $i$ in parallel, we compress the two entries $X(i)$ and $X(i + 1)$ into a single entry with the value of maximum($X(i)$, $X(i + 1)$). The length of $X$ is reduced by a factor of 2 from one level of recursion to the next. Thus $X$ is reduced to having a single element after a logarithmic number of steps. The following example illustrates the technique in the case of finding the maximum:

$$[3, 7, 8, 3, 9, 2, 3, 1] \rightarrow [7, 8, 9, 3] \rightarrow [8, 9] \rightarrow [9]$$

Notice that for this example the compression technique amounts to the balanced binary tree method. The various general techniques presented in this section are not entirely disjoint. However, the compression technique has much wider applicability. For example, within graph algorithms we can use the

*Figure 1.4*

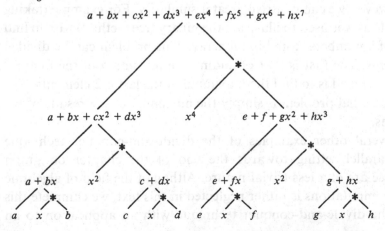

$$a + bx + cx^2 + dx^3 + ex^4 + fx^5 + gx^6 + hx^7$$

technique to compress a graph recursively into a single (super-) vertex. A particular characteristic of the graph is computed for larger and larger parts of the graph. These parts have a diameter of $O(2^k)$ after $k$ stages in each of which certain neighbouring vertices are compressed into common supervertices. We see a typical application of this type in the algorithm for finding the connected components of a graph in chapter 2.

*Obtaining a single element from a set*

There is often a need in computations to obtain a single element (on a 'do not care which' basis) from a given set. The means of doing this depends often upon the data structure in which the elements are stored. For example, given a circular list of elements, suppose that we wish to number (or rank) the elements consecutively around the list starting at some vertex and that it does not matter which one. The obvious solution would be, for only one element $i$ of the circular list, to re-assign $next(i)$ according to $next(i) \leftarrow i$. Then $i$ becomes the tail of the list whilst the head of the list is the original value of $next(i)$. Thus the circular list becomes a conventional list. We can then employ the list-ranking procedure already described before reconstituting (if necessary) the circularity of the list.

To identify a single element of a circular list is difficult unless we have some additional information concerning its elements. Fortunately, for the applications in this text, this is always the case. For example, it may be that the circular list is a list of the vertices of a graph. In this case the vertices usually carry an index (from 1 to $n$, where $n$ is the number of vertices of the graph) and this has nothing to do with the relative positions of the vertices on the list. Then a particular list element can be picked out because its index has a certain value (say, 1). If the list is not circular then these problems do not arise. We can just take, for example, the element at the head of the list as our ('do not care which') selection. A similar remark applies to vectors or to multi-dimensional arrays.

In whatever way the elements of a set are stored, it is invariably the case that there is some constant-parallel-time process by which a single element may be selected.

## 1.3 Reducing the number of processors

Suppose that we have already designed an algorithm working in parallel time $t$ using $p$ processors. Here we presume that $p$ is equal to the maximum number of operations executed within the same parallel step.

Consider, as a first example, the algorithm for finding the maximum of $n$ numbers using the balanced binary tree method. As we described it, this algorithm executes in $O(\log n)$ time using $p \geqslant n/2$ processors. Notice that $n/2$ processors are only actually required in the first step of the algorithm. In the second step only $n/4$ are active, in the third $n/8$ and so on. In a very short time most of the processors are in fact idle. This would suggest that perhaps it is possible to reduce the number of processors required without detriment to the complexity. Suppose that we have $p < n/2$ processors. Now consider partitioning the $n$ numbers whose maximum is to be found into $p$ groups. Let $p - 1$ of these groups contain $\lceil n/p \rceil$ elements and the remaining group contains $n - (p-1)\lceil n/p \rceil$ ($\leqslant \lceil n/p \rceil$) elements. We assign a processor to each of the groups. For all of the $p$ groups in parallel, each processor now finds the maximum (in sequential style) within its group. There will be at most $\lceil n/p \rceil - 1$ comparisons to be made to find the maximum within any group. Thus we can reduce the original problem of size $n$ to a similar problem of size $p$ within $\lceil n/p \rceil - 1$ time units. This can now be solved in $\log p$ time using the balanced binary tree method. Thus, overall, we can find the maximum of $n$ numbers stored in an array in $\lceil n/p \rceil - 1 + \log p$ time using $p < n/2$ processors. Notice that if we set $p = n/\log n$ then we obtain a computation time of $O(\log n)$ and we thus have an optimal parallel algorithm.

There is a general theorem which relates the number of processors to the parallel time and to the total number of basic operations $m$ that have to be carried out.

*Theorem* 1.1 (Brent)
Let $A$ be a given algorithm with a parallel computation time of $t$. Suppose that $A$ involves a total number of $m$ computational operations. Then $A$ can be implemented using $p$ processors in $O(m/p + t)$ parallel time.

*Proof*
Let $m(i)$ be the number of computational operations performed (in parallel) in step $i$ of $A$, the algorithm provided. Using $p$ processors this can be simulated in $m(i)/p + 1$ time. Now summing over all $i$, $1 \leqslant i \leqslant t$, we get the stated parallel computation time because $m = m(1) + m(2) + \cdots + m(t)$. $\qquad\Box$

The proof of Brent's theorem entails two implementation problems. These are firstly how to compute the $m(i)$ and secondly how to group (for fixed $i$) the $m(i)$ operations into $p$ groups. In general these problems may prove difficult;

however, there are no great difficulties for the applications of the theorem within the algorithms presented later in this text.

Let us return for a moment to the optimal parallel algorithm described earlier in this section for finding the maximum of $n$ elements. Many optimal parallel algorithms are possible for similar computations for a set of elements stored in an array. Notice that the assignment of processors to groups of elements in the first phase of this style of algorithm is relatively easy given that they are stored in an array. Let the array be indexed from 0 to $n - 1$. Essentially a processor can be made to start scanning the array at each indexed position $i\lceil n/p\rceil$ for $0 \leqslant i \leqslant p - 1$. Each such processor scans the contiguous elements indexed from $i\lceil n/p\rceil$ to $i\lceil n/p\rceil + p - 1$. It is not easy to obtain similar optimal parallel algorithms for elements stored in a list. This is because the elements so stored are not indexed as they are in an array. It is then not possible to make an assignment of processors in the same way in the first phase of the algorithm. Recently Cole and Vishkin [3] described a quite general result related to processor re-scheduling. They proved that if $n$ jobs are given (each requiring no more than $\log n$ time) and the total number of jobs is bounded by $n$, then the computation may be simulated in $\log n$ time using $n/\log n$ processors on a P-RAM. The method, for example, allows us to rank the elements of a list by an optimal parallel algorithm ($\mathrm{O}(\log n)$ time using $n/\log n$ processors). A discussion of Cole and Vishkin's method, which is rather sophisticated, is beyond the scope of this book. Incidentally, their method also provides a way to improve the efficiency of certain parallel computations (for example, finding the blocks and the biconnected components) on sparse graphs. The algorithms presented in chapter 2 for these problems are optimal for dense graphs where the size of the input is $\mathrm{O}(n^2)$ as provided by an adjacency matrix description.

## 1.4 Examples of fast parallel computations on vectors and lists

We provide here four example algorithms, experience of which should prove useful.

*Example 1* (Prefix computation)
Let $n$ numbers be stored in a vector $A$ in locations $A(n), A(n + 1), \ldots, A(2n - 1)$. The prefix computation computes the values

$A(n)$, $A(n)©A(n+1)$, $A(n)©A(n+1)©A(n+2),\ldots,$ where $©$ is an associative binary operation. The calculation is also sometimes referred to as a partial-sums computation. As we see more graphically later, the following algorithm uses the balanced binary tree method. Let $n$ be a power of 2 (otherwise we add a minimum number of dummy elements to achieve this). Then the following statements, where $n = 2^m$, perform the desired computation for the case when $© = +$.

> **for** $k \leftarrow m - 1$ **step** $-1$ **to** 0 **do**
>     **for** all $j$, $2^k \leqslant j \leqslant 2^{k+1} - 1$, **in parallel do** $A(j) \leftarrow A(2j) + A(2j + 1)$
> $B(1) \leftarrow A(1)$
> **for** $k \leftarrow 1$ **to** $m$ **do**
>     **for** all $j$, $2^k \leqslant j \leqslant 2^{k+1} - 1$, **in parallel do**
>         $B(j) \leftarrow$ **if** $j$ is odd **then** $B((j - 1)/2)$ **else** $B(j/2) - A(j + 1)$

At the end of the computation the value of $A(n) + A(n + 1) + \cdots + A(n + j)$, for $0 \leqslant j \leqslant n - 1$, is stored in location $B(n + j)$. The computation runs in O($\log n$) time and, as we have described it, uses $n$ processors. With the numbers initially stored in an array as already described, we can easily achieve the same time complexity with O($n/\log n$) processors. The reduction in the number of processors can be attained in the same way as it was for the maximum-finding algorithm at the beginning of the last section. The same algorithmic structure can be used for any other binary associative function. Typical examples of the associative operation $©$ are maximum, minimum, multiplication and addition.

*Figure 1.5*

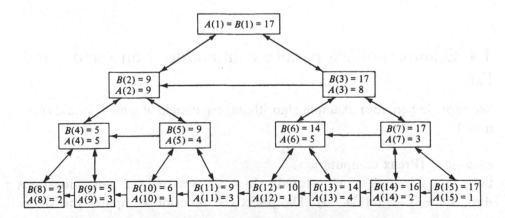

The algorithm is perhaps more easily understood with reference to the balanced binary tree of the computation. Figure 1. shows such a tree for an example partial-sums computation in which the operation $\copyright$ is addition. The elements over which the prefix computation is to be performed are stored in $A(8)$ to $A(15)$. The arcs in the figure show the flow of information. In the first phase of the computation, and in three parallel steps proceeding up the tree, for each non-leaf node we compute the sum of all its leaf descendants. The second phase of the computation takes three parallel steps proceeding from the root to the leaves. In each such step, $A(j+1)$ is required to compute $B(j)$ for each odd $j$. The horizontal arcs in the figure indicate this. Finally the required values of the partial sums are stored in $B(8)$ to $B(15)$.

*Example 2* (Minima of intervals)
Suppose that we are given a vector $x(i)$ of integers and a vector $int(i) = [l(i) \mathrel{..} r(i)]$ of intervals, both of size $n$, $1 \leqslant i \leqslant n$. We show how to compute, for each $i$, $\min\{x(k) \mid k \in int(i)\}$. Again we shall employ the balanced binary tree method and take (without loss of generality) $n$ to be a power of 2.

Let the $n$ elements of the vector $x$ be stored at the leaves of a balanced binary tree. The first phase of the algorithm computes, for each node, the minimum of the values stored at its leaf descendants. These minima are for particular (so-called 'good') intervals determined by the structure of the binary tree. An example of this phase of the algorithm is provided by figure 1.6. If the leaves of the tree are indexed from left to right respectively by the integers 1 to 8, then here (for $i \leqslant j$ and $1 \leqslant i, j \leqslant 8$) $min[i \mathrel{..} j]$ is the minimum of the elements stored in the interval $[i \mathrel{..} j]$. Each such interval appearing at a node of the tree is a

*Figure 1.6*

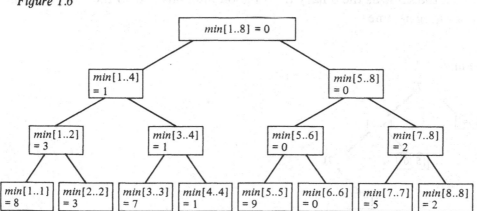

good interval, all other intervals are not good. Thus $[1 .. 7]$ is not a good interval. The second phase of the algorithm now assigns a processor to each of the (in general not 'good') intervals $[l(i) .. r(i)]$ and proceeds to find a decomposition of the interval into 'good' intervals. The decomposition of $[1 .. 7]$ into such intervals is shown in figure 1.7, where the good intervals are enclosed in rectangles.

The reader may wish to produce a description of the whole algorithm in 'coded' form. Our description is nevertheless sufficient to see that the problem of finding the minimum for each of the intervals can be solved in O(log $n$) time using $n$ processors. The only difficulty of obtaining this complexity is the partitioning of a bad interval into good intervals. We indicate how this may be done in logarithmic sequential time as follows. We use the balanced binary tree of good intervals as a substrate for the computation. We place the bad interval at the root and then divide it into two intervals. The point of division is the same as the division point of the current good interval into its son intervals. The two intervals obtained from the bad interval are then passed to the sons of the root. These intervals have their (at most one in each case) limits modified in an obvious way. Then the process is repeated. Figure 1.8 shows this process in a schematic manner. If the limits of an interval generated by this process coincide with the limits of the good interval at the current node of the binary tree, then no further partitioning of this interval is required. In this way a tree of intervals (into which the original bad interval is partitioned) is built up. In this tree no node has more than two grandchildren. In fact it is just this observation that provides a constant bound on the amount of computation required at a given depth in the tree. In figure 1.8, $P_r$ and $P_l$ denote the two paths which are traced from the root in this process and off which there are spurs (branch paths of length 1) to good intervals belonging to the partition. The depth of the tree is at most the same as the binary tree of good intervals and so the computation takes O(log $n$) time.

*Figure 1.7*

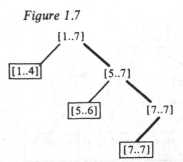

*Example 3* (Doubling technique revisited)

The doubling technique which we have already used in order to rank the elements of a list may be employed for many similar $O(\log n)$-parallel-time computations. We provide some additional examples here. For this purpose we first reproduce the essential part of the doubling procedure that we previously employed. Here we have replaced the parameter 'length' by a general one called '*value*' and $\copyright$ is a general binary operator. We presume that, for each $k$, $value(k)$ has been initialised to a suitable value. Again, for each element $k$, $k$ points to the element $P(k)$. The final element of the list points to itself. Thus, if the condition $P(k) \neq P(P(k))$ is not true, then $k$ is the final element of the list. The following is then the typical structure of a doubling computation.

> **repeat** $\log n$ **times**
>     **for** all $k \in L$ **in parallel do**
>       **if** $P(k) \neq P(P(k))$ **then**
>         **begin**
>           $value(k) \leftarrow value(k) \copyright value(P(k))$
>           $P(k) \leftarrow P(P(k))$
>         **end**

Now suppose that we replace '*value*' by '*minimum*' and that $\copyright$ is the binary minimum operator. If, for each list element $k$, we have the initial assignments that $minimum(k) \leftarrow k$, then it is easy to see that after the computation $minimum(1)$ stores the value of the minimum element of the list. We can similarly find the maximum element.

*Figure 1.8*

$\boxed{\phantom{xx}}\!\!\diagdown$ : A bad interval for which $r(i)$ is not an $r(i)$ for a good interval

$\square$ : A good interval

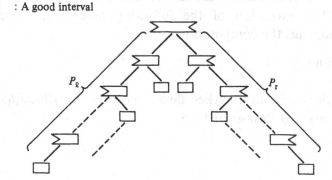

Suppose that we wish to find a particularly distinguished element with a certain property. Perhaps it is the only '*green*' one for example. We can first suitably initialise the elements, for example as follows.

**for** all $k \in L$ **in parallel do** *value*($k$) ← **if** *colour*($k$) = *green* **then** 1 **else** 0

Then using a maximum computation causes maximum(1) to point to the distinguished element.

Many similar computations are possible. Our final example here sets up an application for example 4. Suppose that we wish to divide a list (as near as possible) into two lists of equal length. Let Ⓒ be addition modulo 2. Then, if we initially set *value*($k$) ← 1, after the computation *value*($k$) is either 0 or 1 depending upon the parity of the distance from the element to the end of the list. We can regard *value*($k$) as being a mark (of either 0 or 1) on the element $k$. The two required lists can then be computed according to example 4.

*Example 4* (Sublist computation)
Given a list of length $n$, we imagine that some of its elements are marked. For each element $i$ of the list, *next*($i$) points to the next element. We take the final element to point to itself. The problem is to construct a sublist of the marked elements. The following is first executed.

**repeat** log $n$ **times**
    **for** all $i$ **in parallel do**
        **if** *next*($i$) is not marked **then** *next*($i$) ← *next*(*next*($i$))

After this (with the possible exception of its first and last elements) the list starting at the first element of the initial list is the required sublist. We adjust the first and last elements as follows. The first element of the sublist is either the element currently at its head (*head*(*list*)) if this is marked, otherwise it is *next*(*head*(*list*)). The last element is the current last element if it is marked, otherwise it is the element of the current sublist which does not point to a marked element. Thus execution of the following makes the suitable adjustments and completes the computation.

**for** all $i$ **in parallel do**
    **begin**
    **if** $i$ = *head*(*list*) **then if** $i$ is not marked **then** *head*(*list*) ← *next*(*head*(*list*))
    **if** *next*($i$) is not marked **then** *next*($i$) ← $i$
    **end**

**Bibliography**

[1] A. Aho, J. Hopcroft and J. Ullman. *The Design and Analysis of Computer Algorithms*. Addison-Wesley (1974).

[2] H. Alt, T. Hagerup, K. Melhorn and F. Preparata. Deterministic simulation of idealised parallel computers on more realistic ones. *Proceedings of the 12th Symposium on Mathematical Foundations of Computer Science* (1986). Lecture Notes in Computer Science 233 (eds. J. Grunska, B. Rovan and J. Wiedermann). Springer-Verlag, 199–208.

[3] R. Cole and U. Vishkin. Approximate and exact parallel scheduling with applications to list, tree and graph problems. *FOCS 1986*.

[4] S. Cook. The classification of problems which have fast parallel algorithms. *FCT 1983*.

[5] S. Fortune and J. Wyllie. Parallelism in random access machines. *STOC 1978*, 114–18.

[6] Z. Galil. Efficient algorithms for finding maximal matchings in graphs. *ACM Computing Surveys* **18**, 1 (1986), 23–38.

[7] G. Kindervater and J. Lenstra. An introduction to parallelism in combinatorial optimisation. Report OS-R8501, Centre for Mathematics and Computer Science, Amsterdam (1985).

[8] J. Ullman. *Computational Aspects of VLSI*. Computer Science Press (1983).

[9] P. van Emde Boas. The second machine class: models of parallelism. *Parallel Computers and Computations* (eds. J. van Leeuwen and J. K. Lenstra). CWI Syllabus, Centre for Mathematics and Computer Science, Amsterdam.

[10] J. von zur Gathen. Parallel arithmetic computations: a survey. *Proceedings of the 12th Symposium on Mathematical Foundations of Computer Science* (1986). Lecture Notes in Computer Science 233 (eds. J. Grunska, B. Rovan and J. Wiedermann). Springer-Verlag, 93–112.

# CHAPTER 2

# GRAPH ALGORITHMS

This chapter is concerned with computational problems in graph theory. In particular we restrict attention to some of the problems which are known to be in *NC* and which are therefore solvable in polylogarithmic time using a polynomial number of processors. The area of graph theory has provided perhaps the largest arena for research into parallel computations so that the literature in this field is particularly rich. Apart from the wish to be representative of the main stream of recent work, our choice in problem selection was influenced both by the desire to illustrate commonly used techniques and also by the convenience of making some algorithms contribute to the solutions of subsequent problems.

We assume that the reader is familiar with the notion of a graph and with commonly used definitions in graph theory. Elementary graph theory is a basic tool of computer science so that our assumption is likely to be valid; otherwise there are many introductory texts, for example [17], which may be consulted.

The chapter is divided into sections, each covering a selection of similar or related problems. In section 2.1 we present a number of basic algorithms associated with trees. These algorithms are often required to solve subtasks of larger problems. Moreover, it is often the case that an efficient parallel algorithm has been contrived by manipulating some tree structure to solve the problem in hand. In section 2.2 we present solutions to a number of problems all concerned, one way or another, with questions of connectivity. In section 2.3 we present a solution to the problem of finding an Eulerian circuit of a graph and subsequently this is applied as a subtask in solving the problem of finding a maximal matching. In the same section (as a subtask to finding Eulerian circuits) we also see a commonly applied algorithmic technique known as Euler partitioning. A further application of this technique is seen in an algorithm which finds an optimal edge-colouring of a bipartite graph in section 2.4. In fact section 2.4 is devoted entirely to problems of colouring (either the vertices or the edges of) various classes of graph. In particular there are several examples of the well-known algorithmic technique of divide-and-conquer applied in a parallel setting.

## 2.1 Parallel computations on trees

The computation of various tree functions is a common feature in many efficient parallel graph algorithms. It is often the case for particular algorithms that polylogarithmic efficiency is obtained simply because the algorithm has been contrived to perform certain subtasks on a tree. In this context, we present here some basic computations on trees.

### 2.1.1 THE EULER TOUR TECHNIQUE ON TREES

The novel parallel algorithmic methodology described here, known as the Euler tour technique, was described by Tarjan and Vishkin in [44]. As we shall see, using it enables several useful computations to be performed. An Eulerian circuit is a cycle which traverses every edge of a graph precisely once. By an elementary theorem, a directed connected graph contains a (directed) Eulerian circuit (and is therefore called Eulerian) if and only if, for every vertex $v$, $indegree(v) = outdegree(v)$. Conceptually, given a tree the technique first replaces each edge by two anti-parallel edges. The resulting graph is thus Eulerian because $indegree(v) = outdegree(v)$ for each vertex $v$. Constructing an Eulerian circuit can be the start of many useful computations. The construction is as follows.

We suppose that the tree is given in adjacency list representation. Such a tree $T$ and its representation are shown in figures 2.1(a) and (b). Without any further work we can regard this representation as consisting of a list, for each vertex $v$, of the edges directed from $v$. The directed edge $(i, j)$ appears in $i$'s list and $(j, i)$ appears in $j$'s list. In constructing the Eulerian circuit, we first make the adjacency list for each vertex circular by causing the final item to point back to the first. For all such lists the final item can be found in $O(\log n)$ parallel time using $O(n)$ processors by means of the standard doubling technique. We can now construct the Eulerian circuit. For this we need to define, for each edge $(i, j)$, $tournext(i, j)$ which is the edge following $(i, j)$ in the Eulerian circuit. If $next(i, j)$ is the next edge after $(i, j)$ on the circular adjacency list for $i$, then we execute

**for** all (directed) edges **in parallel do** $tournext(i, j) \leftarrow next(j, i)$

This takes $O(\log n)$ parallel time using $O(n)$ processors, again employing doubling to find the $next(j, i)$ on the (circular) adjacency lists. The list of edges defined by tournext does indeed represent an Eulerian circuit because the list is constructed in such a way that any exit edge from a particular vertex can only be repeated after all other exits have been used in circular order. For the example tree of figure 2.1 we obtain the Eulerian circuit indicated in figure 2.1(c). Clearly, and in general, this tour corresponds to the order of advancing and retreating along edges during a depth-first searching of the tree starting at an arbitrary vertex. If we break the Eulerian cycle at an arbitrary edge, fixing some edge $(i, j)$ as a first edge of the list so formed, vertex $i$ becomes the root at which the depth-first traversal of the tree may be imagined to start. Tarjan and Vishkin called such a list a *traversal list* of the tree. As they showed in [44] this list may be employed for various computations, some of which we now describe.

### 2.1.2 THE TREE-ROOTING AND RELATED PROBLEMS

We show how to transform an undirected unrooted tree into a rooted tree. For each vertex $v$ (except the root) we find *father*($v$). Moreover, the tree may be easily orientated to provide either an out-tree (in which every vertex except the root has indegree of 1) or an in-tree (in which every vertex except the root has outdegree of 1). We also show how to compute the number of descendants, $nd(v)$, of each vertex $v$. These problems are solved using the traversal list described in the previous section.

Let the first edge on this list be $(i, j)$ so that vertex $i$ becomes the root. We rank the elements of the traversal list using the list-ranking algorithm of

*Figure 2.1*

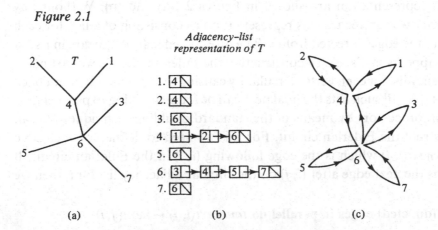

*Adjacency-list representation of T*

1. $\boxed{4}\boxed{\phantom{x}}$
2. $\boxed{4}\boxed{\phantom{x}}$
3. $\boxed{6}\boxed{\phantom{x}}$
4. $\boxed{1} \rightarrow \boxed{2} \rightarrow \boxed{6}\boxed{\phantom{x}}$
5. $\boxed{6}\boxed{\phantom{x}}$
6. $\boxed{3} \rightarrow \boxed{4} \rightarrow \boxed{5} \rightarrow \boxed{7}\boxed{\phantom{x}}$
7. $\boxed{6}\boxed{\phantom{x}}$

(a)                              (b)                              (c)

chapter 1. By *rank*(*r*, *s*) we denote the rank of the edge (*r*, *s*). Thus *rank*(*i*, *j*) = 1. (Notice that here, by the rank of an element, we choose conveniently to mean its distance from the beginning of the list. In chapter 1 we used the same term to mean its distance to the end of the list.) Of two edges (*k*, *l*) and (*l*, *k*), the one of lower rank is marked as the advance edge from *k* to *l*, and the one of higher rank is marked as the retreat edge from *l* to *k*. For each advance edge (*i*, *j*), in parallel, we set *father*(*j*) = *i*. The set of advance edges constitutes an out-tree whilst the retreat edges provide an in-tree. The number of descendants of each vertex *i*, except the root, can be found by executing

**for** all *i* **in parallel do** $nd(i) \leftarrow (rank(i, father(i)) - rank(father(i), i) + 1)/2$

A simple inductive argument on the size of $nd(i)$ proves that the formula used here for $nd(i)$, which is the number of descendants of *i* including *i* itself, is correct.

For the operations in this section that cannot be done in constant time using $O(n)$ processors, the standard doubling technique ensures that no more than $O(\log n)$ time is required.

### 2.1.3 PREORDER AND POSTORDER NUMBERING OF VERTICES

In the traversal list advance edges (*i*, *j*) occur in preorder on *j*. We can compute the sublist of advance edges (*i*, *j*), and thus the list of endpoints of these edges. The elements of this list are then ranked and this gives the preorder numbering of vertices. A similar computation will number the vertices in postorder. For each vertex *j*, except the root, there is exactly one retreat edge (*j*, *i*), and the retreat edges appear in the postorder on *j*.

### 2.1.4 THE BINARY RELATIONS 'IS A DESCENDANT OF' AND 'IS AN ANCESTOR OF'

Node *i* is an ancestor of *j* if and only if $preorder(i) \leqslant preorder(j) < preorder(i) + nd(i)$. Hence the relations 'is an ancestor of' and 'is a descendant of' for all pairs of vertices are computable in $O(1)$ time if the preorder numbering and number of descendants of all vertices are known.

### 2.1.5 THE MINIMUM (MAXIMUM) VALUE IN THE SUBTREE ROOTED AT EACH NODE

Let *M* be a vector of dimension *n* such that $M(i)$ contains the value stored in the tree at the node with preorder number *i*. For node *i*, the elements

$M(preorder(i))$ to $M(preorder(i) + nd(i) - 1)$ contain the values stored at the descendant nodes of $i$. For each $i$ we can compute the minimum value associated with nodes in such an interval using the same technique as that employed in example 2 in section 1.4. This takes logarithmic time using $O(n)$ processors.

### 2.1.6 REMARKS ON TREE TECHNIQUES FOR GENERAL GRAPHS

Sequential algorithms often employ some form of graph traversal which is equivalent to tracing the edges of a spanning tree of the graph. Perhaps, from a sequential complexity point of view, the most successful and commonly used form of graph traversal is the depth-first search. During the search the graph is decomposed into a (depth-first) tree and non-tree edges. Unfortunately, it seems (see chapter 7) that the problem of finding a depth-first search tree is hardly parallelisable. Hence many fast parallel computations in graph theory avoid depth-first search computation. The problem of finding the connected components of a graph exemplifies this.

  Some classes of graph have a structure strongly related to trees. Two such examples are outerplanar graphs and Halin graphs. As we shall see later in this chapter, algorithmic advantage can be made of this fact in the production of efficient parallel algorithms.

  When a spanning tree of a graph is found or when the graph is represented as a tree of simpler components, various functions on the tree can be efficiently computed to solve a problem for the whole graph. This supports the view that the tree is a very important structure in designing efficient parallel graph-algorithms.

## 2.2 Paths, spanning trees, connected components and blocks

We present five algorithms in this section all of which, in some sense, solve problems concerned with connectivity. These problems are often also encountered as subtasks of larger problems and we shall be making use of the algorithms presented here in this way later in the chapter. Two vertices of a graph are said to be connected if there is a path between them. Concerning paths between vertices we are most commonly concerned to find the shortest paths (either in terms of the number of edges that have to be traversed or, in the case of weighted graphs, in terms of the sum of the edge weights of the edges traversed). In subsection 2.2.1 we describe an efficient parallel shortest-paths algorithm. This binary relation of being 'connected' is an equivalence relation on the vertex set of a graph and the subgraph induced by each equivalence class is a connected component of the graph. In subsection 2.2.2 we deal with the problem of finding the connected components of a graph whilst in subsection 2.2.3 we show that a slight modification to this algorithm provides an efficient way to obtain a spanning tree of a graph. If a connected component contains no articulation point (that is, a vertex whose removal will disconnect the component) then the component is said to be a block. In a block (with at least three vertices) there are at least two vertex-disjoint paths between any pair of vertices. A block is therefore sometimes referred to as a two-connected component. In subsection 2.2.4 we describe an algorithm which finds the blocks of a graph.

## 2.2.1 SHORTEST PATHS

The following algorithm to find the shortest paths between every pair of vertices of a weighted graph is essentially due to Kucera.[32] The algorithm takes as input the edge-weight matrix $M$ of a graph and outputs the matrix $M'$ defined as follows:

$$M'(i, j) = 0, \qquad i = j$$
$$M'(i, j) = \min\{M(i_0, i_1) + M(i_1, i_2) + \cdots + M(i_{k-1}, i_k)\}, \qquad i \neq j$$

where the minimum is taken over all possible sequences $i_0, i_1, i_2, \ldots, i_k$ for which $i = i_0$ and $j = i_k$. Obviously, $M'(i, j)$ is the length of the shortest path from $i$ to $j$. The algorithm consists essentially of an iterated step. Within each iteration, the search for a (possibly) shorter path between each pair of vertices is extended to consider all possible paths utilising up to twice the number of currently considered edges. Thus a logarithmic number of iterations is sufficient. The following detailed description of the algorithm utilises the auxiliary matrices $m_{ij}$ and $q_{ijk}$ where $i$, $j$ and $k$ range from 1 to $n$.

1. **for all** $i, j$ **in parallel do** $m(i, j) \leftarrow M(i, j)$
2. **repeat** $\log_2 n$ **times**
   **begin**
   **for all** $i, j, k$ **in parallel do** $q(i, j, k) \leftarrow m(i, j) + m(j, k)$
   **for all** $i, j$ **in parallel do** $m(i, j) \leftarrow \min\{m(i, j), q(i, 1, j), q(i, 2, j), \ldots, q(i, n, j)\}$
   **end**
3. **for all** $i, j$ **in parallel do**
   **if** $i \neq j$ **then** $M(i, j) \leftarrow m(i, j)$ **else** $M(i, j) \leftarrow 0$

It is an easy exercise to show, by induction on $t$, that, after $t$ iterations and for $i \neq j$, $m(i, j)$ is given by $m(i, j) = \min\{M(i_0, i_1) + M(i_1, i_2) + \cdots + M(i_{k-1}, i_k)\}$, where the minimum is over all sequences $i = i_0, i_1, i_2, \ldots, i_k = j$ for which $k \leqslant 2^t$. Since we only consider positive edge weights a minimum-length path will be a simple path utilising no more than $n$ edges. Thus after $t = \log n$ all possible minimum path lengths will have been considered.

Statements 1 and 3 can be executed in constant time using $n^2$ processors. Within statement 2, each minimum can be computed in $O(\log n)$ time using $O(n/\log n)$ processors (a suitable algorithm is described in chapter 1). For each iteration there are $n^2$ such minima to be computed. Over all iterations, these minima can thus be found in $O(\log^2 n)$ time using $O(n^3/\log n)$ processors. The assignments to the $q(i, j, k)$ within statement 2 take constant time for each iteration using $n^3$ processors. Overall, on a P-RAM, we therefore have an $O(\log^2 n)$ algorithm using $n^3$ processors, which places the problem in *NC*. In fact it is easy to see that the number of processors can be reduced to $O(n^3/\log n)$ without detriment to the true complexity. The description of Kucera[32] was for the W-RAM model of computation. As we saw in chapter 1, within this model the minimum of $n$ numbers can be found in constant time using $n^2$-processors. His implementation of this shortest-paths algorithm therefore requires $O(\log n)$ time using $n^4$ processors.

### 2.2.2 CONNECTED COMPONENTS OF A GRAPH

Given the adjacency matrix $A$ of an undirected graph $G = (V, E)$, where $V = \{1, 2, \ldots, n\}$, we describe an algorithm which finds the connected components. Specifically, the output from the algorithm is a vector $C$ of length $n$ such that $C(i) = C(j) = k$ if and only if vertex $i$ is in the same component as vertex $j$. Moreover $k$ is the numerically smallest label of any vertex in the same component. We first show, following Hirschberg *et al.*,[20] how $C$ may be found in $O(\log^2 n)$ time using $O(n^2/\log n)$ processors. We then briefly describe the improvement of Chin *et al.*,[10] that the same time bound may be achieved with a reduction in the number of processors to $O(n^2/\log^2 n)$. This represents a nice example of the idea contained within Brent's theorem described in chapter 1. The improved algorithm is optimal in the sense that the product of the running time with the number of processors is of the order of the running time ($O(n^2)$) for the fastest sequential algorithm using the adjacency matrix as input.

The algorithm works by iterating, $\log n$ times, the two-step sequence outlined below. Before the first iteration $C$ is initialised so that $C(i) = i$, $0 \leqslant i \leqslant n$. The effect of each iteration is to modify $C$, in effect to merge vertices recursively into larger and larger pseudo-vertices. At any stage all those vertices $j, k, l, \ldots$ of the original graph for which $C(j) = C(k) = C(l) = \cdots = i$, where $i$ is in the set $V$, constitute a pseudo-vertex labelled $i$. It will be convenient occasionally to refer to any such vertex $i$ as a p-vertex. Thus if $i$ labels a pseudo-vertex then $i$ is a p-vertex. Moreover, for any vertex $j$ which is not a p-vertex, we say that $i = C(j)$ is the p-vertex of $j$. It is an invariant of the algorithm that a p-vertex $i$ is that vertex with the numerically smallest label in the pseudo-vertex $i$. Each successive iteration reduces the number of pseudo-vertices for each component by at least half until a single pseudo-vertex is associated with each component. We illustrate the algorithm by applying it to the single-component graph of figure 2.2. The algorithm deals with all components in parallel.

Before describing the individual steps of each iteration we need to define the notion of a $k$-tree-loop. A $k$-tree-loop, $k \geqslant 0$, is a weakly connected digraph (that is, a digraph in which for every pair of vertices $i$ and $j$ there exists a path from $i$ to $j$ or a path from $j$ to $i$) in which every vertex has outdegree of 1 and such that there exists exactly one circuit which has length $k + 1$. Removal of any one edge of this circuit results in an in-tree (that is, a tree in which every vertex except the root has an outdegree of 1).

The input to each iteration, described by the following steps, is the current vector $C$. The adjacency matrix (in this initial form of the algorithm) is unchanged throughout the computation. If we interpret $(i, C(i))$ as an edge of a digraph then it is an invariant of the algorithm that $C$ describes a set of special 0-tree-loops called clubs. A club is a 0-tree-loop in which all the edges are incident with the root and this is that vertex with the numerically smallest label in the club. Thus a pseudo-vertex may be thought of as a club.

*The two-step sequence*

*Step 1*

This step starts with a parallel assignment to a vector $T$.

1. **for** all vertices $i$ **in parallel do** $T(i) \leftarrow \min_j \{C(j) \mid A(i, j) = 1, C(j) \neq C(i)\}$

*Figure 2.2*

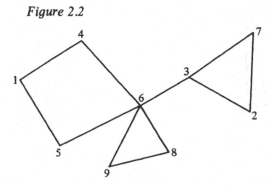

If here $\min_j$ is over the empty set then $C(i)$ is assigned to $T(i)$. The effect of this statement is to assign to $T(i)$ the p-vertex of smallest numerical value of vertices (if they exist) which are adjacent to vertex $i$ but which are in different pseudo-vertices. If $i$ is not adjacent to vertices in different pseudo-vertices then $T(i)$ is assigned the p-vertex of $i$. We now execute

> 2. **for** all vertices $i$ **in parallel do** $T(i) \leftarrow \min_j \{ T(j) \mid C(j) = i, T(j) \neq i \}$

If here $\min_j$ is over the empty set then $C(i)$ is assigned to $T(i)$. If $i$ is a p-vertex then the last statement sets $T(i)$ to be the smallest p-vertex of vertices which are adjacent to vertices in pseudo-vertex $i$, whilst if $i$ is not a p-vertex (i.e. $i \neq$ any $C(j)$) then $T(i)$ becomes the p-vertex of $i$. In general if all the vertices of the component under examination have not been merged to a single pseudo-vertex then $(i, T(i))$ may be thought of as a directed edge between distinct vertices. For our example this now provides the digraph consisting of 1-tree-loops illustrated in figure 2.3.

In fact figure 2.3 also represents $T$ immediately after statement 2 because in the first iteration this statement does not change $T$. This is the case whatever the input because the only $j$ satisfying $C(j) = i$ will be $i$ itself and $C(i) \neq i$.

Any club associated with a graph component containing a single p-vertex is clearly just reproduced in $T$ in step 1. On the other hand, if the component has more than one p-vertex then $T$ will always describe a set of 1-tree-loops for the component. We can see this as follows. Each pseudo-vertex of such a component contains at least one vertex adjacent to a vertex of another pseudo-vertex. Considering $T$, the net effect of step 1 is then to cause each p-vertex to point to precisely one other distinct p-vertex, whilst vertices which are not p-vertices point to their own p-vertices. Consider the digraph components described by $T$ and induced by p-vertices only. Each such component must contain a loop, because every vertex has an out-edge. Moreover such a

*Figure 2.3*

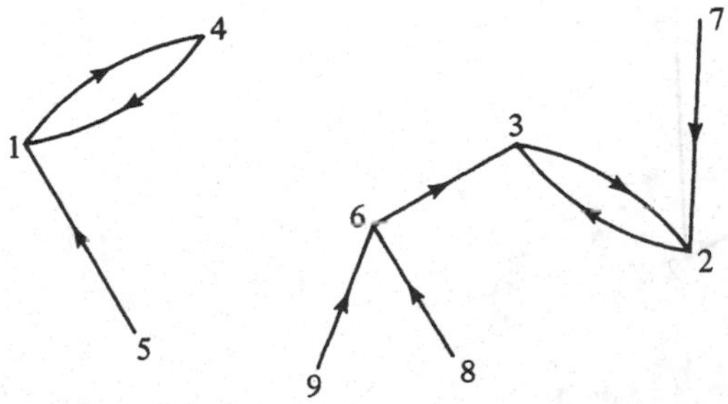

component cannot have more than one loop, otherwise there would exist some p-vertex $i$ with two different $T(i)$. Finally the loop of such a component can only be of length 2. Otherwise (if it were of length 1) $i$ on the loop would not be distinct from $T(i)$ or (if it were of length greater than 2) for some vertex $i$ on the loop $T(i)$ could not be the smallest p-vertex of vertices adjacent to vertices in pseudo-vertex $i$. Thus in $T$ the p-vertices, of a graph component containing more than one p-vertex, always induce 1-tree-loops. Therefore so do all the vertices in such a component, since non-p-vertices merely point to p-vertices. Also, notice that the smallest p-vertex in a 1-tree-loop must lie on the loop.

## Step 2

In this step we merge all vertices in the same tree loop, specifically we merge them into that p-vertex which has the numerically least label. If we interpret $T$ as a function and if we make the usual definition of $T^k(i) - T^1(i) = T(i)$ and $T^k(i) = T(T^{k-1}(i))$ for $k > 1$ – then, for $k \geqslant n - 2$, $T^k(i)$ will be one of the two vertices, say $u$ and $w$, on the loop of the 1-tree-loop containing $i$. We merge vertices of the 1-tree-loop into the vertex with numerically smallest label and use the fact that $(T(u) = w$ and $T(w) = u)$ to help us do this. For this reason we first copy $T$ into the auxiliary vector $B$ –

   3. **for** all vertices $i$ **in parallel do** $B(i) \leftarrow T(i)$

– before executing the statement

   4. **repeat** log $n$ **times**
       **for** all vertices $i$ **in parallel do** $T(i) \leftarrow T(T(i))$

which uses the standard doubling technique to set $T(i) = T^k(i)$. For our example the graphical representation of $T$ is now shown in figure 2.4. This displays, typifying the general case, a set of clubs. Execution of the following statement achieves our objective.

   5. **for** all vertices $i$ **in parallel do** $C(i) \leftarrow \min\{B(T(i)), T(i)\}$

*Figure 2.4*

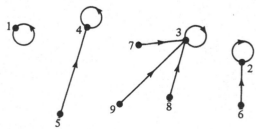

The vector $C$ now describes a set of pseudo-vertices which forms the input for the next iteration.
**end** of the two-step sequence

For our example the output from the first iteration of the two step sequence is illustrated in figure 2.5.

A second iteration of steps 1 and 2 now reduces our example component to a single pseudo-vertex. During this process and after step 1 we obtain the 1-tree-loop of figure 2.6, so that step 2 will now produce the club (pseudo-vertex) rooted at vertex 1.

*Lemma 2.1*
The above algorithm finds the connected components of an undirected graph.

*Proof*
Conceptually, the input to the next iteration of the algorithm may be thought of as the graph induced by the pseudo-vertices output from the last iteration. In such a graph there is an edge between the pseudo-vertices $i$ and $j$ iff there exist two vertices $k$ and $l$ such that $C(k) = i$, $C(l) = j$ and $A(k,l) = 1$. (In this sense, the effect of the first iteration on the component illustrated in figure 2.1 is to produce the graph consisting of the single edge $(1,2)$. The second iteration reduced this component to a single pseudo-vertex.) In general we now see that for such a graph component, containing more than one pseudo-vertex, an

*Figure 2.5*

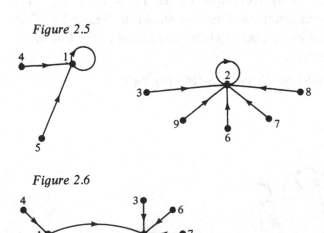

*Figure 2.6*

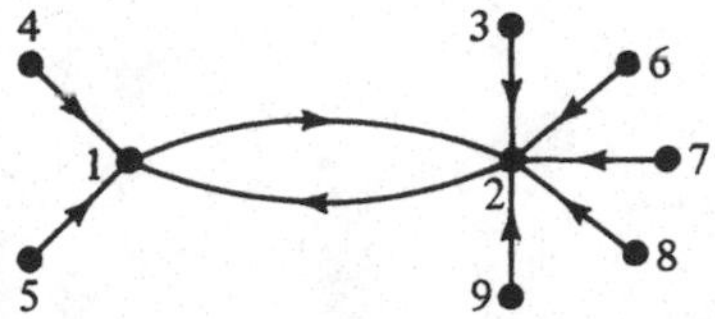

iteration of (step 1, step 2) will reduce the number of pseudo-vertices by at least a factor of 2. It will then follow that $\log_2 n$ iterations of (step 1, step 2) will be sufficient to merge the vertices into a single pseudo-vertex. As we say in the description of the algorithm, the effect of step 1 is for $T$ to describe a set of 1-tree-loops and each of these consists of a 1-tree-loop of p-vertices plus other vertices pointing to the p-vertices. Each such tree-loop therefore contains at least two p-vertices. Step 2 merges all vertices in the same 1-tree-loop into a single pseudo-vertex. Thus for the next iteration the number of pseudo-vertices of our component is at least halved. This completes the proof. □

Consider now the complexity of the algorithm. Statements 1 to 5 are iterated $\log n$ times. A single execution of statement 4 also requires $\log n$ iterations. Thus, no matter how many processors are available, the algorithm requires at least $O(\log^2 n)$ time. We show first that this time bound can be achieved with $O(n^2)$ processors. Notice that with at least $n$ processors statements 3 and 5 take $O(1)$ time as does the initialisation of the vector $C$ before the first execution of statement 1. With a similar number of processors statement 4 takes $O(\log n)$ time. We just need to show that each of the statements 1 and 2 can be implemented to run in $O(\log n)$ time using $O(n^2)$ processors. Not surprisingly, these implementations are similarly achieved so we just describe that for statement 1. The following detail this statement more precisely.

1(a). **for** all $i, j$, $1 \leqslant i, j \leqslant n$, **in parallel do**
     $Temp(i, j) \leftarrow$ **if** $A(i, j) = 1$ **and** $C(i) \neq C(j)$ **then** $C(j)$ **else** $\infty$
1(b). **for** all $i$, $1 \leqslant i \leqslant n$, **in parallel do** $Temp(i, 1) \leftarrow \min_{1 \leqslant j \leqslant n}\{Temp(i, j)\}$
1(c). **for** all $i$, $1 \leqslant i \leqslant n$, **in parallel do**
     $T(i) \leftarrow$ **if** $Temp(i, 1) = \infty$ **then** $C(i)$ **else** $Temp(i, 1)$

In step 1(a), for each vertex $i$, the numbers whose minimum is to be found are stored in the $i$th row of the array $Temp$. In this regard, if vertex $j$ either is not adjacent to $i$ or is in the same pseudo-vertex, then $Temp(i, j)$ is allocated some number greater than $n$ (denoted by $\infty$). Step 1(b), for each row in parallel, finds the minimum number in the row and places it in location $Temp(i, 1)$. Finally 1(c) assigns the required values to the $T(i)$. With $n^2$ processors step 1(a) takes $O(1)$ time, whilst the same time bound can be achieved for step 1(c) with only $O(n)$ processors. Considering step 1(b), by assigning a processor to each of the $n$ elements of a row (and for each of the $n$ rows) the minima can be found by straightforward recursive doubling in $O(\log n)$ time. Thus, overall, the algorithm can certainly be made to run in $O(\log^2 n)$ time using $O(n^2)$ processors.

Obviously, the method used to find the minimum is wasteful of processors. Indeed, we could better employ the standard prefix computation described in chapter 1 to find the minimum for each row in parallel. This will require $O(n/\log n)$ processors per row and $O(\log n)$ time, that is, $O(n^2/\log n)$ processors in all for the same time bound. Step 1(a) can then be executed in $O(\log n)$ time simply by making parallel assignments to all the elements of $n/\log n$ columns of the array *Temp* in each time step. Step 1(c) requires constant time with only $O(n)$ processors. Hence, $O(n^2/\log n)$ processors are sufficient to ensure that the algorithm runs in $O(\log^2 n)$ time. However, we can improve the bound on the number of processors even further as we briefly describe in the following paragraphs.

### An optimal algorithm for connected components of a graph

The improved version of the previously described algorithm presented here is also optimal. As described by Chin *et al.*,[10] this improvement is achieved by a closer emulation of the algorithmic conception used in the proof of lemma 2.1. This is that the input to each iteration can be thought of as the graph induced by the set of pseudo-vertices output from the last iteration. If $P$ denotes the set of pseudo-vertices, then after $k$ iterations we have that $|P| \leqslant n/2^k$, because their number is at least halved in each iteration. Clearly we might expect to take advantage of this reduction in the problem size as the algorithm proceeds. In the implementation described so far this is not done. For example in a statement like 2(b), after $k$ iterations, the minima for each $i$ need really be found only over $|P|$ elements instead of $n$. Of course, in order to set this up properly, certain additional housekeeping operations will be required. Putting consideration of these aside for the moment, let us consider the possible advantage from a saving of processors point of view. We suppose that we have $nK$ processors (that is, $K$ for each row of the array *Temp*) and let us reconsider the complexity of computing a statement such as 2(b). We saw in chapter 1 that, given $K$ processors, we can compute the minimum of $n$ elements in $T$ units of time where:

$$T = \begin{cases} \lceil n/K \rceil - 1 + \lceil \log_2 K \rceil & \text{if } K < \lfloor n/2 \rfloor \\ \lceil \log_2 n \rceil & \text{if } K \geqslant \lfloor n/2 \rfloor \end{cases}$$

We take $K$ to be fixed and after the $k$th iteration we have that '$n$' $= n/2^k$. We consider the total time, over *all* iterations, required to compute the minima. Before the first iteration we suppose that '$n$' is more than twice the number of processors, then after a number of iterations, say $t$, we suppose that '$n$'

becomes less than this number. Because $|P|$ is at least halved in each iteration, $|P|$ is at most $2K$ after $t = \log_2 n - \log_2 K$ iterations. Therefore the total time required to compute a statement such as 2(b), over all iterations, is bounded by $T'$, where

$$T' = \sum_{k=0}^{t-1} (\lceil (\lfloor n/2^k \rfloor)/K \rceil - 1 + \log K) + \sum_{k=t}^{\log n - 1} \log(n/2^k)$$
$$\leqslant \lceil 2n/K \rceil + t \log K + \log^2 K$$
$$= O(n/K + \log n \cdot \log K)$$

If we now set $K = n/\log^2 n$ so that the number of processors is $(n/\log n)^2$, we see that $T'$ is $O(\log^2 n)$. Thus, without incurring time penalties, we improve the bound on the number of processors required to compute 2(b) by a factor of $\log n$. Encouraged by this observation, let us look briefly at the housekeeping operations required by this approach.

Within the computation we take the pseudo-vertices to be represented by p-vertices. Which vertices are currently p-vertices can be denoted within a vector called *Flag*. Thus $Flag(i) = 1$ if $i \in P$, otherwise $Flag(i) = 0$. Initially $Flag(i) = 1$ for all vertices $i$, and at the commencement of an arbitrary iteration we set $P \leftarrow \{i \mid Flag(i) = 1\}$. Anticipating that part of the housekeeping we will need to describe is to modify the adjacency matrix so that, for current pseudo-vertices $i$ and $j$, $A(i, j) \leftarrow 1$ if there exist vertices $k \in i$ and $l \in j$ such that $A(k, l) = 1$, we see that statements 1 and 2 of our previous description of the algorithm can be replaced by

**for** all $i \in P$ **in parallel do** $T(i) \leftarrow \min_{j \in P} \{j \mid A(i, j) = 1\}$

If here $\min_{j \in P}$ is over the empty set, then $i$ is assigned to $T(i)$. As before, this creates a set of 1-tree-loops but now only over the current set of p-vertices. Remember that all other vertices $k$ have $C(k) =$ some p-vertex. A detail of executing this statement is that we need to be able to assign processors to only those vertices in $P$. This can be achieved here (and at other relevant points in the implementation) by the use of an auxiliary vector, of dimension $n$, in which all vertices are stored. Using a suitable algorithm from chapter 5, we can then sort the elements of this auxiliary vector according to the values in *Flag*. In this way, in $O(\log n)$ time using $n$ processors, we can ensure that the first $|P|$ elements of the auxiliary vector are the elements of $P$ by virtue of the fact that for these and only these $Flag(i) = 1$. Thus, in the operation of min, $j \in P$ would be replaced by 'the first $|P|$ elements' of the auxiliary array. Having created the set of 1-tree-loops, we notice that if $T(i) = i$ then $i$ will correspond to an isolated pseudo-vertex and so represents a component of the input graph which does not have to be reduced any further. For any such vertex $i$, we therefore set $Flag(i) = 0$. In this description of our algorithm we have so far described how the original step 1 is modified. Moreover, we saw in the previous paragraph how this can be implemented to run in $O(\log^2 n)$ time using $(n/\log n)^2$ processors. Let us now proceed to modify step 2. Statements 3, 4 and 5 remain the same except that, in each, the injunction '**for** all vertices $i$ . . .' is replaced by '**for** all $i \in P$ . . .'. The pseudo-vertices input to the current iteration now form a set of clubs as required; the new set of pseudo-vertices will consist of those vertices $i$ for which $C(i) = i$. However, we still need in step 2 to take care of those other vertices of the original graph which were not representative of pseudo-vertices before this iteration. This is easily done by remembering that each such vertex $j$ has $C(j) = $ some pseudo-vertex input to the current iteration; because of this we just need to execute

> **for** all vertices $i$ **in parallel do** $C(i) \leftarrow C(C(i))$

in order to update the p-vertices of these vertices (this statement does not change $C(i)$ for those vertices which were pseudo-vertices input to the current iteration). The final, and additional, requirement of our modified form of step 2 is to update the adjacency matrix as implied earlier and to reassign to some elements of *Flag*. To update the adjacency matrix we first execute

> **for** all $i \in P$ **in parallel do**
>     **for** all $j \in P$, $C(j) = j$, **in parallel do** $A(i, j) \leftarrow \mathbf{OR}_{k \in P}\{A(i, k) \,|\, C(k) = j\}$

The effect of this statement is to set $A(i, j) = 1$ if $A(i, k) = 1$ for some $k$ which is merged into $j$. We complete the update of the adjacency matrix by now executing

> **for** all $j \in P$, $C(j) = j$, **in parallel do**
>     **for** all $i \in P$, $C(i) = i$, **in parallel do** $A(i, j) \leftarrow \mathbf{OR}_{k \in P}\{A(k, j) \,|\, C(k) = i\}$

and the effect of this statement is to make the assignment $A(i, j) \leftarrow 1$ if $A(k, j) = 1$ for some $k$ merged into $i$. We need to consider the complexity implications of updating the adjacency matrix in this way. Consider the first of these two steps required for the update. The second can be considered in a similar manner. Given the adjacency matrix and two pseudo-vertices $i$ and $j$, the first step requires that we assign to each $A(i, j)$ the result of *or*-ing together those elements in the $i$th row which are in columns corresponding to current pseudo-vertices and which are to be merged into pseudo-vertex $j$. Now **or**, like **min**, is a binary associative operation so that we can think of a similar computation (and therefore complexity analysis) to that applied in the case of our modified treatment of the original statements 1 and 2. As before we consider that we have $nK$ processors ($K$ for each row of the adjacency matrix) and we are here required to compute several associative functions within one row of the matrix, whereas previously one such result had to be computed within a row of the array called *Temp*. Now, in chapter 1, we saw that (provided the arguments for each such function are in contiguous locations) we can compute the result of several associative functions over a total of $p$ arguments within the same time bound as computing a single associative function over $p$ arguments. In order to get the arguments for each function into contiguous locations, we can equivalently order the elements of a vector of the vertices according to the auxiliary parameter $C(i) * Flag(i)$. We associate such a parameter with each vertex $i$. The ordering can be accomplished in O($\log p$) time using $p$ processors. It may then be used to reference columns of the adjacency matrix in the required manner. This is because, within the array, the vertices will be arranged in contiguous subsets each with the same $C$-value and with $Flag(i) = 1$, whilst all those with $Flag(i) = 0$ will be arranged together (they all have $C(i) * Flag(i) = 0$) at the end of the array. Thus we can see, at least in principle, that the updating of the adjacency matrix may be achieved by a similar computation (and therefore with a similar complexity analysis) as that employed in our modified treatment of statements 1 and 2 (step 1) of the algorithm. In fact, not surprisingly, the details yield the same result that summing over all iterations the updating of the adjacency matrix can be achieved in O($\log^2 n$) time using $(n/\log n)^2$ processors. All other steps of the algorithm are easily seen to be achievable within the same constraints and so, overall, we have the result that the connected components of a graph may be found in O($\log^2 n$) time using O($n^2/\log^2 n$) processors.

### 2.2.3 SPANNING FOREST

We show here that a straightforward modification of the connected components algorithm provides a parallel method of finding a spanning forest (that is, a set of spanning trees, one tree for each component) as a by-product of that algorithm. Moreover, this is achievable without incurring additional complexity penalties. Thus, as Chin *et al.*[10] demonstrated, a spanning forest may be found in O($\log^2 n$) time using O($n^2/\log^2 n$) processors.

Consider the 1-tree-loops generated by step 1 of the algorithm of subsection 2.2.2. These are described by a set of directed edges $(i, T(i))$, one from each vertex $i$. In fact, for the algorithm as modified in the last stages of its description, one from each pseudo-vertex $i$. Let $E'$ be the set of directed edges of such a 1-tree-loop and let $e \in E'$ be that directed edge from the vertex $j$ for which $C(j) = j$ after step 2 of the algorithm. Then, treating edges as being undirected, the set $E = E' - e$ forms a tree spanning the pseudo-vertices of the 1-tree-loop. This observation provides the algorithmic insight we need. Through it the algorithm can be made to construct a spanning tree inductively for each component of the graph. A set $E$ at a particular iteration spans pseudo-vertices generated in the previous iteration, and each of these pseudo-vertices has an associated spanning-tree of the (pseudo-) vertices absorbed into that pseudo-vertex and so on. Essentially, we therefore need to augment the algorithm with statements which on the one hand collect edges of the 1-tree loops over all iterations (by modifying step 1) and on the other hand perform some housekeeping. In particular, whenever the adjacency matrix is updated with an assignment such as $A(i, j) \leftarrow 1$, we must at the same time record one (there are possibly several) of the edges between the pseudo-vertices $i$ and $j$. Such an edge might be $(s, t)$ where $s$ and $t$ are vertices of the original graph and $s$ is presumed to have been absorbed into $i$ and $t$ into $j$. Should $(i, j)$ be an edge of a 1-tree-loop in the next iteration then $(s, t)$ becomes an edge of the spanning tree. It is a straightforward but tedious exercise to elaborate the modifications in encoded form, we therefore omit that detail. We illustrate the uncomplicated principle of the algorithm taking the graph of figure 2.2 as input. The set of 1-tree-loops generated by step 1 of the algorithm in the first iteration is shown in figure 2.3. Because in this first iteration $C(1) = 1$ and $C(2) = 2$ after step 2 of the algorithm, these 1-tree-loops give rise to the edges of figure 2.7 being included in the set of spanning tree edges. At the end of the first iteration the set of pseudo-vertices becomes $\{1, 2\}$ and the adjacency matrix update assigns $A(1, 2) = 1$ because we have that $A(4, 6) = 1$ and that $A(5, 6) = 1$ before the update. We suppose that, of the two edges $(4, 6)$ and $(5, 6)$, $(4, 6)$ is chosen to record proper endpoints of the edge between pseudo-vertices 1 and 2. The input to the second iteration is the graph induced by the pseudo-vertices 1 and

*Figure 2.7*

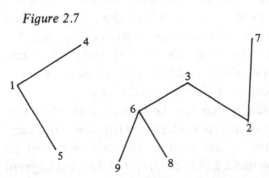

2. Step 1 then generates the 1-tree-loop consisting of the two (directed) edges $(1, 2)$ and $(2, 1)$. After step 2 in this iteration $C(1) = 1$ so that $(2, 1)$ becomes the spanning tree of the graph input to this final iteration. Because the endpoints of $(2, 1)$ are proper pseudo-vertices they have to be replaced by vertices of the original graph. The edge $(4, 6)$ was chosen for this purpose and so this edge is added to those in figure 2.7 to obtain the complete spanning tree of the original input.

### 2.2.4 MINIMUM-WEIGHT SPANNING FOREST

Given a weighted graph, we outline here a parallel algorithm to find a spanning forest (that is, a spanning tree for each component of the graph) such that the sum of the edge weights of the forest is a minimum. The algorithm is due to Sollin[9] and for its particularly effective implementation we follow Chin *et al.*[10] In fact the algorithm is an adaptation of the connected components algorithm and the algorithm to find a spanning tree. The input to the algorithm is the edge-weight matrix $M$.

The connected components algorithm is modified so that in step 1, instead of choosing an edge from each vertex to a neighbouring vertex with least numerical label, we choose that edge from each vertex which has least weight. Using an essentially similar argument to that employed at the end of step 1 of the connected components algorithm, we can see that a set of 1-tree-loops will also be obtained here. Otherwise, the algorithm proceeds essentially as the algorithm to find a spanning tree. The following lemma establishes the validity of the algorithm.

*Lemma 2.2*
The proposed algorithm finds a minimum-weight spanning forest.

*Proof*
The algorithm clearly finds a spanning tree for each component. We prove that for each component $G_c = (V_c, E_c)$ of the graph the spanning tree so constructed is of minimum weight. This is done by showing that, at each iteration, the edges added to the tree $T$ under construction belong to a tree of minimum weight. In the first iteration suppose that an edge $(i, j)$ from $i$ is added to $T$. We now see that the assumption that $(i, j)$ does not belong to a minimum-weight spanning tree leads to a contradiction. Let $T_m$ be a minimum-weight spanning tree which does not therefore contain $(i, j)$. There is precisely one path from $i$ to $j$ in $T_m$; let us denote this by $P$. Then $P + (i, j)$ forms a circuit containing another edge, say

$(i, k)$, from $i$. Now the algorithm chooses an edge of least weight from $i$ such that $w(i, j) \leqslant w(i, k)$. Let us consider the tree $T'_m = T_m - (i, k) + (i, j)$. We have that $w(T_m) \geqslant w(T'_m)$ because $w(i, j) \leqslant w(i, k)$, and so $T'_m$ must also be a tree of minimum weight. Thus we have a contradiction because $(i, j) \in T'_m$. The same argument can be applied at each successive stage so that on completion of the algorithm we have a minimum-weight spanning tree. That completes the proof.                                                                                          □

The algorithm has the same complexity and processor requirements as the two preceding algorithms and so we can find a minimum-weight spanning tree in $O(\log^2 n)$ time using $O(n^2/\log^2 n)$ processors.

For the purposes of illustrating the algorithm we again take as input the graph of figure 2.2 and add edge weights as follows: $w(1, 4) = 1$, $w(1, 5) = 2$, $w(2, 3) = 1$, $w(2, 7) = 3$, $w(3, 6) = 4$, $w(3, 7) = 9$, $w(4, 6) = 9$, $w(5, 6) = 10$, $w(6, 8) = 5$, $w(6, 9) = 5$ and $w(8, 9) = 6$. With these edge weights, the set of 1-tree-loops obtained after step 1 of the first iteration is again illustrated in figure 2.3. Thus figure 2.7 again shows the set of (weighted) tree edges added at this stage to the minimum-weight tree under construction. The input to the second iteration is, conceptually, the (weighted) graph induced by the set of pseudo-vertices output from the previous iteration, in this case the set $\{1, 2\}$. In updating the edge-weight matrix an edge chosen between pseudo-vertices $i$ and $j$ is an edge of minimum weight between these pseudo-vertices. In our example there are two edges between the pseudo-vertices 1 and 2, namely $(4, 6)$ and $(5, 6)$, and of these $(4, 6)$ has minimum weight. Thus $(4, 6)$ is chosen to provide proper endpoints for the edge connecting pseudo-vertices 1 and 2 before the second iteration. In this second and final iteration the only 1-tree-loop generated by step 1 consists of the (directed) edges $(1, 2)$ and $(2, 1)$. The edge $(2, 1)$ thus forms the weighted spanning tree (because $C(1) = 1$ after step 2) in this final iteration. Thus $(4, 6)$ is added to the edges of figure 2.7 to obtain the minimum-weight spanning tree of the example graph we took as input.

### 2.2.5 TWO-CONNECTED COMPONENTS OF A GRAPH

The algorithm we briefly outline here is due to Tarjan and Vishkin.[44] Given an undirected connected graph $G = (V, E)$ the algorithm first constructs any spanning tree $T$ of $G$. We have already described a suitable algorithm to find $T$. Using $T$ an auxiliary graph $G'$ is constructed. For every edge of $G$ there corresponds a vertex of $G'$ and the construction is such that two vertices of $G'$ are in the same connected component if and only if the corresponding two edges of $G$ are in the same block. The problem of finding the blocks of a graph is thus reduced to the problem of finding the connected components of some auxiliary graph, and for this we can use the algorithm described earlier. We shortly describe the construction of $G'$. In order to illustrate this we make use of the graph $G$ shown in figure 2.8(a); in (b) we see the blocks of $G$.

Central to our description is the construction of the auxiliary graph $G'$. We root $T$ (denoting the root by $r$) and label the vertices according to their preorder numbering which is found using a previously described algorithm. We similarly compute the number of descendants $nd(v)$, for each vertex $v$. We also compute the functions $low(v)$ and $high(v)$ for each vertex $v$: $low(v)$ is the lowest node adjacent to a descendant of $v$ (throughout 'a descendant of $v$' includes $v$) and $high(v)$ is the highest vertex adjacent to a descendant of $v$. For every edge of $G$ there is a corresponding (and similarly labelled) vertex of $G'$. There is a path between vertices of $G'$ if and only if the corresponding edges of $G$ lie on a common vertex-disjoint cycle. Any such cycle of $G$ can be expressed as the ring-sum of cycles from a cycle basis. As is well known, a cycle basis for $G$ is a set of cycles each member of which is formed by a non-tree edge $(i, j)$ and the unique path in (any spanning tree) $T$ between $i$ and $j$. With this background, and starting with no edges in $G'$, it can be seen that the following statements ensure that there is a path between vertices of $G'$ if and only if the corresponding edges of $G$ are in the same two-connected component.

1. **for** all non-tree edges $(u, w)$, $u < w$, $w \neq r$, **in parallel do** add $((u, w), (w, father(w)))$ to $G'$

Figure 2.8

G

The blocks of G

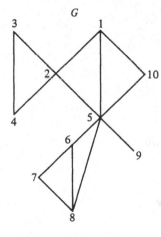

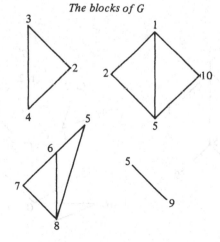

(a)                                        (b)

2. **for** all non-tree edges $(v, w)$, $v \neq r$, $w \neq r$ and of $v$ and $w$ neither is a descendant of the other, **in parallel do** add $((v, father(v)), (w, father(w)))$ to $G'$

3. **for** all tree edges $(v, w)$, $v \neq r$, $v < w$, and some edge of $G$ joins a descendant of $w$ with a non-descendant of $v$ $\{low(w) < v$ or $high(w) > v + nd(v)\}$, **in parallel do** add $((v, w), (v, father(v)))$ to $G'$

Figure 2.9(a) shows a spanning tree $T$ of our example graph $G$. Using the above rules to construct $G'$ we obtain this auxiliary graph as illustrated in figure 2.9(b). The cost of the algorithm is dominated by the cost of finding the spanning tree of $G$ and the connected components of $G'$. Hence we can find the blocks of a graph in $O(\log^2 n)$ time using $O(n^2/\log^2 n)$ processors on a P-RAM.

## 2.3 Eulerian circuits and maximal matchings

An Eulerian circuit of a graph is a circuit which traverses every edge of the graph precisely once. A graph containing an Eulerian circuit is called Eulerian. As is well known, an undirected connected graph $G$ is Eulerian if and only if the degree of every vertex of $G$ is even. Similarly, if $G$ is a connected digraph then $G$ is Eulerian provided that, for every vertex $v$, $indegree(v) = outdegree(v)$. In section 2.3.1 we describe an algorithm to find an Eulerian circuit of a graph, provided such a circuit exists. As we shall see, the algorithm is applicable both to directed and to undirected graphs. We use the Eulerian circuit algorithm in subsection 2.3.2 as a subprocedure in an algorithm which finds a maximal matching of a graph. A matching of a graph is a subset of its edges such that no

*Figure 2.9*

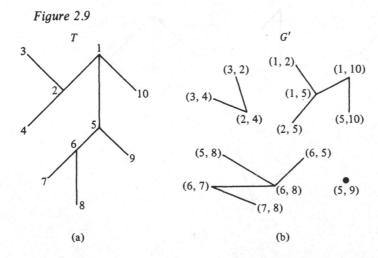

(a)                                                    (b)

two of the edges in the subset have a common endpoint. A maximal matching is a matching which is not a proper subset of any other matching. The description of the Eulerian circuit algorithm also includes a description of the algorithmically useful technique of obtaining a so-called Euler partition of a graph. An Euler partition is a partitioning of the edges of a graph into edge-disjoint cycles and paths. Numbering the edges alternately with 0 and 1 along these paths and cycles allows a decomposition of a graph into two graphs (the first (second) consists of the edges labelled 0 (1)) in each of which the maximum vertex degree is approximately halved. Recursive application of this technique has logarithmic depth and hence its algorithmic usefulness. This is exemplified in the algorithm which finds optimal vertex colourings of outerplanar graphs described in subsection 2.4.1.

### 2.3.1 EULERIAN CIRCUITS

Given a graph $G = (V, E)$, where $V = \{1, 2, \ldots, n\}$, the algorithm we describe finds an Eulerian circuit of $G$. The algorithm, due to Atallah and Vishkin,[6] was originally described using a different model of computation, namely a W-RAM. Therefore within that description (as we explicitly indicate at the end of our presentation) the time complexity is improved by a factor of $\log n$. The input is a list of the edges of the graph; these are stored in a vector called *EDGE* of dimension $m = |E|$. The algorithm presumes that the input is an Eulerian directed graph. For an undirected graph we can use the same algorithm, provided we undertake some preprocessing. We describe this preprocessing immediately, the object of which is to ascribe a direction to each edge of the Eulerian undirected graph in such a way that the resultant digraph is also Eulerian.

So, given an undirected graph $H = (V, E)$ we first obtain a digraph $H'$ by replacing each edge $(i, j)$ by two anti-parallel directed edges $(i, j)$ and $(j, i)$. $H'$ is stored as a set of edges in the vector *EDGE'* of dimension $2|E|$. We have to decide which of these two edges will replace $(i, j)$ of $H$. Notice that any vertex $v$ of $H$ will be of even degree because $H$ is Eulerian. Let the edges directed from $v$ in $H'$ be $(v, v_0), (v, v_1), \ldots, (v, v_{d-1})$, where $d$ is the outdegree of $v$. For the purpose of sorting the elements of *EDGE'* we define the minimum of two edges $(i, j)$ and $(k, l)$ to be $\min\{(i, j), (k, l)\} \leftarrow$ **if** $(i < k)$ **or** $(i = k$ **and** $j < i)$ **then** $(i, j)$ **else** $(k, l)$. After sorting, which takes $\log m$ time with $m$ processors (see chapter 5), the edges directed from $v$, for each $v$, will be in contiguous locations in *EDGE'*. Within each such set of contiguous locations we can easily add the auxiliary labels 0 to $d - 1$ on edges directed from (each) $v$ within the same complexity constraints. For each edge of $H'$ we now define a distinct successor, thus partitioning the edges into circuits. We use the vector $SUCCESSOR$, also of dimension $2|E|$, to record successor edges. For each odd number $i$ and each $v$ (in parallel) we set

$$SUCCESSOR((v_i, v)) \leftarrow (v, v_{i+1})$$

and

$$SUCCESSOR((v_{i+1}, v)) \leftarrow (v, v_i)$$

where the subscripts are modulo $d$. These assignments create a representation of a set of cycles such that, for every cycle $C$, there is an anti-parallel cycle $C'$. If for each $C$ we eliminate one of $C$ and $C'$ then we will have achieved our purpose, because it will then be the case that exactly one of $(i, j)$ and $(j, i)$ in $H'$ (for all $(i, j)$ in $H$) will have been eliminated and in such a way that for every vertex $v$ of $H'$ the outdegree of $v$ will equal its indegree. To this end, we first copy the vector $EDGE'$ into $EDGE''$ and then for each edge $e$ in parallel we execute the following.

> **repeat** $\log_2 m$ **times**
> **begin**
> $EDGE''(e) \leftarrow \min\{EDGE''(e), EDGE''(SUCCESSOR(e))\}$
> $SUCCESSOR(e) \leftarrow SUCCESSOR(SUCCESSOR(e))$
> **end**

where the operation min is as defined before. The effect of these operations is to place in $EDGE''(e)$ that edge of minimum value on the circuit containing $e$. For each edge $(i, j)$ in $EDGE'$ we now, in parallel, if $EDGE''((i, j)) > EDGE''((j, i))$ replace $(i, j)$ by 'null'. In this way one and only one of $(i, j)$ and $(j, i)$ is eliminated with the required effect that the remaining edges in $EDGE'$ describe an Eulerian digraph. To complete the preprocessing we need to clean up the representation by placing the non-null entries in $EDGE'$ into the vector $EDGE$ in readiness for processing by the main algorithm. This is easily done by associating the auxiliary values of 1 with non-null elements of $EDGE'$ and 0 with null elements. Then, for each non-null element, a parallel partial-sums computation (as described in chapter 1) establishes the location of $EDGE$ to which the non-null element of $EDGE'$ is to be assigned. The whole of this preprocessing for undirected graphs can be achieved in O($\log n$) time with $m$ processors.

We now describe the algorithm the input of which is presumed to be a digraph described by the set of edges stored in the array $EDGE$. We illustrate the algorithm with respect to the directed graph of figure 2.10.

*Step 1*

We obtain a lexicographic ordering of the elements of *EDGE* defined as follows. Given two edges $(i, j)$ and $(k, l)$ then $(i, j) < (k, l)$ if $j < l$ or $(j = l$ and $i < k)$. For our example graph, the vector *EDGE* becomes

| (2,1) | (4,1) | (3,2) | (7,2) | (1,3) | (6,3) | (3,4) | (5,4) | (1,5) | (6,5) | (2,6) | (4,6) | (5,7) |
|---|---|---|---|---|---|---|---|---|---|---|---|---|

We now take a copy of *EDGE* into a vector called *SUCCESSOR*, also of dimension *m*, and there reorder the elements according to the lexicographic order defined as $(i, j) < (k, l)$ if $i < k$ or $(i = k$ and $j < l)$. For our example, *SUCCESSOR* becomes

| (1,3) | (1,5) | (2,1) | (2,6) | (3,2) | (3,4) | (4,1) | (4,6) | (5,4) | (5,7) | (6,3) | (6,5) | (7,2) |
|---|---|---|---|---|---|---|---|---|---|---|---|---|

*EDGE* and *SUCCESSOR* together define a set of edge-disjoint cycles for any digraph. On any cycle, the edge following the edge stored in *EDGE(i)* is to be found in *SUCCESSOR(i)*. For our example the edges are thus partitioned into two edge-disjoint cycles, as is readily seen. For later computational clarity we associate a pointer *P(i)* with each address *SUCCESSOR(i)*. Here we initialise *P(i)* to point to *SUCCESSOR(j)* where *j* is the address in *EDGE* of the edge stored in *SUCCESSOR(i)*. This initialisation is very simply achieved. During the sorting process each edge (finally located at *SUCCESSOR(i)*) merely has to carry with it a record of its original position (*P(i)*) in the vector. In the chapter on sorting we see that *m* elements can be sorted in O(log *m*) time using *m* processors on a P-RAM. Thus overall this step of the algorithm takes O(log *n*) time (O(log *m*) = O(log *n*) because *m* is at most quadratic in *n*) using *m* processors.

*Figure 2.10*

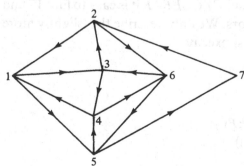

*Step 2*

In this step we construct an auxiliary graph in which some of the nodes represent the cycles output from step 1. For this reason we need to identify the cycle to which any edge belongs. We represent a cycle by one of its edges, namely that one of least lexicographic order (in the sense that $(i, j) < (k, l)$ if $i < k$ or if $(i = k$ and $j < l)$). We compute the required representation within the vector $CYCLEREP$. At the end of this step $CYCLEREP(i)$ will store the (edge representing the) cycle to which $EDGE(i)$ belongs. The following achieves our purpose.

> **for** all $i$, $1 \leqslant i \leqslant m$, **in parallel do** $CYCLEREP(i) \leftarrow SUCCESSOR(i)$
> > **repeat** $\log m$ **times**
> > > **for** $1 \leqslant i \leqslant m$ **in parallel do**
> > > > **begin**
> > > > $CYCLEREP(i) \leftarrow \min\{CYCLEREP(i), CYCLEREP(P(i))\}$
> > > > $P(i) \leftarrow P(P(i))$
> > > > **end**

For our example graph $CYCLEREP$ becomes

| (1,3) | (1,5) | (1,3) | (1,5) | (1,3) | (1,5) | (1,5) | (1,5) | (1,5) | (1,5) | (1,5) | (1,5) | (1,5) |
|---|---|---|---|---|---|---|---|---|---|---|---|---|

Using the standard doubling technique this takes $O(\log n)$ time using $m$ processors. We are now in a position to compute the main output from this step, namely a bipartite graph $G'$. By $C$ we denote the set of edges representing cycles which form the entries of $CYCLEREP$. In the following the members of $C$ play the role of nodes. If $V$ is the set of vertices of the graph input to the overall algorithm, then $G' = (V', E')$ is defined as follows:

$V' = V \cup C$
$E' = \{(u, v) \mid u \in V, v \in C$ and $u$ is in the circuit represented by $v\}$

For our example, $G'$ is shown in figure 2.11 which distinguishes the subsets of vertices $V$ and $C$. In fact, given $EDGE$ and $CYCLEREP$ it is easy to find $V'$ and $E'$ in $O(\log n)$ time using $O(m)$ processors. We only describe the (slightly more difficult) step of computing $E'$. We first execute

> **for** all $i$, $1 \leqslant i \leqslant m$, **in parallel do**
> > **for** $EDGE(i) = (u, v)$ **do**
> > > **begin**
> > > $EDGE'(2i - 1) \leftarrow (u, CYCLEREP(i))$
> > > $EDGE'(2i) \leftarrow (v, CYCLEREP(i))$
> > > **end**

which, in constant time, places in the vector $EDGE'$ (of dimension $2m$) the edges of $E'$. However, each such edge appears at least twice in the vector. This is because two consecutive edges on a given cycle have a vertex in common. The problem of copies of edges is further exacerbated because each member of $V$ may appear several times in a given cycle. In our example, the vertices 4, 5 and 6 each appear twice on the circuit represented by $(1, 5)$. We can eliminate copies of edges by first lexicographically sorting the contents of $EDGE'$. The effect of this is to place in contiguous locations of $EDGE'$ all copies of the same edge. We then eliminate copies by executing

**for all** $i$, $1 \leqslant i < 2m$, **in parallel do**
    **if** $EDGE'(i) = EDGE'(i + 1)$ **then** $EDGE(i) \leftarrow \infty$

where $\infty$ denotes an arbitrary value lexicographically greater than any member of $E'$. A further sorting of $EDGE'$ then places the elements of $E'$ in the first $|E'|$ addresses of $EDGE'$; these are then readily transferred to a vector of precise dimension.

As we have already indicated, for any $(u, v) \in E'$, $u$ may appear several times in $v$. Now step 3 of the algorithm requires, apart from $G'$, for every such $(u, v)$ one arbitrarily chosen representative edge $(i, u) = CERTIFICATE(u, v)$ on $v$, which 'certifies' the edge $(u, v)$. Again, a proper application of sorting easily renders $CERTIFICATE(e)$ for all $e \in E'$ and we therefore omit the details. Unless any vertex $u$ appears more than once on a given cycle $v$, $CERTIFICATE(u, v)$ can only be one edge. In our example there are just three vertices, 4, 5 and 6, which appear more than once on a given cycle, namely the cycle $(1, 5)$. In what follows we shall take $CERTIFICATE(4, (1, 5)) =$

*Figure 2.11*

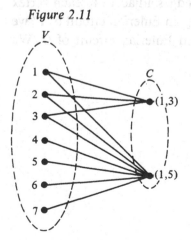

$(3, 4)$, $CERTIFICATE(5, (1, 5)) = (1, 5)$ and $CERTIFICATE(6, (1, 5)) = (2, 6)$.

Overall step 2 takes $O(\log n)$ time using $O(m)$ processors.

### Step 3

Here we first use the algorithm of subsection 2.2.3 to find a spanning tree $T$ of the bipartite graph $G'$ output from the previous step. This takes $O(\log^2 n)$ time using $O(n^2/\log^2 n)$ processors. For later purposes we take figure 2.12 to describe $T$ for our example input. We now define $T'$ to be the graph obtained from $T$ by replacing each edge $(i, j)$ by the two directed and anti-parallel edges $(i, j)$ and $(j, i)$. The graph $T'$ contains an Eulerian circuit because the indegree for each vertex equals its outdegree. In the next step of the algorithm an Eulerian circuit of $T'$ is established in the manner described in section 2.1.1 using the Euler tour technique on trees. In this respect notice that a traversal list of $T$ is equivalent to an Eulerian circuit of $T'$. We wish to find an Eulerian circuit of $T'$ with specific properties and for this reason we shall need to carefully specify a circular order of the edges adjacent to each vertex of $T'$ in the subset $C$.

### Step 4

In this step we compute a large cycle $L$ whose edges alternate between edges of $T'$ and edges of the graph $G$ input to the algorithm. The cycle $L$ will have the property that the edges of $G$ and the edges of $T'$ will both appear on $L$ in the order of, respectively, an Eulerian circuit of $G$ and an Eulerian circuit of $T'$. As the Euler tour technique on trees shows, as long as we define *any* circular order of edges adjacent to each vertex of $T'$ we obtain an Eulerian circuit of $T'$. We shall see that a particular circular order of those edges adjacent to each vertex $w$ in the subset $C$ of $T'$ ensures that in establishing an Eulerian circuit of $T'$ we also obtain $L$ with its embedding of the required Eulerian circuit of $G$. We

*Figure 2.12*

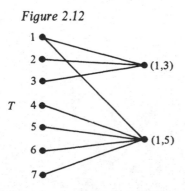

therefore now define this circular order for each such $w$. Consider then a particular $w$ of degree $d$ in $T$. By $(v_0, w)$, $(v_1, w)$, ..., $(v_{d-1}, w)$ we denote the edges adjacent to $w$ in $T$, where $v_0, v_1, \ldots, v_{d-1}$ are, of course, real vertices. On the cycle $w$, for $0 \leqslant \alpha \leqslant d - 1$, the edge $(i_\alpha, v_\alpha)$ denotes $CERTIFICATE(v_\alpha, w)$ and $(v_\alpha, j_\alpha)$ denotes $SUCCESSOR(i_\alpha, v_\alpha)$ after step 1 of the algorithm. We now modify the vectors $EDGE$ and $SUCCESSOR$ as output from step 1 so that they will describe $L$. We add to $EDGE$ the edges of $T'$ and, for each $w \in C$ and $0 \leqslant \alpha \leqslant d - 1$, we make the following assignments: $SUCCESSOR(v_\alpha, w) \leftarrow (v_\alpha, j_\alpha)$. We change each $SUCCESSOR(i_\alpha, v_\alpha)$ as output from step 1 as follows: $SUCCESSOR(i_\alpha, v_\alpha) \leftarrow (w, v_\alpha)$. The only undefined elements of $SUCCESSOR$ are now for the edges $(w, v_\alpha)$. In $T$, we take $v_\alpha$ to be adjacent to $w_0, w_1, \ldots, w_{d-1}$ in making the following assignments: $SUCCESSOR(w_i, v_\alpha) \leftarrow (v_\alpha, w_{i+1 \,(\mathrm{mod}\, d)})$. As we now show, the required cycle $L$ is at this point described by $EDGE$ and $SUCCESSOR$.

We can see that the assignments made to $EDGE$ and $SUCCESSOR$ implicitly provide a circular order to the edges adjacent to each vertex of $T'$ (in the spirit of the Euler tour technique) as follows. For each real vertex (that is, one not representing a cycle) this is trivially so. For each vertex $w$ representing a cycle, the implicit successor of $(v_\alpha, w)$ in $T'$ is obtained as follows. Tracing the path defined by $SUCCESSOR$, starting with $(v_\alpha, w)$, we proceed first to $(v_\alpha, j_\alpha)$ and then traverse edges around the cycle $w$ (as defined by $SUCCESSOR$) until an edge $(i_\beta, v_\beta)$ is encountered which is $CERTIFICATE(w, v_\beta)$ for some $(w, v_\beta) \in T$. It is possible that $(v_\alpha, j_\alpha) = (i_\beta, v_\beta)$. $SUCCESSOR$ then leads us from $(i_\beta, v_\beta)$ to $(w, v_\beta)$. Thus, in $T'$, the implicit successor to $(v_\alpha, w)$ is $(w, v_\beta)$. Since $w$ is a cycle, the method we have just described for determining the implicit successor of any edge $(v_\alpha, w)$ of $T'$ describes also a circular order of the edges about $w$ in the spirit of the Euler tour technique on trees. It follows that $L$ will contain the edges of $T'$ in the order of an Eulerian circuit. Now consider that digraph which is $T'$ except that each circuit $w$ is expanded into the circuit defined by $SUCCESSOR$ after step 1; here we take the edges from and to $v$ of $T'$ which is not a circuit vertex to be to and from that copy of $v$ on $w$ which is the endpoint of $CERTIFICATE(v, w)$. For our example input this graph, and the cycle $L$, are shown schematically in figure 2.13. The expanded cycle vertices $(1, 3)$ and $(1, 5)$ are indicated by sequences of dashed edges which we understand are directed around the cycles in clockwise fashion. Every edge of the input $G$ appears on precisely one of these cycles each of which is partitioned into segments entered by an edge $(v_\alpha, w)$ and left by an edge $(w, v_\beta)$, where $v_\alpha$ and $v_\beta$ are real vertices of $T'$. Now because $L$ contains the edges of $T'$ in the order of an Eulerian circuit, it follows that in $L$ each (and all) of these segments of circuit edges is not traversed a second time until all of the other segments have been traversed. It therefore also follows that the edges of the input graph *G* are contained in *L* in the order of an Eulerian circuit.

Step 4 of the algorithm, namely the augmentation of *EDGE* and *SUCCESSOR* which now describe *L*, takes constant time with *n* processors.

### Step 5

In this final step of the algorithm we erase from *L* the edges of *T'*, so leaving the desired Eulerian circuit of the input graph *G*. This is easily accomplished by noting that the edges of *T'* only come in consecutive pairs within the cycle *L*. Thus our purpose is achieved by executing the following.

> **repeat 2 times**
> > **for** all $e \in EDGE$ **in parallel do**
> > > **if** $SUCCESSOR(e) \in T'$ **then**
> > > > $SUCCESSOR(e) \leftarrow SUCCESSOR(SUCCESSOR(e))$

This takes constant time with $O(m)$ processors and completes our description of the algorithm.

Overall the implementation of the algorithm as we have described it requires $O(\log^2 n)$ time using $O(m)$ processors on a CREW P-RAM. In the original description of Atallah and Vishkin[6] an $O(\log n)$ time is achieved in a different model of the computation, namely a W-RAM. The only difference from the

*Figure 2.13*

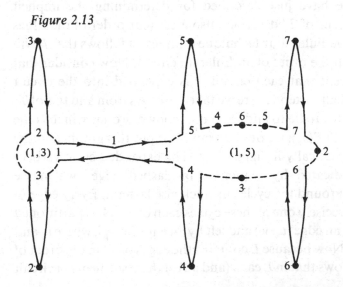

algorithmic description point of view is that, within the W-RAM model, an $O(\log n)$ procedure to find a spanning tree of the graph $T$ can be used at step 3. The spanning tree procedure was described by Tarjan and Vishkin in [44].

### 2.3.2 MAXIMAL MATCHINGS

We describe an algorithm due to Israeli and Shiloach[24] which finds a maximal matching of a graph given its adjacency list representation. The complexity of the algorithm is essentially determined by the use of a subprocedure to find Eulerian circuits (subsection 2.3.1). Their description is within the W-RAM model of computation which provides a time-complexity of $O(\log^3 m)$ with $m + n$ processors, whilst within the P-RAM model (see the brief discussion at the end of the last section) we require $O(\log^4 m)$ time.

The algorithm consists of at most $\log_{3/2} n$ phases. We denote the $i$th phase by $F_i$. The input to $F_i$ is a graph $G_i$ for which a matching $M_i$ (which is not necessarily maximal) is found; then $G_{i+1}$ is constructed from $G_i$ by removing the edges of $M_i$ and all their incident edges. The final maximal matching is the accumulation of the edges in all the $M_i$. The input to the initial phase is the graph for which we are to find a maximal matching. Our algorithmic description concentrates on the so-called *DEGREE SPLIT* procedure because each phase of the algorithm consists of at most $1 + \lceil \log \Delta(G) \rceil$ applications of *DEGREE SPLIT*. Here $G$ is the graph input to the phase and $\Delta(G)$ is the maximum vertex degree of $G$. We need the following definition before describing the procedure *DEGREE SPLIT*. If $k$ is the smallest integer (there are in fact at most two) satisfying $2^k \leqslant \Delta(G) \leqslant 2^{k+1} + 1$ then an active vertex of $G$ is defined to be any vertex $v$ for which $d(v) \geqslant 2^k$. Notice that $k = \lfloor \log \Delta(G) - 2 \rfloor$.

### The procedure DEGREE SPLIT

$G(i, j)$ denotes the graph input to the $j$th application of this procedure within the $i$th phase of the algorithm. Thus $G(1, 1)$ is the graph input to the algorithm. We presume $G(i, j)$ to be in adjacency list representation.

### Step 1

The active vertices of $G(i, j)$ are found. This is achieved by first finding in parallel the degree $d(v)$ of each vertex $v$ of the graph using the method of recursive doubling on the adjacency list for each $v$. This takes $O(\log(\Delta(G(i, j))))$ time using $O(m)$ processors, where $\Delta(G(i, j))$ is the maximum vertex degree of $G(i, j)$. The maximum degree is then found in $\log n$ time using $n$ processors, also by recursive doubling along a vector containing the $d(v)$. Overall this step takes $O(\log n)$ time using $O(m)$ processors.

### Step 2

The graph $G^*(i, j)$ is constructed. This graph is constructed as follows. We first obtain that graph induced by all those edges of $G(i, j)$ for which at least one endpoint is an active vertex (in constant time using $m$ processors), then for every vertex of odd degree in this graph (if there be any) we add an edge to an introduced vertex $v$. Here the degrees of the vertices are found as in step 1. The result is $G^*(i, j)$. Notice that $G^*(i, j)$ need not be a connected graph and that each component of $G^*(i, j)$ contains an Eulerian circuit because the construction ensures that every vertex has even degree. This observation depends upon an elementary theorem of graph theory that the number of vertices of odd degree in any graph is even. Overall this step takes $\log n$ time and $m$ processors.

### Step 3

Use the algorithm of subsection 2.3.1 to find in parallel an Eulerian circuit of each component of $G^*(i, j)$. This takes $O(\log^2 n)$ time and $m + n$ processors. The bound on the number of processors arises from the fact that $G^*(i, j)$ may have $m + n$ edges, the (possible) additional $n$ are those with the introduced vertex $v$ as endpoint.

### Step 4

Tracing the Eulerian circuit in each component of $G^*(i, j)$ label the edges 0 and 1 alternately. In any component not containing $v$ we start at any vertex and label the first edge with 1. In the component containing $v$ (if it exists) we start the trace at $v$ and begin the labelling with 0. This step can be implemented in $\log m$ time using $m$ processors. For example, we can use a partial-sums computation (chapter 1) to rank the edges in each Eulerian circuit in parallel and then we label odd edges (in this ranking) with one label and even edges with the other.

### Step 5

In this final step we remove the edges of $G(i, j)$ which become labelled with a 0 in step 4. If the graph resulting from this removal of edges is not a matching then it is $G(i, j + 1)$, otherwise it is $M_i$. This step takes constant time with $m$ processors.

Overall each application of the procedure *DEGREE SPLIT* takes $O(\log^2 n)$

time using $m + n$ processors. Before completing the description of the algorithm and verifying it, we illustrate one phase of the algorithm. In particular we shall apply the procedure *DEGREE SPLIT* to the graph $G(1, 1)$ of figure 2.14 and we repeat this process until a matching is produced. Applying *DEGREE SPLIT* to this graph we obtain the active vertices in step 1. These are 1, 3, 4, 5 and 9 because $\Delta(G(1, 1)) = 6$ and thus $k = 2$. Step 2 yields the graph $G^*(1, 1)$ shown in figure 2.15. Also shown there are the Eulerian circuits for each component (denoted by EC under each component) as established in step 3. In the figure the edges drawn from vertices of odd degree to the introduced vertex $v$ are indicated by dashed lines. The alternate labelling of the edges with 0 and 1 as required in step 4 is also shown in figure 2.15. Step 5 of the procedure now produces $G(1, 2)$ which is shown in figure 2.16. Now $G(1, 2)$ is input to *DEGREE SPLIT*. Every vertex of this graph will be active because $\Delta(G(1, 2)) = 3$, $k = 0$ and the degree of every vertex lies between 1 and 3. The graph $G^*(1, 2)$ is shown in figure 2.17. Also shown there is an Eulerian circuit (EC) and the corresponding alternate labelling of the edges with 0 and 1 as required. Figure 2.18(a) shows $G(1, 3)$, the graph obtained by the removal of those edges labelled 0 from $G(1, 2)$. We now submit $G(1, 3)$ to the procedure *DEGREE SPLIT* because a matching has not yet been obtained. Again, every

*Figure 2.14*

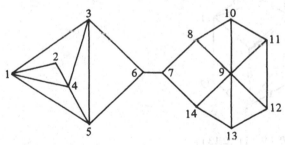

*Figure 2.15*

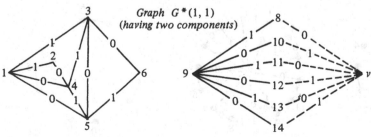

Graph $G^*(1, 1)$
(*having two components*)

EC = ( 1 3 6 5 3 4 2 1 4 5 1)       EC = ($v$ 8 9 10 $v$ 11 9 12 ... 14 $v$)

vertex is active and $G^*(1, 2)$ is shown in figure 2.18(b). Also shown in that figure is the alternate labelling of edges with 0 and 1; here we take the Eulerian circuit to be the sequence of clockwise loops back to $V$ starting $(V\,1\,2\,V\,3\,\ldots)$. The output to this application of *DEGREE SPLIT*, obtained by removing the edges labelled 0 in figure 2.18(b) from the graph $G(1, 3)$, is the required matching from this phase as shown in figure 2.18(c).

*Figure 2.16*

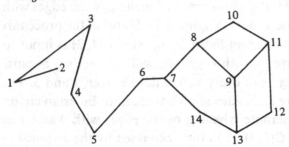

*Figure 2.17*

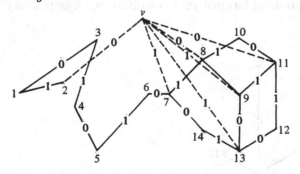

EC = $(v\,2\,1\,3\,4\,5\,6\,7\,v\,8\,7\,14\,13\,9\,11\,10\,8\,9\,v\,11\,12\,13\,v)$

*Figure 2.18*

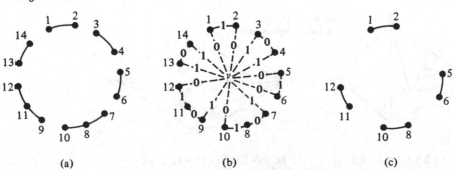

(a)                          (b)                          (c)

Before proceeding further with our example, we investigate the number of applications of *DEGREE SPLIT* that are required in order that the graph input to one phase of the algorithm is reduced to a matching.

*Lemma 2.3*

If $G$ is the graph input to a phase of the algorithm then at most $1 + \lceil \log \Delta(G) \rceil$ applications of *DEGREE SPLIT* are required to produce a matching.

*Proof*

$G$ is a graph such that $2^k \leqslant \Delta(G) \leqslant 2^{k+1} + 1$ for some (smallest) integer $k$. Let $G_1$ denote the graph output from a single application of *DEGREE SPLIT*. If $v$ is an active vertex of $G$ we then have that $2^{k-1} \leqslant d_{G_1}(v) \leqslant 2^k + 1$ because, in all cases, as is easily seen,

$$\lfloor d_G(v)/2 \rfloor \leqslant d_{G_1}(v) \leqslant \lfloor d_G(v)/2 \rfloor + 1$$

It also follows that all of the vertices that are active in $G$ remain active in $G_1$. Moreover, if $G_j$ denotes the graph output after $j$ applications of *DEGREE SPLIT*, then they remain active for all $j$, $1 \leqslant j \leqslant k$. For every active vertex $v$ in $G_k$ we have that $1 \leqslant d_{G_k}(v) \leqslant 3$ and since $\Delta(G_k) \leqslant 3$ every vertex with non-zero degree must be active. Only two more (at most) applications of *DEGREE SPLIT* are then required to reduce the degree of each vertex to at most 1 thus yielding a matching. Given the previously stated value of $k$ the lemma then follows.     □

Before showing that a logarithmic number of phases are sufficient to produce a maximal matching for any graph, we proceed to produce a maximal matching for our example. One more phase of the algorithm will be sufficient. We accumulate edges for the final matching from each phase. In this respect the first phase produced the edge set $\{(1,2),(5,6),(8,10),(11,12)\}$. The input to the second and final phase is obtained by removing edges in this set together with their incident edges from the graph $G(1,1)$. This graph, $G(2,1)$, is shown in figure 2.19(a). All vertices are active in this graph and $G^*(2,1)$ is shown in figure 2.19(b). Also shown there is an Eulerian circuit (EC) with the corresponding alternate labelling of the edges with 0 and 1. The graph obtained by removing these edges which are labelled 0 from $G(2,1)$ is shown in figure 2.19(c). This graph is a matching and so the second phase is complete. The edge set $\{(3,4),(7,14),(9,13)\}$ is added to the maximal matching under construction. Moreover there can be no more phases required because if we subtract these edges along with their incident edges from $G(2,1)$ we obtain an empty graph.

Thus the final maximal matching is given by the edge set $\{(1,2), (5,6), (8,10),$ $(11,12), (3,4), (13,14)\}$.

In order to complete our description of the algorithm we have to show that a logarithmic number of phases will be sufficient to find a maximal matching. By $G_j$ we denote the graph input to $F_j$, the $j$th phase. The essence of the proof is to show that if $G_{i+1}$ is not an empty graph then it has a vertex cover $C_{i+1}$ which satisfies $|C_{i+1}| \leqslant 2|C_i|/3$. Taking $C_1 = V$, it will then follow that $|C_i| = 0$ when $i = \log_{3/2}|V|$. In other words, after a logarithmic number of phases, $G_i$ will have no edges.

### Theorem 2.1

A logarithmic number of phases of the maximal matching algorithm are sufficient to produce a maximal matching.

### Proof

By $A_i$ we denote the set of vertices which become active during $F_i$. From within the proof of lemma 2.3 we note that $A_i$ is precisely the set of vertices which are active within the $k$th application of *DEGREE SPLIT* in the $i$th phase. It follows that $A_i$ is a vertex cover of $G_i$ because, if this were not the case, there would exist some edge $(u, v)$ such that neither $u$ nor $v$ become active during $F_i$. But this is a contradiction because in any phase, as we pointed out in the proof of lemma 2.2, every vertex with non-zero degree is active in the $k$th application of *DEGREE SPLIT*. Before showing that there exists a vertex cover $C_{i+1}$ which satisfies $|C_{i+1}| \leqslant 2|C_i|/3$, we first need to see that at least half the vertices of the particular vertex cover $A_i$ can be made to be incident with edges of $M_i$. In other words, if $A_i/G_{i+1}$ denotes the subset of $A_i$ in $G_{i+1}$, we first prove that we can ensure that $|A_i/G_{i+1}| \leqslant |A_i|/2$.

In the $i$th phase, the matching $M_i$ is produced after two more applications of *DEGREE SPLIT* to the graph $G^k$ produced after the $k$th application. Without

*Figure 2.19*

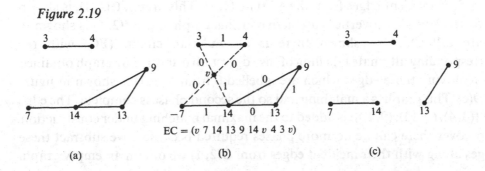

$EC = (v\ 7\ 14\ 13\ 9\ 14\ v\ 4\ 3\ v)$

(a)                          (b)                          (c)

loss of generality we can take $G^k$ to be a connected graph. We modify *DEGREE SPLIT* in these last two applications in the following way. Instead of removing the edges labelled 0, we remove whichever constitutes the smaller set: the edges labelled 0 or the edges labelled 1. This guarantees that $|M_i| \geqslant |E^k|/4$, where $E^k$ is edge set of $G^k$. If $|E^k| \geqslant |A_i|$ then $M_i$ contains at least $|A_i|/4$ edges, both endpoints of each belong to $A_i$ and so at least half of the vertices of $A_i$ are incident with edges of $M_i$. If $|E^k| < |A_i|$ then $G^k$ is a tree (it is connected). In this case we remove any edge from $G^k$ (along with its adjacent edges) which has a leaf as an endpoint and add this edge to $M_i$. Now since $\Delta(G^k) \leqslant 3$ this removal creates at most two trees from $G^k$. We denote these by $T_1$ and $T_2$, where $T_1$ has $n_1$ vertices and $T_2$ has $n_2$. If $T_1$ and $T_2$ are each subjected to the modified procedure *DEGREE SPLIT*, then together they contribute at least $((n_1 - 1) + (n_2 - 1))/4$ edges to $M_i$. Hence, together with the vertices of the first edge, we have at least $|A_i|/2$ vertices in $M_i$. Thus we have seen that by modifying the last two applications of *DEGREE SPLIT* we can ensure that $|A_i/G_{i+1}| \leqslant |A_i|/2$.

We now prove that for all $i$, $1 \leqslant i \leqslant \log_{3/2}|V|$, the graph $G_i$ has a vertex cover $C_i$ satisfying $|C_i| \leqslant (\frac{2}{3})^{i-1}|V|$. This we do by induction on $i$, proving that $|C_{i+1}| \leqslant 2|C_i|/3$. For $i = 1$ we take $|C_i| = |V|$ which provides a basis for the induction. As the induction hypothesis we assume the statement to be true for $i$ ($> 1$) and show that it follows for $i + 1$. We consider two cases. The first is that $|A_i| \leqslant 4|C_i|/3$. Now, as we have seen, at the end of the *ith* phase at least half the vertices in $A_i$ are removed. The result then follows immediately because $A_i/G_{i+1}$ is a vertex cover of $G_{i+1}$ with the claimed property: $|A_i/G_{i+1}| \leqslant |A_i|/2 \leqslant (4|C_i|/3)/2 = 2|C_i|/3$. The second case is that $|A_i| \leqslant 4|C_i|/3$. Again at least half of the vertices of $A_i$ are removed at the end of the *ith* phase and these are those vertices which are endpoints of edges in $M_i$. Now $C_i$ is a vertex cover of $G_i$ and so at least one endpoint of every edge of $M_i$ is a member of $C_i$. It follows that at least one quarter of the edges of $A_i$ are in $C_i$. Now $C_i/G_{i+1}$ is a vertex cover of $G_{i+1}$ with the claimed property because $|C_i/G_{i+1}| \leqslant |C_i| - |A_i|/4 \leqslant |C_i| - (4|C_i|/3)/4 = 2|C_i|/3$. That completes the proof of the theorem. □

Given that each application of the procedure *DEGREE SPLIT* takes $O(\log^2 n)$ time using $m + n$ processors, that each phase of the algorithm requires at most $1 + \lceil \log \Delta(G) \rceil$ applications of *DEGREE SPLIT* (lemma 2.2) and that a logarithmic number of phases are required (theorem 2.1) we see that we have overall an $O(\log^4 n)$ algorithm in the P-RAM model of computation.

## 2.4 Colouring of graphs

In this section we describe a number of algorithms concerned with the
colouring of the vertices or the edges of various classes of graphs. In such
colourings it is understood that the vertices (edges) are to be coloured in such a
way that no two adjacent vertices (edges) are to be similarly coloured and that
within this constraint we are concerned to minimise the number of colours
used. If the number of colours used is the smallest possible, then the colouring
is said to be optimal. As is well known, the question of how to produce optimal
or near optimal colourings is often of interest in problems of scheduling or
timetabling.

We shall see several examples of a general approach to designing fast parallel
algorithms for problems dealing with well-structured objects. The approach is
to reflect their structure in the divide-and-conquer technique in such a way that
the resulting algorithms are recursive. The first step in the technique is a
decomposition of the input graph into similarly structured graphs whose sizes
are some constant proportion (less than 1) of the size of the input graph. The
second step is a recursive and parallel application of the same algorithm to
each of the new graphs *independently*. This independence may result in some
inconsistencies between graphs when the input graph is reconstructed. In these
colouring algorithms the inconsistencies might, for example, be that different
colours have been assigned to different copies (in separate graphs) of the same
vertex or edge. The third step of the algorithm removes these inconsistencies by
making suitable adjustments to the colouring of (some of) the graphs which are
to be recombined. The classes of graphs for which we use this approach are
bipartite, outerplanar and Halin graphs. As we shall see, for each of these
classes it is possible to take a member of the class and to decompose it into two
or more smaller examples of the same class. Thus these graphs are well suited
to the algorithmic approach we have outlined.

A bipartite graph is a graph $G = (V, E)$ for which it is possible to partition the
vertices into two subsets $V_1$ and $V_2$, where $V_1 \cup V_2 = V$ and $V_1 \cap V_2 = \varnothing$, such
that there is no edge with both endpoints in $V_1$ or both endpoints in $V_2$. An
outerplanar graph has a planar embedding in which all the vertices appear on
the boundary of a single face. Without loss of generality we can take this to be
the external face because an elementary theorem provides that given any face $f$
of a planar embedding there exists another embedding in which $f$ is the
external face. A Halin graph is planar and consists of a tree $T$ with no vertices
of degree 2 and a circuit $C$ (called the skirt) which consists precisely of a
sequence of all the leaf vertices of $T$.

We can construct a graph in which each vertex corresponds to an internal face of a particular outerplanar graph and which has an edge between such face vertices if and only if the corresponding faces are adjacent. The graph so constructed is a tree and is a partial dual of the outerplanar graph. (In fact it is the graph obtained from the dual by deleting the vertex corresponding to the external face of the outerplanar graph.) Algorithmically, we take advantage of this so-called *tree of faces* when colouring outerplanar graphs.

It is well known that the minimum number of colours with which it is possible to edge-colour a graph so that no two adjacent edges are similarly coloured is either $\Delta$ or $\Delta + 1$, depending upon the graph. Throughout this section $\Delta$ is the maximum vertex degree of the graph. The problem of determining whether or not a graph is $\Delta$-edge-colourable is *NP*-hard.[22] However, it is known that bipartite, outerplanar and Halin graphs (except for odd cycles) are all $\Delta$-edge-colourable. We shall see that the problems of finding optimal edge colourings of bipartite, Halin and outerplanar graphs are in *NC*. The problem of optimally vertex-colouring an arbitrary graph is also well known to be *NP*-hard. However, polynomial-time sequential algorithms are known for the classes of graph mentioned. We shall see that the problems of optimally vertex-colouring the classes of graphs mentioned are also in *NC*. Notice that a tree is a special case of a bipartite graph. However, as we shall also see, especially efficient algorithms are possible for optimal colouring of trees.

## 2.4.1 EDGE-COLOURING OF BIPARTITE GRAPHS

The algorithm we outline, essentially a parallelisation of that described by Gabow and Kariv,[16] finds an optimal edge-colouring for any bipartite graph. The key subalgorithm employed here also happens to be our first example to use the divide-and-conquer approach outlined earlier.

We first describe this key subalgorithm which is designed to find an optimal edge-colouring for a bipartite graph whose maximum degree, $\Delta$, is an integral power of 2. Such a graph $G$ may be recursively divided into two bipartite graphs $G_1$ and $G_2$ both of which have maximum degrees which are also integral powers of 2. In one such decomposition, the maximum degree of the input graph is exactly halved in the two graphs which are output. This is achieved using a so-called Euler partition of the graph. Every graph has an Euler partition, that is a partition of the edges of the graph into edge-disjoint paths and cycles so that each vertex of odd degree is the endpoint of exactly one path. We can find such a partition for a connected graph $G$ in $\log n$ parallel time using $O(m)$ processors. If $G$ is Eulerian we can employ the method described in (the preamble to and including) step 1 of the algorithm to find an Eulerian circuit. This produces a partitioning of the edges into edge-disjoint cycles. If $G$ is not Eulerian we add a dummy vertex $v$ and an edge from $v$ to each vertex of odd degree to get a graph $G^*$. We then obtain a partitioning of the edges of $G^*$ into edge-disjoint cycles, then if we drop the edges added in constructing $G^*$ from $G$ (possibly only some of) these cycles become paths. The graphs $G_1$ and $G_2$ are then obtained by labelling edges 0 or 1 alternately along each path and cycle using the technique of recursive doubling. This takes $O(\log n)$ time using $O(m)$ processors. All edges labelled 0 constitute $G_1$ and those labelled 1 form $G_2$. Assume now that, recursively, $G_1$ and $G_2$ are coloured and each uses the $\Delta/2$ colours denoted by $1, 2, 3, \ldots, \Delta/2$. In reconstructing $G$ we obtain a $\Delta$-colouring (and remove colouring inconsistencies) by renaming the colours for $G_2$ simply by numerically adding the number $\Delta/2$ to the colour assigned to each of its edges in parallel constant time. A recursive outline of the Euler-colouring procedure which produces an optimal edge-colouring of a bipartite graph in which $\Delta$ is an integral power of 2 is thus provided by

> **procedure** *Euler-colour*$(G)$
> **begin**
> $\{G$ has maximum degree $\Delta\}$
> **if** $\Delta = 1$ **then** colour all edges of $G$ with the colour 1 **else**
>   **begin**
>   find an Euler partition of $G$
>   using the Euler partition divide $G$ into two graphs $G_1$ and $G_2$ with
>       maximal degrees $\Delta/2$
>   **for** $G = G_1$ and $G = G_2$ **in parallel do** *Euler-colour*$(G)$
>   reconstruct $G$ from $G_1$ and $G_2$ renaming colours in $G_1$ so that $G_1$
>       and $G_2$ use disjoint colour sets
>   **end**
> **end**

Provided $\Delta$ is an integral power of 2, the procedure clearly produces a $\Delta$-edge-colouring which is optimal. Also the recursion has depth $\log_2 n$ and so overall the procedure takes $O(\log^2 n)$ time using $O(m)$ processors. Figure 2.20 illustrates (from left to right) one decomposition stage of the algorithm for an example graph whose maximum degree is an integral power of 2. The edges of $G_1$ are the dashed edges. After one more recursive call of the procedure *Euler-colour*, each of $G_1$ and $G_2$ uses the colour set $\{1, 2\}$. The colours in $G_2$ are automatically renamed 3 and 4 by adding $\Delta/2$ to the colour of each edge.

We now make use of the procedure *Euler-colour* to optimally edge-colour any bipartite graph. By $d$ we denote the maximal power of 2 not exceeding $\Delta$. During the course of the algorithm the set of edges $E$ is partitioned into two sets $C$ (of coloured edges) and $U$ (of uncoloured edges). Initially $E = U$. The algorithm essentially consists of a **while** statement and each iteration of its body enlarges a partial $\Delta$-colouring of the graph. Within each iteration a subgraph $G'$ of maximum degree $d$ is constructed. We edge-colour $G'$ using *Euler-colour*. Now, as we shall see, we can ensure that $G'$ contains at least a certain constant proportion of uncoloured edges and so all edges of the graph become coloured after a logarithmic number of iterations. By an $\alpha\beta$ colouring of an (uncoloured) edge $(i, j)$ we mean assigning the colour $\alpha$ to $(i, j)$ at $i$ and the colour $\beta$ to $(i, j)$ at $j$. A pairwise colouring in any iteration is an $\alpha\beta$ colouring of all the (uncoloured) edges such that no colour appears more than once at any vertex (taking edges previously coloured together with current $\alpha\beta$ colourings). Given the adjacency list for each vertex such a colouring is easily achieved locally at each vertex in $\log n$ parallel time with $O(m)$ processors. For some uncoloured edges this may mean (legitimately) that $\alpha = \beta$, if this happens we take the edge to be coloured $\alpha$. We can now enlarge on the details of the algorithm as follows.

**Algorithm** {to edge-colour a bipartite graph}
**begin**
**while** $U$ is non-empty **do**
  **begin**
    1.  pairwise colour the graph

Figure 2.20

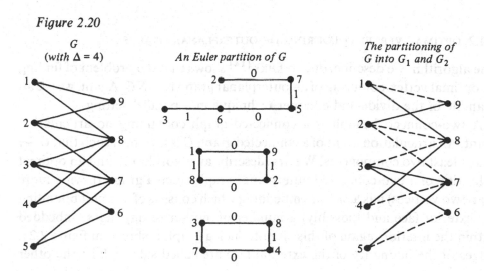

2.  find the set $S$ of at most $d$ colours such that at least $\frac{1}{6}$ of the uncoloured edges are assigned a colour pair $\alpha\beta$ with both $\alpha, \beta \in S$

3.  erase all (pairs of) colours $\alpha\beta$ on uncoloured edges if $\alpha \notin S$ or $\beta \notin S$ {these edges will not be coloured in this iteration}

4.  {Let $G'$ denote the subgraph of $G$ containing each edge whose colours (either a single colour assigned in a previous iteration or both $\alpha$ and $\beta$ from the current pairwise colouring) are in $S$} erase all colours in $G'$ and edge-colour $G'$ (obtaining a $d$-colouring) using *Euler-colour*, if the maximal degree of $G'$ is less than $d$ then add some dummy edges to $G'$

**end**

**end**

We presume for the moment that the set $S$ in step 2 exists; then the set $U$ is reduced in each iteration by a factor of $\frac{1}{6}$. Thus a logarithmic number of iterations of the **while** statement body are sufficient to obtain a complete colouring. In each iteration we apply the procedure *Euler-colour* and so overall (assuming that finding $S$ is not too costly) the algorithm requires $O(\log^3 n)$ time using $O(m)$ processors. Consider now the existence and the computation of $S$. Divide the set of $\Delta$ colours, $\{1, \ldots, \Delta\}$, into four subsets $S_i, i = 1, 2, 3$ and $4$. The $S_i$ are all of the same size (or their sizes differ by at most 1 if $\Delta$ is not a multiple of 4). There are 6 pairs $(S_i, S_j)$ of distinct sets. Hence there must exist a pair of sets $(S_i, S_j)$ such that at least $\frac{1}{6}$ of the pairwise coloured edges with $\alpha \neq \beta$ have $\alpha \in S_i$ and $\beta \in S_j$. We set $S \leftarrow S_i \cup S_j$. The set $S$ has at most $d$ colours because, for any $i$ and $j$, $|S_i| + |S_j| \leqslant d$. Moreover, it is easy to compute $S$ in $O(\log n)$ time using $O(m)$ processors.

### 2.4.2 OPTIMAL VERTEX-COLOURING OF OUTERPLANAR GRAPHS

The algorithm we describe, due to Diks,[14] shows that the problem of finding an optimal vertex-colouring of an outerplanar graph is in $NC$. Again, we see an example of the divide-and-conquer technique in a parallel setting.

A two-connected graph is a connected graph containing no articulation point. An articulation point of a connected graph $G$ is a vertex $i$ such that $G - i$ has at least two components. We first describe an algorithm to find an optimal colouring of a two-connected outerplanar graph. Such a graph (having more than two vertices) has a planar embedding which consists of a circuit bounding the exterior face and (possibly) a number of (non-crossing) edges embedded within the interior region of this circuit. Such a graph is shown in figure 2.21. Edges of the boundary of the external face are called sides, whilst the other edges are called diagonals. As is easily seen, for such a graph with $n$ vertices and $m$ edges, $m \leqslant 2n - 3$. Also such a graph has just one Hamiltonian circuit (that is, a circuit passing precisely once through each of the vertices) which is simply the circuit bounding the external face. For convenience we call two-connected outerplanar graphs (with $n$ vertices) $n$-gons.

*Procedure to optimally colour n-gons*

The input to the procedure consists of the set of edges (sides and diagonals undistinguished) of the $n$-gon stored in a vector of dimension $m$. The output is, for every vertex $i$, the colour of that vertex given by *colour*$(i)$. In step 1 we find the outerplanar realisation of the $n$-gon. Specifically, we compute that permutation of the vertices which corresponds to the order in which they appear around the boundary of the external face.

*Step 1.1*

In this step we determine which of the edges are sides. The following observation allows this to be done in an efficient manner. The edge $e = (i, j)$ is a side of the $n$-gon $G$ if and only if $G - \{i, j\}$ is connected. The following achieves our purpose.

> **for** all edges $(i, j)$ **in parallel do**
>     **if** $G - \{i, j\}$ is connected **then** in the vector of edges mark $(i, j)$ as a side

Each $G - \{i, j\}$ can be constructed in constant time with $n$ processors and for each the test for connectedness can be achieved in $O(\log^2 n)$ time using $O(n^2/\log^2 n)$ processors using the algorithm described earlier in this chapter. In fact that algorithm produces an array $C$ such that $C(i) = C(j)$ if and only if vertices $i$ and $j$ are in the same component. For each test the (strictly)

*Figure 2.21*

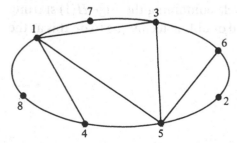

additional step required to check for connectedness, namely that $C(i) = C(j)$ for all $i$, is easily achieved in constant time with $n$ processors. Since $m \leqslant 2n - 3$, overall this step takes $O(\log^2 n)$ time using $O(n^3/\log^2 n)$ processors on a P-RAM.

## Step 1.2

In this step we construct two anti-parallel (directed) Hamiltonian cycles of the $n$-gon. Given the vector of edges (with sides marked in step 1.1) we first, in constant time with $n$ processors, construct the vector $H$ which has twice the length and which for each edge $(i, j)$ contains the anti-parallel edges $(i, j)$ and $(j, i)$, each marked if $(i, j)$ happens to be a side edge. We now lexicographically order the elements of $H$ in $O(\log n)$ time using $O(n)$ processors employing the algorithm described in the chapter on sorting. From the point of view of this sorting let $(i, j)$ and $(k, l)$ be two elements of $H$. Then $(i, j) < (k, l)$ if $(i, j)$ is marked and $(k, l)$ is not. Whilst if both $(i, j)$ and $(k, l)$ are marked (or both unmarked) then $(i, j) < (k, l)$ if $i < k$ or ($i = k$ and $j < l$). After the ordering, the first $2n$ locations of the vector are occupied by marked edges. For our example (figure 2.21) these will be $(1, 7)$, $(1, 8)$, $(2, 5)$, $(2, 6)$, $(3, 6)$, $(3, 7)$, $(4, 5)$, $(4, 8)$, $(5, 2)$, $(5, 4)$, $(6, 2)$, $(6, 3)$, $(7, 1)$, $(7, 3)$, $(8, 1)$, $(8, 4)$. For each of these edges we now define a successor. This will, in effect, create two antiparallel Hamiltonian cycles. The following statement achieves this.

> **for** all $k$, $1 \leqslant k \leqslant 2n$, **in parallel do**
>   **for** $H(k) = (i, j)$ **do**
>     $successor(H(k)) \leftarrow$ **if** $s \neq i$ where $H(2j) = (r, s)$ **then**
>                                                                  $H(2j)$ **else** $H(2j - 1)$

This takes constant time with $O(n)$ processors. Thus overall this step requires $O(\log n)$ time using $O(n)$ processors.

## Step 1.3

In this step we compute $P(i)$ for each vertex $i$, where $P(i)$ is the position of vertex $i$ in tracing the (directed) Hamiltonian cycle containing the edge $H(1)$ starting at vertex 1. Essentially we use the standard doubling technique to do this as the following details show.

> **for** all $k$, $1 \leqslant k \leqslant 2n$, **in parallel do**
>   **begin**
>   $distance(H(k)) \leftarrow 1$
>   **repeat** $\log n$ **times**

```
for successor(H(k)) = (i, j) do
    if i ≠ 1 then
        begin
        distance(H(k)) ← distance(H(k)) + distance(successor(H(k)))
        successor(H(k)) ← successor(successor(H(k)))
        end
    if successor(H(k)) = H(1) then P(j) ← distance(H(k)) where H(k) = (i, j)
end
```

Step 1.3 takes $O(\log n)$ time using $O(n)$ processors. This completes all the substeps of step 1 of the algorithm in which we have computed that permutation of the vertices (vertex $i$ appears in position $P(i)$) which corresponds to the order in which they appear around the boundary of the external face.

Without loss of generality, we can assume in what follows that $P$ is the identity function, that is that $P(i) = i$ for all $i$, $1 \leqslant i \leqslant n$. In step 2 of the algorithm each side is presumed to be directed as follows: $(i, i + 1)$ for $1 \leqslant i \leqslant n - 1$ and the remaining edge in the direction $(n, 1)$. Each diagonal $(i, j)$ of the original $n$-gon is replaced by two antiparallel edges $(i, j)$ and $(j, i)$. The (internal) faces of the $n$-gon can then be thought of as directed cycles, each (directed) edge belonging to exactly one such cycle. In step 2 we first compute, for each edge $(i, j)$, $next(i, j)$ which is the next edge on the cycle (face) containing $(i, j)$. For our example, shown now in figure 2.22, we have the $next(1, 2) = (2, 3)$, $next(3, 6) = (6, 1)$, $next(1, 6) = (6, 7)$ and so on. This computation is a necessary preliminary to computing the so-called tree of faces of the $n$-gon. In this tree each vertex corresponds to an internal face of the $n$-gon and there is an edge between two vertices if the corresponding faces have an edge (specifically a diagonal) in common. Note that every directed cycle contains exactly one edge $(i, j)$ such

*Figure 2.22*

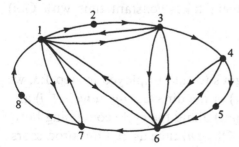

that $i > j$. For each cycle this edge is called the main edge and will be used to represent the cycle later. In step 2 we compute the tree of faces. Each vertex of the tree is represented by a main edge and we construct the tree in directed form. The root of the tree will be $(n, 1)$. For other main edges $(i, j)$, we compute *father*$(i, j)$ in the tree. Notice that the main edge of a cycle containing $(j, i)$ is the father of the main edge $(i, j)$.

*Step 2.1*

In this step we compute *next*$(i, j)$ for each $(i, j)$ of the directed $n$-gon and then find *main*$(i, j)$ which is the main edge of the cycle to which $(i, j)$ belongs. A vector, of dimension $2m - n$, of the edges of the directed $n$-gon is easily constructed in constant time using $O(n)$ processors given the vector of edges of the $n$-gon input to the whole algorithm. We now order the elements of the vector in $O(\log n)$ time using $O(n)$ processors making use of an algorithm described in the chapter on sorting. We sort according to the following order between pairs. Letting $(i, j)$ and $(k, l)$ be such a pair, $(i, j) < (k, l)$ if $i < k$ or $(i = k$ and $(l < j < i$ or $j < i < l$ or $i < l < j))$. Within the ordered vector *rank*$(i, j)$ is the rank of $(i, j)$ and *rank*$^{-1}(i)$ is the edge with rank $i$. Consider the edges directed from a particular vertex $i$. The effect of the ordering (suppose that the vertices $1, 2, 3, \ldots$ appear in clockwise order around the (directed) $n$-gon) is to order these particular edges as follows: $(i, j_1), (i, j_2), \ldots, (i, j_d)$ where $d$ is the outdegree of $i$, $(i, j_d)$ is the side edge directed from $i$ and $j_1, j_2, \ldots, j_d$ is the anticlockwise order in which these vertices appear about $i$. The virtue of this is that *next*$(i, j)$ for all $(i, j)$ is very simply constructed as follows.

> **for** all $(i, j)$ of the directed $n$-gon **in parallel do** compute *rank*$(i, j)$
> **for** all $i$, $1 \leqslant i \leqslant 2m - n$, **in parallel do** compute *rank*$^{-1}(i)$
> **for** all $(i, j)$ of the directed $n$-gon **in parallel do**
>   **if** $(i, j)$ is a side **then** *next*$(i, j) \leftarrow$ *rank*$^{-1}($*rank*$(i, j) + 1)$ **else**
> $$rank^{-1}(rank(j, i) + 1)$$

Note that *next*$(n, 1) \leftarrow$ *rank*$^{-1}(1)$. The sorting of the vector of edges of the directed $n$-gon ensures that the first two of these statements take $O(\log n)$ time using $O(n)$ processors. The third statement takes constant time with $O(n)$ processors.

*Step 2.2*

In this step, in a manner entirely analogous to that employed in step 1.3, we now compute for each directed edge $(i, j)$ of the directed $n$-gon *main*$(i, j)$ and *dist*$(i, j)$, the distance from $(i, j)$ to *main*$(i, j)$ along the cycle containing both. Using the doubling technique this takes $O(\log n)$ time using $O(n)$ processors.

*Step 2.3*

In this step we compute the tree of faces of the *n*-gon. This is done as follows.

> **for** all diagonals $(i, j)$ of the directed *n*-gon **in parallel do**
> **if** $(i, j)$ is a main edge (that is, $i > j$) **then** *father*$(i, j) \leftarrow$ *main*$(j, i)$

This takes constant time using O($n$) processors. Figure 2.23 shows the tree of faces for our example of figure 2.22. The directed edges are $((i, j), father(i, j))$ where $(i, j)$ is the main edge representing the cycle which is a node of the tree. This is the final stage of step 2 and we are now in a position to start the process of colouring vertices.

*Step 3*

In this step we colour the vertices of each cycle. Within each cycle no two adjacent vertices are similarly coloured; however, vertices may appear in more than one cycle and the various copies may be differently coloured. This inconsistency is dealt with in a later step. We use the colours *A*, *B* and *C*. For each edge $(i, j)$ of the directed *n*-gon, we compute *colour*$(i, j)$ which is the colour of vertex $i$ on the cycle containing $(i, j)$. Each cycle of even length uses two colours whilst odd-length cycles use three colours as follows.

> **for** all edges $(i, j)$ of the directed *n*-gon **in parallel do**
> **begin**
> **if** *dist*$(i, j)$ is even **then** *colour*$(i, j) \leftarrow A$ **else** *colour*$(i, j) \leftarrow B$
> **if** *colour*$(i, j) =$ *colour*$(next(i, j))$ **then** *colour*$(i, j) \leftarrow C$
> **end**

*Figure 2.23*

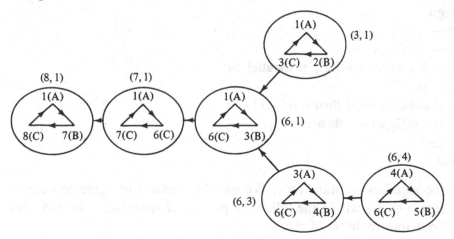

Notice that if $colour(i, j) = colour(next(i, j))$ then $(i, j)$ can only be a main edge and the circuit containing $(i, j)$ must be of odd length. For our example, we have that each cycle is of odd length (all are of length 3) and the colouring of vertices produced by this step is shown (in brackets after each vertex) in figure 2.23. This produces many colouring conflicts, for example vertex 3 is coloured $A$ in circuit $(6, 3)$, $B$ in circuit $(6, 1)$ and $C$ in circuit $(3, 1)$.

## Step 4

In this step we resolve the problem of the non-equivalence of colours of copies of the same vertex in different cycles. Consider two faces corresponding to cycles $C_1$ and $C_2$ which have a common diagonal $(i, j)$. Suppose that $C_1$ is the father of $C_2$ in the tree of faces. By $col(C, i)$ we denote the colour of vertex $i$ in circuit $C$. We ensure agreement between the colours of copies of the vertices $i$ and $j$ in the two cycles by interchanging colours on $C_2$ (the *son* of $C_1$) as follows.

```
if col(C₁, i) ≠ col(C₂, i) then
    begin
    R ← col(C₁, i)
    S ← col(C₂, i)
    for all vertices v on C₂ in parallel do
        begin
        if col(C₂, v) = R then col(C₂, v) ← S
        if col(C₂, v) = S then col(C₂, v) ← R
        end
    end
if col(C₁, j) ≠ col(C₂, j) then
    begin
    R ← col(C₁, j)
    S ← col(C₂, j)
    for all vertices v on C₂ in parallel do
        begin
        if col(C₂, v) = R then col(C₂, v) ← S
        if col(C₂, v) = S then col(C₂, v) ← R
        end
    end
```

This process takes constant time. We use this method of agreeing colours between two cycles within the following process of removing colour clashes throughout the whole set of cycles.

**repeat** log $n$ **times**
1. **for** all cycles **in parallel do** find their depths in the tree of faces
2. **for** all cycles at odd depth **in parallel do**
   **begin**
   agree colours between each cycle and its father
   merge each cycle with its father
   **end**

Statement 1 will take O(log $n$) time using O($n$) processors if we use the standard doubling technique, doubling on the relation *father*. Within statement 2 we interchange colours (if necessary) in the cycle at odd depth in order to get agreement with its father. This takes constant time with O($n$) processors to handle all such cycles in parallel if we employ the previously described technique of agreeing colours between pairs of cycles. In step 2 we also effectively merge each cycle at odd depth in the tree of faces with its father. The merging of cycles involves (for each pair) a constant number of pointer changes (next-edge pointers) and the removal of two (anti-parallel) diagonals. For our example, the application of this step is shown in figure 2.24: (a) shows the tree of faces after one iteration, (b) after two iterations and finally in (c) we have reduced the tree of faces to a single cycle in which all the vertices appear. In effect the height of the tree of faces is halved within each iteration of statement 2

Figure 2.24

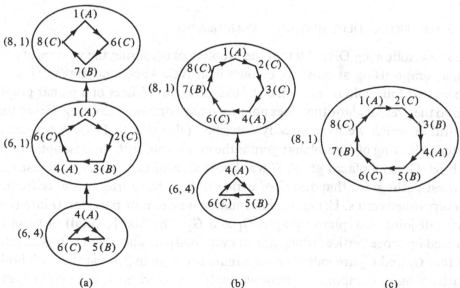

(a)                                    (b)                                    (c)

and so a logarithmic number of repetitions is sufficient to agree colours across all cycles. Overall this step takes $O(\log^2 n)$ time using $O(n)$ processors.

Given the above procedure, we can quickly sketch the algorithm to vertex-colour general outerplanar graphs. The outline is as follows.

1.  Find the biconnected components of the outerplanar graph.
2.  Construct and orientate the tree of biconnected components.
3.  In parallel, colour each biconnected component.
4.  Use the tree of biconnected components to agree colours between components.

For the first step we use the algorithm described earlier in the chapter. For step 2 the tree of biconnected components consists of a node for each biconnected component and an edge between nodes if the corresponding biconnected components have copies of the same articulation point. As is easily seen the corresponding graph is indeed a tree. We can then root and orientate this tree – an appropriate algorithm was described at the beginning of this chapter. Step 3 uses the *n*-gon colouring procedure to colour those components which are *n*-gons (those components which have more than two vertices). All other components are a single edge and two colours are sufficient to colour the endpoints. In step 4 we use essentially the same technique as that used in step 4 of the *n*-gons procedure (in a simpler form, because two components will only ever share a single vertex so that at most one colour exchange will ever be required within components at odd depths of the tree).

### 2.4.3 SIX-VERTEX-COLOURING OF PLANAR GRAPHS

We show, following Diks,[14] that the problem of colouring the vertices of any planar graph using at most six colours is in *NC*. Appel and Haken[2] have shown that four colours are sufficient to colour the vertices of a planar graph and so the present algorithm does not produce an optimal colouring. Given the algorithm which we have already described (also due to Diks) for optimal vertex-colouring of outerplanar graphs the present algorithmic description can be brief. Given a planar graph $G$ we choose an arbitrary vertex $v$ and use the shortest-paths algorithm described earlier to find the shortest distance from $v$ to every other vertex. Using this information we can now partition $G$ into two vertex-disjoint outerplanar graphs $G_1$ and $G_2$. The first (second) of these is induced by those vertices which are an even (odd) distance from $v$. It is easy to see that $G_1$ and $G_2$ are indeed outerplanar, although in general they will both consist of many components. Now we apply the algorithm for optimal vertex-colouring of outerplanar graphs to $G_1$ and $G_2$ in parallel. This uses (at most) three colours for each of these graphs. Taking disjoint colour sets for $G_1$ and $G_2$ ensures that $G$ can be reconstructed without two adjacent vertices having the same colour. Thus a six-colouring of $G$ is obtained. In the P-RAM model of computation this takes $O(\log^2 n)$ time using $O(n^4)$ processors.

### 2.4.4 OPTIMAL EDGE-COLOURING OF OUTERPLANAR GRAPHS

Following Gibbons and Rytter,[19] we describe an algorithm which produces an optimal edge-colouring of an outerplanar graph in polylog time. This is yet a further exemplification of the divide-and-conquer technique applied in parallel. We first concentrate on two-connected outerplanar graphs as we did when describing optimal vertex-colouring of outerplanar graphs earlier. In fact we shall assume familiarity with the terminology introduced in section 2.4.2 and with the first two steps of the algorithm described there. Those steps described how sides and diagonals can be identified, how we can obtain a planar realisation of the graph and how the so-called tree of faces (and the faces of the graph themselves) can all be computed in $O(\log^2 n)$ time using a polynomial (of low order) number of processors on a P-RAM. Our description therefore presumes the availability of these structures and information.

We first show how to obtain an optimal colouring for two-connected outerplanar graphs with a maximum degree of 3. Such a graph is shown in figure 2.25 with the faces labelled $F_1, F_2, \ldots, F_{10}$. Notice that no two diagonals can have a common endpoint. If the faces of the graph are edge-coloured independently then many edges will be coloured inconsistently because one edge can belong to two distinct faces. Even if each edge is coloured consistently in this sense and has the same colour in both faces, the whole colouring can still

Figure 2.25

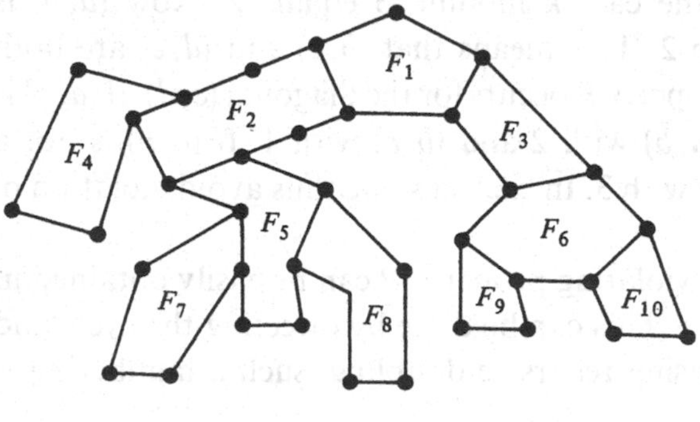

be improper, because two distinct but similarly coloured sides in different faces
can have a common endpoint in $G$. We start with a correct colouring of each
face independently and step by step we shall remove inconsistencies between
faces. We ensure that the following crucial invariant holds and this will enable
us to remove inconsistencies between faces.

*Property P*

Each face $C$ is properly coloured as a cycle and, if in $C$ there are three
consecutive edges $e_1, e_2, e_3$ such that $e_2$ is a diagonal, then these edges are
coloured by three distinct colours.

In [38] it was shown that each cycle can be (independently) coloured to satisfy
property $P$. Here we parallelise the method described there. The first step of
our algorithm consists then of simultaneously and independently colouring all
faces to satisfy property $P$. For a given face we start from the edge joining this
face to its father face and colour its edges consecutively using the colours $1, 2, 3$
in rotational order. If the face has no father then we start from any edge
common with some other face. After colouring in this manner, consider how
property $P$ may be violated. Different cases need to be reviewed depending
upon the value of $k$ modulo 3. If $k$ modulo 3 is 0 then property $P$ must be
satisfied for all possible sets of three consecutive edges, so we need only
consider the cases of $k$ mod 3 being 1 or 2. Let the colouring of edges around the
face start at the edge $(c, d)$ which is coloured 1; then $(d, e)$ is coloured 2, $(e, f)$ is
coloured 3, $(f, g)$ is coloured 1 and so on. Consider the colours assigned in this
process to the final two edges to be coloured. In other words, consider the
colours that get assigned to the edges $(a, b)$ and $(b, c)$. If $k$ modulo 3 equals 1,
then $(a, b)$ is coloured 3 and $(b, c)$ is coloured 1. If the edge $(c, d)$ is now
recoloured with 3, then no violation of property $P$ can occur. This is because
the edge $(b, c)$ cannot be a diagonal because the maximum degree is 3 and $(c, d)$
is a diagonal. Now consider the case $k$ modulo 3 equals 2. Now $(a, b)$ is
coloured with 1 and $(b, c)$ with 2. This means that $(b, c)$ and $(d, e)$ are both
coloured 2 and a violation of property $P$ occurs for the diagonal $(c, d)$. If $(a, b)$ is
a diagonal then we recolour $(a, b)$ with 2 and $(b, c)$ with 1. If $(a, b)$ is not a
diagonal then we recolour $(b, c)$ with 3. In each case we thus avoid violation of
property $P$.

   For one face a colouring not violating property $P$ can be easily obtained in
$\log n$ time using $O(n)$ processors. This can be done by directing the cycle and
breaking it at vertex $c$. Then, using recursive doubling, such a numbering is

achieved for the (open) list by computing distances from each element to the end of the list modulo 3. Then some constant-time operations, as described, may be required to remove outstanding violations of property $P$. Hence the initial independent colouring of all the faces can be done in logarithmic time with $O(n^2)$ processors, where $n$ processors are required for each face. Let $G$ be the two-connected outerplanar graph with $\Delta = 3$ shown in figure 2.25. Then figure 2.26 shows the tree of faces (which we shall denote by $TF$) in which each node is a face of the graph. These faces are imagined to have been coloured as shown following the process just described.

Now consider resolving colouring inconsistencies just between two faces $C$ and $C'$, where $C$ is the father of $C'$ in $TF$. Let $(a, b)$ be the diagonal edge shared by $C$ and $C'$. Also let $(e, a)$, $(a, b)$, $(b, f)$ be consecutive edges in $C$ coloured $x_1, y_1, z_1$, respectively, and let $(d, a)$, $(a, b)$, $(b, c)$ be consecutive edges of $C'$ coloured $x, y, z$ respectively. The situation is depicted in figure 2.27. We can ensure that no colouring inconsistencies will arise between these two faces if for edges of $C$ only we recolour as follows. If the edge is coloured $x_1$ then we recolour it with $z$, if the edge is coloured $y_1$ then we recolour it with $y$ and if the edge is coloured $z_1$ then we recolour it with $x$. In other words we perform the colour reassignment $(x_1, y_1, z_1) \leftarrow (z, y, x)$ in $C$. Of course, it may already be the case that $x_1 = z$ for example. Whatever the situation, resolving colouring inconsistencies between two faces such as $C'$ and $C$ is easily done in constant time.

*Figure 2.26*

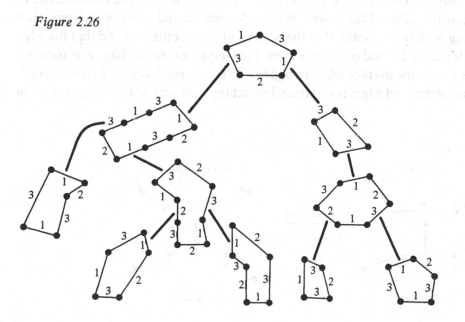

Notice that the recolouring operation is well defined if property $P$ holds, and this operation preserves that property. Thus property $P$ is an invariant as we remove colouring inconsistencies across the whole of the tree of faces. This is achieved using exactly the same methodology as that employed in the second half of step 4 of the optimal vertex-colouring of two-connected outerplanar graphs. In other words, we resolve inconsistencies between faces at odd depths with their father faces and then merge these faces. Each such operation halves the height of the tree $TF$. Thus a logarithmic number of iterations of this process will suffice to remove all colouring inconsistencies. Notice that the colouring must be optimal because $\Delta = 3$ and exactly three colours are employed. If $\Delta < 3$ an optimal colouring is easily found in $O(\log n)$ time with $O(n)$ processors. Thus we have the following lemma.

### Lemma 2.4
We can obtain an optimal colouring of any two-connected outerplanar graph with $\Delta \leqslant 3$ in $\log^2 n$ time using $O(n^2)$ processors. $\qquad\qquad\square$

### Optimal edge-colouring of general outerplanar graphs ($\Delta > 3$)

Let $G$ be a biconnected outerplanar graph with $\Delta > 3$. Such a graph is shown in figure 2.28. The outerplanar graph *reduced*($G$) is obtained in the following way. We find a node $c$ of degree 2. It is easy to see that at least two nodes of degree 2 must exist. Let $H = (c, b), (b, d), (d, e), (e, f), \ldots, (q, a), (a, c)$ be the sequence of consecutive sides of the $n$-gon. We mark each second edge of this sequence starting with $(b, d)$. Notice that the edge $(c, b)$ is never marked and that the edge $(a, c)$ is marked if and only if $n$ is even. Each node, except perhaps $c$, is incident with exactly one marked edge. In figure 2.28 the marked edges are emboldened. The set of marked edges is a maximal matching (possibly not covering the node

*Figure 2.27*

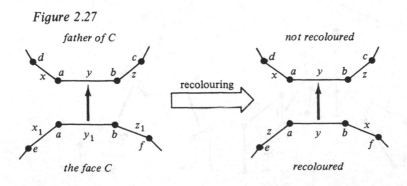

*c*). We denote this set by $M(G)$. Then the graph *reduced*$(G)$ is given by removing all edges in $M(G)$ from $G$. Notice that, given an optimal colouring of *reduced*$(G)$, we can obtain an optimal colouring of $G$ simply by providing the same new colour for all the edges of $M(G)$. This is because the maximum degree of *reduced*$(G)$ is exactly 1 less than that for $G$, since every vertex of maximum degree in $G$ will be an endpoint of one edge in $M(G)$. We also have the following lemma.

*Lemma 2.5*

Let *reduced*$(G)$ have $m'$ edges where $G$ is a biconnected outerplanar graph having $\Delta > 3$ and $m$ edges. Then *reduced*$(G)$ can be constructed in O($\log n$) parallel time with O($n$) processors and $m' \leqslant \frac{3}{4}m$.

*Proof*

There are at least $(n-1)/2$ edges in $M(G)$ and all of them are removed. The maximal number of edges of the outerplanar graph is $2n - 3$. This proves that $m' \leqslant \frac{3}{4}m$. A suitable node $c$ can be found and the marking of edges carried out in $\log n$ time with $n$ processors using recursive doubling. This completes the proof. □

Notice that after the removal of $M(G)$ the maximum degree of $G$ decreases by 1; however, degrees in biconnected components can decrease by more than 1. For example the maximal degree of biconnected components after deleting edges of $M(G)$ in figure 2.28 decreases by 2, as can be seen in figure 2.29 which shows the tree of biconnected components. Notice that this tree can be found in O($\log^2 n$) time using O($n^2/\log^2 n$) processors by utilising a previously described algorithm to find the blocks of a graph. Let $TB$ denote the tree of biconnected components. We use the tree $TB$ to agree colour inconsistencies between the

Figure 2.28

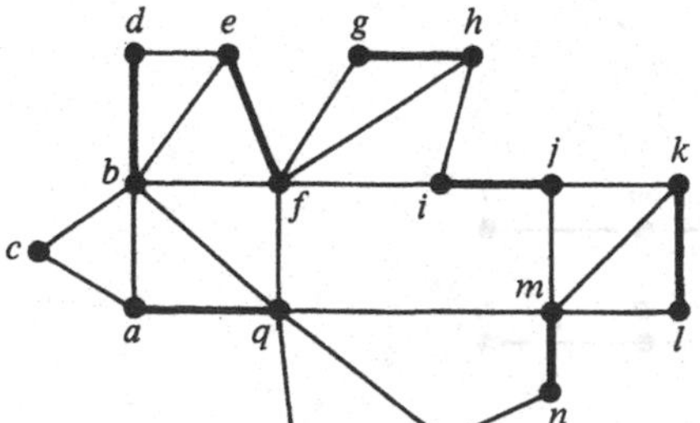

two connected components which we presume to have been independently coloured. The method we use is the familiar one of iterating the process of making components at odd levels in the tree agree with their fathers and then merging these components with their fathers. This halves the height of the tree in each iteration and so a logarithmic number of iterations is sufficient. Therefore we just need to see how we can bring about agreement between a biconnected component and its father. Let $\Delta$ be the maximum degree of *reduced*($G$) for which $TB$ has been constructed. We assume that each biconnected component is already edge-coloured using colours from within the set $\{1, \ldots, \Delta\}$. Consider a father vertex $F$ in $TB$ and an articulation point $v$ which $F$ has in common with the sons $S_1, S_2, \ldots, S_r$. Let $P(S_i)$ denote the set of colours present at $S_i$ in $F$ and let $d(S_i)$ be the degree of $v$ in $S_i$. The problem is to extract from the set $\{1, \ldots, \Delta\} - P(F)$ a number of disjoint subsets with cardinalities $d(S_i)$ for all $i$, $1 \leqslant i \leqslant r$. Then taking a one-to-one correspondence between colours in the subset with cardinality $d(S_i)$ and colours in $P(S_i)$ will define a colour exchange in $S_i$ which for all $i$ will remove inconsistencies. This is because no colour in $\{1, \ldots, \Delta\}$ can then appear more than once at $v$. Within a single iteration in which the height of $TB$ is halved, this agreeing of colours between all components at odd levels with their fathers can be achieved in $O(\log n)$ time using $n^2$ processors. The details, although tedious, are not difficult and so we omit them. Thus we can remove colouring inconsistencies over the whole of $TB$ in $O(\log^2 n)$ time using $n^2$ processors.

*Figure 2.29*

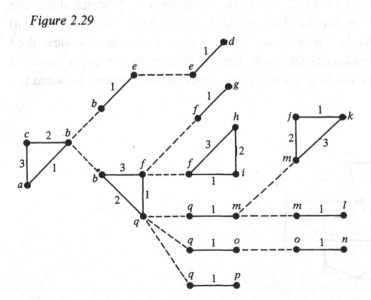

If we call this process *ADJUST*, then the procedure for optimally edge-colouring a biconnected outerplanar graphs with maximum degree $\Delta$ is

    procedure *edge-colour*$(G, D)$
    begin $\{\Delta \geqslant 3$, $G$ is a biconnected graph,
                    the procedure colours $G$ using colours from $[1 \ldots D], D \leqslant \Delta\}$
    if $\Delta \leqslant 3$ then use the algorithm described earlier for this case else
        begin find $M(G)$
        colour every edge in $M(G)$ with the colour $D$
        $G \leftarrow reduced(G)$
        find the biconnected components of $G$ and construct $TB$
        for all biconnected components $X$ in parallel do *edge-colour*$(X, D - 1)$
        *ADJUST*
        end
    end

We illustrate the procedure *ADJUST* with reference to the tree of biconnected components shown in figure 2.29. We take the root of the tree to be the component which is the circuit $(a, b, c)$. Let the edges of the biconnected components be coloured as indicated in figure 2.29. In figure 2.30(a) the inconsistencies between components at odd levels in the tree have been

*Figure 2.30*

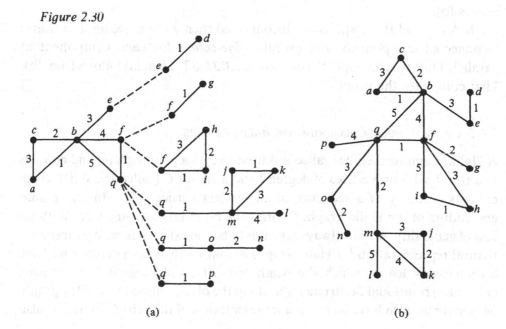

(a)                                                         (b)

removed and components at these odd levels have been merged with their fathers. In figure 2.30(b) the process has been repeated once more and an optimal colouring of *reduced*($G$) has been obtained, where $G$ is the graph of figure 2.28. The edges of $M(G)$ can now be coloured with the colour 6 so that an optimum colouring of $G$ is obtained.

We are now in a position to prove the main result of this section.

*Theorem 2.2*
(a) Every outerplanar graph can be optimally edge-coloured in $O(\log^3 n)$ time with $n^2$ processors.
(b) If $G$ is a biconnected outerplanar graph with $\Delta \geqslant 3$, then *edge-colour*$(G, \Delta)$ optimally edge-colours $G$ in $O(\log^3 n)$ time with $n^2$ processors.

*Proof*
(b) Lemma 2.5 implies that the depth of the recursion is $O(\log n)$. The first operation, if $\Delta > 3$, is the removal of $M(G)$ and this decreases the number of edges by a factor of $\frac{3}{4}$. In one instance of *edge-colour*, for a graph with $n$ vertices all other operations (constructing the tree of biconnected components and the operation *ADJUST*) take $O(\log^2 n)$ time with $n^2$ processors. An optimal colouring is produced because, as we saw earlier, the base cases of the recursion produce optimal colourings and in other cases when $\Delta$ is increased by 1 (with the addition of the edges in $M(G)$) so is the number of colours used. This proves (b).
(a) If $\Delta \geqslant 3$ and the graph is not biconnected then we can decompose $G$ into biconnected components and execute *edge-colour* for each component in parallel. Then we can apply the operation *ADJUST*. Then (a) follows from (b). That completes the proof.                                                                         □

### 2.4.5 OPTIMAL EDGE-COLOURING OF HALIN GRAPHS

A Halin graph (sometimes called a skirted tree) is a planar graph and consists of a tree $T$ with no vertices of degree 2 and a circuit $C$ (called the skirt) which consists precisely of a sequence of all the leaf vertices of $T$. In any planar embedding of the Halin graph, $C$ forms the boundary of some face. Without loss of generality, we can always take this to be the external face. We presume a natural representation for Halin graphs as follows. For each vertex $v$ we have an adjacency list in which the neighbours of $v$ are ordered in their (say, clockwise) rotational occurrence about $v$ in the planar embedding of the graph. Moreover we also have an explicit representation of the skirt $C$ (thus $T$ is also available in a single parallel step by removing skirt edges from the Halin graph). Given an adjacency list representation, we can easily obtain the representation used here in polylog time. Obtaining a planar embedding as represented by a set of faces is in $NC$.[26] The problem of then proceeding to our representation is straightforward although we omit the details. However, observe that $C$ will be a face which has exactly one edge in common with every other face and that if $(u, v), (v, w)$ are consecutive edges of some face (in anticlockwise order) then $u$ and $w$ will be consecutive vertices in our adjacency list representation for $v$. We describe an algorithm due to Gibbons and Rytter.[19]

Before describing our edge-colouring algorithm we note the following fact. Here $nd(v)$ is the number of descendants of $v$ (including $v$) in a rooted tree.

*Fact 1*

For every tree $T$ with $n$ vertices there exists at least one vertex $x$ such that, for every component $K$ of $T - x$, $|K| \leqslant n/2$.

*Proof*

Let $T$ be arbitrarily rooted at some vertex $u$. It is easy to see that at least one vertex $x$ will exist for which $nd(x) > n/2$ and for which $nd(w) \leqslant n/2$ for every son $w$ of $v$. Moreover it is easy to see that $x$ satisfies the thesis. $\qquad\square$

Using the Euler tour technique, we described at the beginning of the chapter how to compute $nd(v)$ for all $v$ in O(log $n$) parallel time with $n$ processors (also *father*($v$) of which knowledge will be presumed later). Hence we can find $x$ efficiently as follows. Given $nd(v)$ for all $v$, we proceed (in parallel) to compute $MND(v)$, defined to be max$\{nd(w) \,|\, w$ is a son of $v\}$. This can be done in logarithmic time using a standard doubling argument. If $nd(v) > n/2$ and if $MND(v) \leqslant n/2$ then $v$ satisfies fact 1. It is possible that $v$ is not unique in this respect. It is a simple matter to identify a single vertex satisfying fact 1 in logarithmic time by, for example, choosing the first such vertex in a locally constructed list of vertices (we assume they have a suitable alphabetic labelling) using, again, a standard doubling argument. Thus a vertex satisfying fact 1 can be found in O(log $n$) time using O($n$) processors.

Given $x$ as defined in fact 1, we imagine (without loss of generality) that $T$ is rooted at $x$. We shall require to find, for each *son*($x$), its leftmost descendant leaf $L(son(x))$ and its rightmost descendant leaf $R(son(x))$. Such vertices are indicated in figure 2.31. In that figure the circuit $C$ of the Halin graph bounds the exterior face. The degree of $x$ is $d$ and its sons are $v_1, v_2, \ldots, v_d$. We can find

$L(v_i)$ and $R(v_i)$ for all $i$, $0 \leqslant i \leqslant d-1$, in $\log n$ parallel time using standard doubling arguments based on leftmost and rightmost sons (in our representation these sons are known, being on either side of $father(v_i)$ in the adjacency list of $v_i$).

### The optimal edge-colouring algorithm

#### Step 1 {Decomposition}

In constant parallel time using $O(m) = O(n)$ processors, we decompose the Halin graph as follows. Remember that, by definition of a Halin graph, $d(v) > 2$ for all $v$. It follows that $d(x) > 2$ and that $L(v) \neq R(v)$ for all $v$ unless $v$ is a leaf, in which case $v = L(v) = R(v)$. If $(u, w)$ is an edge such that $u = L(v_i)$ and $v = R(v_{i+1})$ where subscripts are modulo $d$, then $(u, w)$ is deleted. (In fact, such edges have to be stacked for reconstruction purposes later.) In addition, for each $L(v_i)$ and $R(v_i)$ we add edges $(x, L(v_i))$ and $(x, R(v_i))$. This deletion and addition of edges results in a graph in which $x$ is an articulation point; we complete the decomposition by separating the graph at $x$, passing a copy of $x$ to each component. The decomposition for figure 2.31 is shown schematically in figure 2.32. Notice that each component of the decomposition will be a Halin graph unless $v_i$ is a leaf of $T$. In this case the component associated with $v_i$ will be the multigraph with $n = 2$ and $m = 3$. Notice that, in constant time, we preserve our form of the representation of Halin graphs during the decomposition.

*Figure 2.31*

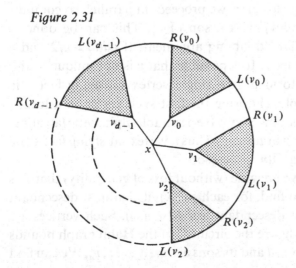

*Step 2* {Recursive application of the algorithm}

> **for** all components created in step 1 **do in parallel**
> **if** the size of the component $> 2$ **then**
> recursively apply the algorithm to this component
> **else** {$n = 2$} colour the edges of this {multigraph}
> component with 1, 2 and 3

*Step 3* {Reconstruction and colouring}
Given an optimum colouring of each of the components of the decomposition
described we can find an optimum colouring of the reconstructed component
as follows. Figure 2.33 schematically illustrates this. For the *i*th component of

*Figure 2.32*

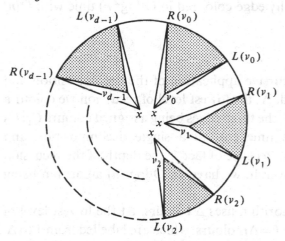

*Figure 2.33*

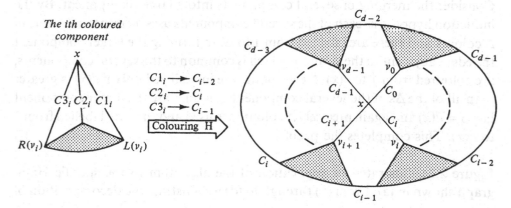

The *i*th coloured
component

$C1_i \longrightarrow C_{i-2}$
$C2_i \longrightarrow C_i$
$C3_i \longrightarrow C_{i-1}$

Colouring H

the decomposition (which contains $v_i$, the $i$th son of $v$), let $C1_i$, $C2_i$ and $C3_i$ (in clockwise rotational order about $x$) be the edge colours present at $x$. For $k = 0, 1, 2, \ldots, d - 1$ we intend that colour $C_k$ be assigned to $e_k = (x, v_k)$ in $H$. In order to achieve this we permute the colours in the $i$th component according to any permutation in which $C1_i$ becomes $C_{i-2}$, $C2_i$ becomes $C_i$ and $C3_i$ becomes $C_{i-1}$. These permutations can be found within our time constraints with little difficulty. These permutations additionally ensure that when $H$ is reconstructed there are no colour clashes on replaced edges because $C3_i$ and $C1_{i+1}$ are replaced by the same colour which is assigned to the skirt edge $(L(v_i), R(v_{i+1}))$ which is replaced after the edges $(x, L(v_i))$ and $(x, R(v_{i+1}))$ have been removed. Such a colouring scheme is shown schematically in figure 2.33. **end** of the algorithm

*Theorem 2.3*
Any Halin graph can be optimally edge-coloured in $O(\log^2 n)$ time with $O(n)$ processors.

*Proof*
Our algorithm is simply the recursive application of the decomposition and reconstruction process described. At the lowest level of recursion we colour a multigraph with $n = 2$ and $m = 3$, the three edges being assigned colours $C_1$, $C_2$ and $C_3$ in constant time. The time cost of a single decomposition and reconstruction phase is $O(\log n)$. Because of fact 1, the depth of the recursion does not exceed $\log n$ and so, overall, we have an $O(\log^2 n)$ algorithm using $O(n)$ processors on a P-RAM.

We need to show that the algorithm uses $\Delta$ colours. At the lowest level of recursion each multigraph uses $3\ (= \Delta)$ colours, which are labelled from 1 to $\Delta$. We therefore have a basis for an inductive proof of this statement for all $n$. Consider the merging of several components into a larger component. By the induction hypothesis each of the several components uses its respective value of $\Delta$ colours and these are labelled from 1 to $\Delta$. In forming the larger component the edges adjacent to the vertex $x$, which is common to the several components, are coloured from 1 to $d(x)$. New colours are introduced only if $d(x)$ is greater than all of the $\Delta$s of the several components. In this case the larger component has $\Delta = d(x)$ and again precisely $\Delta$ colours are used and they are labelled from 1 to $d(x)$. This completes the proof.                                   $\square$

Figure 2.34 illustrates an application of the algorithm to the specific Halin graph shown in (a). From (a) through to (d) we illustrate the decomposition of

Figure 2.34

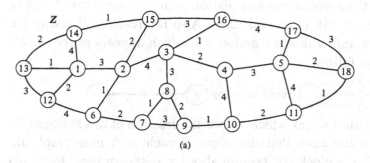

(a)

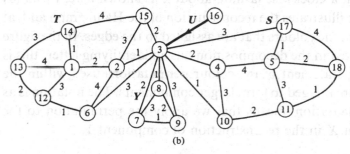

(b)

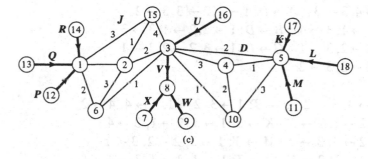

(c)

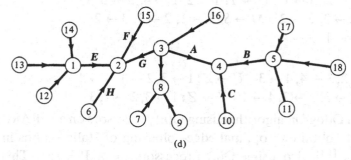

(d)

the graph for successively deeper levels of the recursion. For reasons of clarity we do not separate the graph at the articulation points; at successive levels of the recursion these are (3), (1, 5) and (2, 4). Also for reasons of clarity we represent the multigraph with $n = 2$ and $m = 3$, which appears at the lowest level of recursion, as follows.

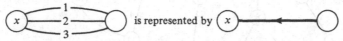

Here $x$ is the articulation vertex which caused the creation of this multigraph. In figure 2.34 we understand that the edges of each such multigraph are coloured 1, 2 and 3 in a clockwise fashion about $x$ as shown here. From (d) back to (a) figure 2.34 illustrates the reconstruction of the Halin graph and, at each level of recursion, the colours that are assigned to the edges. In the figure each component created in the decomposition has an identifying letter; this is used in the following statement of the colour permutations used within the components as they are merged to form larger components. The notation is as follows, $X \rightarrow Y$: 'permutation' means that we apply the permutation to the colours of component $X$ in the reconstruction of component $Y$.

from (d) to (c)

$E \rightarrow J: 1 \rightarrow 2, 2 \rightarrow 4, 3 \rightarrow 3$ $\quad$ $A \rightarrow D: 1 \rightarrow 1, 2 \rightarrow 3, 3 \rightarrow 2$

$\quad F \rightarrow J: 1 \rightarrow 3, 2 \rightarrow 1, 3 \rightarrow 4$ $\quad$ $B \rightarrow D: 1 \rightarrow 2, 2 \rightarrow 1, 3 \rightarrow 3$

$\quad G \rightarrow J: 1 \rightarrow 4, 2 \rightarrow 2, 3 \rightarrow 1$ $\quad$ $C \rightarrow D: 1 \rightarrow 3, 2 \rightarrow 2, 3 \rightarrow 1$

$\quad H \rightarrow J: 1 \rightarrow 1, 2 \rightarrow 3, 3 \rightarrow 2$

from (c) to (b)

$D \rightarrow S: 1 \rightarrow 4, 2 \rightarrow 3, 3 \rightarrow 2$ $\quad$ $J \rightarrow T: 1 \rightarrow 3, 2 \rightarrow 1, 3 \rightarrow 4, 4 \rightarrow 2$

$\quad V \rightarrow Y: 1 \rightarrow 2, 2 \rightarrow 1, 3 \rightarrow 3$ $\quad$ $K \rightarrow S: 1 \rightarrow 3, 2 \rightarrow 1, 3 \rightarrow 4$

$\quad P \rightarrow T: 1 \rightarrow 1, 2 \rightarrow 3, 3 \rightarrow 2$ $\quad$ $W \rightarrow Y: 1 \rightarrow 3, 2 \rightarrow 2, 3 \rightarrow 1$

$\quad L \rightarrow S: 1 \rightarrow 4, 2 \rightarrow 2, 3 \rightarrow 1$ $\quad$ $Q \rightarrow T: 1 \rightarrow 2, 2 \rightarrow 4, 3 \rightarrow 3$

$\quad X \rightarrow Y: 1 \rightarrow 1, 2 \rightarrow 3, 3 \rightarrow 2$ $\quad$ $M \rightarrow S: 1 \rightarrow 1, 2 \rightarrow 3, 3 \rightarrow 2$

$\quad R \rightarrow T: 1 \rightarrow 3, 2 \rightarrow 1, 3 \rightarrow 4$

from (b) to (a)

$S \rightarrow Z: 1 \rightarrow 1, 2 \rightarrow 2, 3 \rightarrow 4, 4 \rightarrow 3$ $\quad$ $U \rightarrow Z: 1 \rightarrow 3, 2 \rightarrow 1, 3 \rightarrow 4$

$\quad T \rightarrow Z: 1 \rightarrow 4, 2 \rightarrow 3, 3 \rightarrow 2, 4 \rightarrow 1$ $\quad$ $Y \rightarrow Z: 1 \rightarrow 3, 2 \rightarrow 2, 3 \rightarrow 1$

We have described an $O(\log^2 n)$ algorithm using $O(n)$ processors on a P-RAM. It is in fact possible to obtain an optimal edge-colouring of Halin graphs in $O(\log n)$ parallel time,[18] also using $O(n)$ processors on a P-RAM. This improved algorithm starts from an optimal edge-colouring of the tree $T$ of the Halin graph in $O(\log n)$ time. Such a colouring is possible using the algorithm described in the following section.

### 2.4.6 OPTIMAL EDGE-COLOURING OF TREES

We show that the problem of optimally edge-colouring a tree $T$ is possible in $O(\log n)$ time using $n$ processors on an EREW P-RAM. The colours used will be denoted by $0, 1, 2, \ldots, \Delta - 1$. First we root $T$ and for each vertex we determine its father and its sons. We can do this within the required constraints using the Euler tour technique described in subsection 2.1.1. In this way each node $v$ (of the original tree) has up to $\Delta - 1$ outgoing edges (directed to the sons of $v$) and (except for the root) exactly one incoming edge.

For each vertex $v$, let us label its outgoing edges by different elements from the set $Q = \{0, 1, 2, \ldots, \Delta - 1\}$. This can be done within our complexity constraints by ranking the list of the sons for each vertex $v$ in parallel. We then give the colour $i$ to the edge ($v$, $i$th son of $v$). By $x \oplus y$ we denote the operation $x + y \,(\mathrm{mod}\, \Delta)$. We shall be using the following obvious fact as a basis for legal colourings. For every element $x \in Q$ all the elements $x$, $x \oplus 1$, $x \oplus 2$, $\ldots$, $x \oplus (\Delta - 1)$ are different. Let $F(v)$ be the sum (under $\oplus$) of all labels of edges on the path from the root to $v$. For each vertex $v$ in parallel we colour the edge entering $v$ by $F(v)$. From the aforementioned obvious fact, it follows that this colouring of tree edges is a legal colouring. Moreover the colouring is optimal because only $\Delta$ colours are used.

In order to claim the complexity constraints, we just need to show how $F$ can be computed efficiently. We can use two different classical methodologies described in chapter 1 for this. The first uses the doubling technique and the second uses a parallel prefix computation.

The first method is simply to compute $F(v)$ by doubling on the pointers which, for each $v$, are initially $father(v)$. This takes $O(\log n)$ time using $n$ processors. In the second method the parallel prefix computation is performed on the traversal list (obtained from the Euler tour technique) of the tree. Let the traversal list be $L$. Each undirected edge $(v, father(v))$ is present twice on $L$, once as $(v, father(v))$ and once as $(father(v), v)$. Let $label(v, father(v)) = -label(father(v), v)$, where $label(father(v), v) =$ the colour assigned to this edge at the beginning of the algorithm. Notice that the sum of labels on any cycle (from a vertex back to itself on $L$) is zero. It is now easy to see the following. If the ingoing edge for the vertex $v$ is $e_k$, then

$$F(v) = label(e_1) \oplus label(e_2) \oplus label(e_3) \oplus \cdots \oplus label(e_k)$$

We can turn $L$ into a vector easily in $\log n$ time using $n$ processors. Thus the computation of $F(v)$, for all $v$, is now a parallel prefix computation (chapter 1) and can also be performed in $O(\log n)$ time using $n$ processors.

Notice the following interesting difference between these two methods of computation. The whole algorithm using the doubling technique, whilst it can be performed on a P-RAM, cannot be implemented on an EREW P-RAM. This is because there are inherent concurrent reads in doubling up the tree. No such problem arises using the traversal computation, and in this form the algorithm can be implemented on the more demanding EREW model within the same complexity constraints.

### 2.4.7 REMARKS ON VERTEX-COLOURING OF BIPARTITE AND HALIN GRAPHS, AND OF TREES

For purposes of completeness, we indicate here that the problems of optimally vertex-colouring bipartite and Halin graphs are both in *NC*. In fact the corresponding algorithms are somewhat simpler than the algorithms described earlier for edge-colouring.

In the case of bipartite graphs we just need compute the distances from an arbitrarily chosen vertex $v$ to all the other vertices. This can be done in $O(\log^2 n)$ time using $n^3$ processors on a P-RAM as we described much earlier in the chapter. Then those vertices an odd distance from $v$ are given colour 0 whilst those at an even distance are given the colour 1.

If the bipartite graph is a tree, then we can use the Euler tour technique to root the tree and to determine *father(v)* for each node $v$. Then we can use the doubling technique (doubling on father) to determine the parity of the distance of nodes from the root. Then each vertex can be coloured as before. In this case however the whole process only takes $O(\log n)$ time using $n$ processors.

For Halin graphs we can proceed as follows. If all but one of the vertices are skirt vertices then the colouring is quite easy. We therefore assume that this is not the case in what follows. It is easy to colour $T$ with two colours 1 and 2 depending on the parity of their distances from the root. Then colour clashes on the skirt $C$ may occur. These are resolved as follows. If $C$ has even length then we colour each second vertex on $C$ in a single parallel step with the colour 3. Otherwise we find a vertex $v$ all of whose sons are skirt vertices. If $L\ (=|C|)$ is odd then there is always such a $v$ with an odd number of sons. For convenience, we imagine that the skirt vertices have been consecutively numbered so that the sons of $v$ are the vertices $1, 2, \ldots, d(v) - 1$, where $d(v)$ is the degree of $v$. In a single parallel step, we colour $v$ with 3, even sons of $v$ with the colour of skirt vertex $L$, odd sons of $v$ with 1 or 2 (whichever is not the colour of skirt vertex $L$) and even non-son-of-$v$ skirt vertices with 3. All steps are easily achieved in $\log n$ time with $O(n)$ processors.

**Bibliographic notes**

Our sources for each of the algorithms described were referenced within the text. In the section dealing with problems of connectivity we used, as elsewhere throughout the text, the P-RAM model of computation. This practice prevented our describing an elegant O(log $n$) algorithm for finding the connected components of a graph due to Shiloach and Vishkin[42] and based on the W-RAM model. Moreover there does not seem to be an obvious way of implementing this algorithm on the P-RAM model. Also in the context of connectivity we might have described an algorithm [47] to strongly orientate a graph. The problem is to orientate the edges of a connected graph in such a way that, for any pair of vertices $i$ and $j$, there is a path from $i$ to $j$ and a path from $j$ to $i$.

We described an algorithm of Diks for six-vertex-colouring planar graphs in section 2.4. Very recently Chrobak, Diks and Hagerup[11] published a parallel algorithm to five-colour planar graphs in O(log $n \cdot$ log* $n$) time with O($n/($log $n \cdot$ log* $n$)) processors on a EREW P-RAM. This is the first parallel algorithm to achieve optimal speed-up for the problem.

Perhaps a notable exception to problems dealt with in this chapter is the problem of planarity testing. Ja'Ja' and Simon[26] have shown that this problem is in *NC*.

**Bibliography**

[1] R. Anderson. A parallel algorithm for the maximal path problem. *STOC 1985*, 3337.

[2] K. Appel and W. Haken. Every planar map is four colourable. 'Part 1: Discharging' and 'Part 2: Reducibility' are successive papers in *Illinois Journal of Mathematics* **21** (1977), 429–567.

[3] M. J. Atallah. Parallel strong orientation of an undirected graph. *Information Processing Letters* **18**, 1 (1984), 37–9.

[4] M. J. Atallah and S. Hambrush. Solving tree problems on a mesh-connected processor array. *FOCS 1985*, 220–31.

[5] M. J. Atallah and S. R. Kosaraju. Graph problems on a mesh-connected processor array. *Journal of the ACM* **31**, 3 (1984), 649–67.

[6] M. Atallah and U. Vishkin, Finding Euler tours in parallel. *Journal of Computer and System Sciences* **29**, 330–7 (1984).

[7] B. Awerbuch, A. Israeli and Y. Shiloach. Finding Euler circuits in logarithmic parallel time. *STOC 1984*, 249–57.

[8] J. Bentley. A parallel algorithm for constructing minimum spanning trees. *Journal of Algorithms* **1** (1980), 51–9.

[9] C. Berge and A. Chouila-Houri. *Programming, Games and Transportation Networks.* Wiley (1965), 179.

[10] F. Y. Chin, J. Lam and I. Chen. Efficient parallel algorithms for some graph problems. *Communications of the ACM* **25**, 9 (1982).

[11] M. Chrobak, K. Diks and T. Hagerup. Parallel 5-colouring of planar graphs. *ICAL 1987*.

[12] S. Cook. The classification of problems which have fast parallel algorithms. *FCT 1983*.

[13] E. Dekel, D. Nassimi and S. Sahni. Parallel matrix and graph algorithms. *SJCOMP* **10** (1981), 657–74.

[14] K. Diks. A fast parallel algorithm for six-colouring of planar graphs. *Proceedings of the 12th Symposium on Mathematical Foundations of Computer Science* (1986). Lecture Notes in Computer Science 233 (eds. J. Grunska, B. Rovan and J. Wiedermann). Springer-Verlag, 273–82.

[15] S. Fiorini. On the chromatic index of outerplanar graphs. *Journal of Combinatorial Theory* (B) **18** (1975), 35–8.

[16] H. Gabow and O. Kariv. Algorithms for edge colouring bipartite graphs and multigraphs. *SIAM Journal of Computing* **11**, 1 (1982), 117–29.

[17] A. M. Gibbons. *Algorithmic Graph Theory*. Cambridge University Press (1985).

[18] A. M. Gibbons, A. Israeli and W. Rytter. Parallel $O(\log(n))$ time optimal edge-colouring of trees and Halin graphs. *Information Processing Letters* **27**, 1 (1988).

[19] A. M. Gibbons and W. Rytter. Fast parallel algorithms for edge-colouring of some tree structured graphs. *FCT 1987*.

[20] D. S. Hirschberg, A. K. Chandra and D. V. Sarwate. Computing connected components on parallel computers. *Communications of the ACM* (1979), 461–4.

[21] P. H. Hochschild, E. W. Mayr and A. Siegel. Techniques for solving graph problems in parallel environments. *FOCS 1983*, 351–9.

[22] I. Holyer. The *NP*-completeness of edge-colouring. *SIAM Journal of Computing* **10** (1981), 718–20.

[23] M. A. Huang. Solving some graph problems with optimal or near optimal speed up on mesh-of-trees networks. *FOCS 1985*, 232–40.

[24] A. Israeli and Y. Shiloach. An improved algorithm for maximal matching. *Information Processing Letters* **33** (1986), 57–60.

[25] A. Israeli and A. Itai. A fast and simple randomized parallel algorithm for maximal matching. *Information Processing Letters* **22** (1986), 77–80.

[26] J. Ja'Ja' and J. Simon. Parallel algorithms in graph theory:planarity testing. *SIAM Journal of Computing* (1982), 314–28.

[27] L. Janiga and V. Koubek. A note on finding minimum cuts in directed planar networks by parallel computations. *Information Processing Letters* **21** (1985), 75–8.

[28] H. J. Karloff, D. B. Shmoys and D. Sovoker. Efficient parallel algorithms for edge colouring problems. *Journal of Algorithms* **8** (1987), 39–52.

[29] R. M. Karp, E. Upfal and A. Wigderson. Constructing a perfect matching is in random *NC*. *STOC 1985*, 22–32.

[30] R. M. Karp and A. Wigderson. A fast parallel algorithm for the maximal independent set problem. *STOC 1984*, 266–72.

[31] D. Kozen, U. V. Vazirani and V. V. Vazirani. *NC* algorithms for comparability graphs, interval graphs and testing for unique perfect matching. *Fifth Conference on Foundations of Software Technology and Theoretical Computer Science*. Lecture Notes in Computer Science. Springer-Verlag (1985).

[32] L. Kucera. Parallel computation and conflicts in memory access. *Information Processing Letters* **14**, 2 (1982), 93–6.

[33] G. F. Lev, N. Pippenger and L. G. Valiant. A fast parallel algorithm for routing in permutation networks. *IEEE Transactions on Computers* **C-30**, 2 (1981), 93–100.

[34] L. Lovasz. Computing ears and branchings in parallel. *FOCS 1985*, 464–7.

[35] M. Luby. A simple parallel algorithm for the maximal independent set problem. *STOC 1985*, 1–10.

[36] S. L. Mitchell and S. T. Hedetniemi. Linear algorithms for edge-colouring trees and unicycle graphs. *Information Processing Letters* **9**, 3 (1979), 110–12.

[37] D. Nassimi and S. Sahni. Finding connected components and connected ones on a mesh connected parallel computer. *SIAM Journal of Computing* **9** (1980), 744–57.

[38] A. Proskurowski and M. Sysło. Efficient vertex- and edge-colouring of outerplanar graphs. *SIAM Journal of Algebraic and Discrete Methods* **7** (1986), 131–6.

[39] M. J. Quinn and N. Deo. Parallel graph algorithms. *ACM Computing Surveys* **16**, 3 (1984).

[40] E. Reghbati and D. Corneil. Parallel computations in graph theory. *SIAM Journal of Computing* **7** (1978), 230–7.

[41] C. Savage and J. Ja'Ja'. Fast efficient parallel algorithms for some graph problems. *SIAM Journal of Computing* **10** (1981), 682–91.

[42] Y. Shiloach and U. Vishkin. An $O(\log n)$ parallel connectivity algorithm. *Journal of Algorithms* **2** (1981), 57–63.

[43] Y. Shiloach and U. Vishkin. An $O(n^2 \log n)$ parallel *MAX-FLOW* algorithm. *Journal of Algorithms* **3** (1982), 128–46.

[44] R. E. Tarjan and U. Vishkin. Finding biconnected components and computing tree functions in logarithmic parallel time. *FOCS 1984*, 12–20, also *SIAM Journal of Computing* **14**, 4 (1985), 862–74.

[45] Y. H. Tsin and F. Y. Chin. Efficient parallel algorithms for a class of graph theoretic problems. *SIAM Journal of Computing* **13** (1984), 580–99.

[46] U. V. Vazirani and V. V. Vazirani. The two-processor scheduling problem is in random *NC*. *STOC 1985*, 11–21.

[47] U. Vishkin. An efficient parallel strong orientation. Technical Report, New York University.

# CHAPTER 3

# EXPRESSION EVALUATION

In this chapter, before going on to look at the parallel evaluation of straight-line programs and briefly at dynamic programming, we show that certain expressions may be computed using optimal parallel algorithms. The main algorithm (section 3.3) is explained in the context of arithmetic expression evaluation. In fact the algorithm does have wider applicability. It can be used for the evaluation of many types of algebraic expressions. In particular we prove that it supplies an optimal parallel means of evaluating algebraic expressions with operations from an algebra whose carrier is of $O(1)$ size. This in turn leads to many applications. In chapter 4, for example, the same algorithm is used to compute certain unusual algebraic expressions whose evaluation corresponds to recognising a particular subclass of context-free languages. An optimal algorithm for another non-standard class of expressions is also described in this chapter. This is for the computation of regular expressions whose results correspond to non-deterministic finite automata.

The input to the main algorithm of this chapter, as described in section 3.3, is an expression tree with its leaves numbered consecutively from left to right. In the next section we describe how, given a string representing an expression, we can obtain the corresponding expression tree. In doing so we describe an optimal parallel algorithms due to Bar-On and Vishkin.[1]

## 3.1 Constructing the expression tree

The input to the algorithm we describe here is a string representing the arithmetic expression which we take to be stored in an array. As an example we take the input expression $(a + b) * (c - (d + e)) + f$. Here the operands are numerical constants and the whole expression would be stored in an array of length seventeen.

We show first how to find the corresponding trees given fully bracketed expressions. In a fully bracketed expression each subexpression is enclosed in the brackets '(', ')'. For example, the fully bracketed expression corresponding to our example is $((((a) + (b)) * ((c) - ((d) + (e)))) + (f))$.

If we wish to find the expression tree for fully bracketed expressions, then it is possible to disregard all elements other than brackets. Hence the tree for our example expression is the same as the tree corresponding to the sequence of brackets $((((()())((()(())))())$. We shall first show how this is possible. Each node of such a tree corresponds to a pair of matching left and right brackets. The sons correspond to matching pairs of brackets contained within the (outer) brackets corresponding to a given node: $((\ldots)(\ldots))$. See for example figure 3.1.

Hence the main task is to compute all such pairs, each pair consisting of an opening bracket and a corresponding closing bracket.

We now define $match(i)$ to be that position in the string at which there is a closing (opening) bracket corresponding to the opening (closing) bracket at position $i$. This function plays a crucial role in the construction of the expression tree.

For our example sequence of brackets we have that $match(1) = 12$ and that $match(3) = 8$.

The expression tree can be quite easily found provided that we know the function $match$ and provided that the expression is fully bracketed. Fully bracketed expressions are a special case of simple expressions. An expression is simple if and only if it is enclosed in brackets and every segment enclosed in brackets is of the form $((E_1) \operatorname{op}_1 (E_2) \operatorname{op}_2 \cdots \operatorname{op}_{k-1} (E_k))$, where $\operatorname{op}_i$ are operations of the same priority (fully bracketed expressions satisfy this requirement with $k = 2$). The subtree corresponding to such a segment is shown in figure 3.2.

We can find the tree corresponding to any simple expression in constant time with $n$ processors as follows. The method is readily simulated in $\log n$ time with

*Figure 3.1*

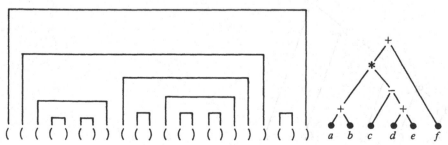

$n/\log n$ processors. We assign a processor to each element of the string. Each matched pair of parentheses encloses a subexpression equivalent to a tree like that of figure 3.2. The root of this subtree is an operator and the subexpression acts like an operand in the enclosing simple expression. We set up pointers to identify each root with its corresponding pair of matched parentheses. The root is easily found for each pair of matched brackets by causing, for example, the processor associated with the right parenthesis to look one position to its left. If that position contains a constant or a variable then the root will be that operator one further position to the left, otherwise the position contains a right parenthesis. The root is then one position to the left of the match for this parenthesis. The processor assigned to any operator may find its left son (the previous operator if it exists in the subexpression, otherwise the operand to the left of the operator) and its right son (the operand to its right) in an obvious manner.

We shall see later how to transform each expression in optimal parallel time to an equivalent simple expression. We now describe how the function *match* may be found with similar efficiency.

First we check to see if the sequence of brackets is a correct one, by which we mean that to each left bracket there corresponds a right bracket and vice versa.

Let one erasing operation consist of erasing a pair () of consecutive left and right brackets. The sequence of brackets is correct if and only if it can be reduced to an empty string. It is easy to see that each sequence $x$ of brackets can be reduced to a sequence which cannot be further reduced and moreover that such a sequence is unique. This irreducible sequence is denoted by *reduced*($x$). For example *reduced*(')(())()((') = ‘))((‘. Generally each irreducible sequence is of the form $)^i(^j$, where $i$ and $j$ are nonnegative integers indicating the number of occurrences of the corresponding brackets. For example, ‘))((’ = ‘)$^2$($^2$‘.

*Figure 3.2.* The subtree corresponding to a simple subexpression $((E_1)\, \mathrm{op}_1(E_2)\, \mathrm{op}_2\cdots(E_k))$

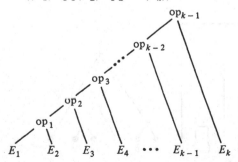

We introduce the operation $\circledR$ for concatenating irreducible sequences: $x \circledR y = reduced(xy)$, which is defined for irreducible $x$ and $y$. For example $')^2('')^3(^2' = ')^4(^2'$. This operation can be defined algorithmically as follows:

$$')^i('^j \circledR ')^k('^l = \text{if } k \geqslant j \text{ then } ')^{i+k-j}('^l \text{ else } ')^i('^{l+j-k}$$

Thus the computation of $\circledR$ can be made in O(1) time on a sequential RAM provided that the integers $i$, $j$, $k$ and $l$ are known. Now, having a sequence of brackets, we can compute its irreducible form as a product of its consecutive symbols, using $\circledR$. This can be done using a regular binary tree. For example, take the sequence $((((())(())(())))$. The corresponding tree of the computation is presented in figure 3.3.

We can see that our example is of a correct string since its irreducible form, which appears at the root, is the empty string. As a useful side effect we have computed a tree of partial results. We shall use this to compute $match(i)$ for a given $i$ in O(log $n$) sequential time.

Assume that there is a left bracket at position $i$. We now describe how we can traverse this tree starting at $i$ and following that unique path in the tree which takes us to the matching right bracket. This traversal takes at most log $n$ moves in a bottom-up phase followed by a similar number of moves in a top-down phase. Whenever we are currently visiting a node which covers the leaves from positions $p$ to $q$ and we are in a bottom-up phase, then the variable $z$ records the reduced form of the substring stored in positions $i+1$ to $q$. In the top-down phase, $z$ records the substring from positions $i+1$ to $p$  1. Initially $z$ is the empty string. This algorithm functions correctly provided that the string is a correct sequence of brackets, which can of course be checked by an inspection

*Figure 3.3*

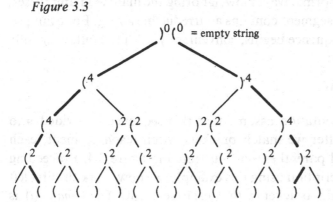

of the value at the root of the tree. One step of the bottom-up phase is

**if** we are at a node which is a right son
    **then** move to its father $\{z$ is not changed$\}$
    **else if** $z$ⓇR[value of the right brother] starts with a right bracket
        **then** move to its right brother and start the top-down phase $\{z$ is not changed$\}$
        **else begin**
            $z \leftarrow z$Ⓡ[value of the right brother]
            move to its father
        **end**

If $l$ and $r$ denote the left and right sons respectively of the currently visited node, then one step of the top-down phase is

    **if** $z$Ⓡ$value(l)$ starts with a right bracket
        **then** move to $l$
        **else begin**
      $z \leftarrow z$Ⓡ$value(l)$
        move to $r$
        **end**

    The tree of partial results can be computed in $O(\log n)$ time with $n/\log n$ processors using the algorithm for the computation of associative functions described in chapter 1.
    The next difficulty is how to compute $match(i)$ for all $i$ in $O(\log n)$ time with $n/\log n$ processors. We divide the string (perhaps augmented with a minimum number of dummy locations to achieve a length which is a power of 2) into segments of length $O(\log n)$. Within each segment we match brackets where possible, using one processor per segment. This is easily achieved in a single pass using a stack in the normal way. Now, ignoring the matched parentheses, we can assume that each segment contains an irreducible string. For example, suppose that the input sequence begins, conveniently, with the following fully matched initial sequence:

    $((()(()())(()()))()(()))()) \cdots$

For convenience of presentation assume that this sequence is divided into segments of length 8. After we match brackets within each segment, each contains four unmatched parentheses as illustrated in figure 3.4. Proceeding with our algorithmic description using this example, we now mark the first left bracket and the last right bracket within each segment. Then $match(i)$ is computed for each position $i$ containing a marked bracket and the computed positions are also marked. All this is indicated in figure 3.4.

The marked positions divide each segment into intervals. We call intervals containing left brackets left intervals, and intervals containing right brackets right intervals. To each left interval there corresponds a right interval. In fact they form a bracket structure. We assign a processor to each left interval. One processor can sequentially compute the function *match* for positions in this interval in $\log n$ time by scanning the positions in the corresponding right intervals.

For example the third bracket (at position 3) is marked and it is the first bracket in the interval $\{3,4\}$. The matching bracket corresponding to 3 is 6, which is the last bracket in the interval $\{5,6\}$. Hence 6 is the match for 3 and 4 is the match for 5. In general if $match(l) = r$ and the left interval $\{l, l+1, \ldots, l+k\}$ corresponds to the right interval $\{r-k, r-k+1, \ldots, r\}$ then $match(l+i) = r-i$, for $1 \leqslant i \leqslant k$.

This gives us an optimal parallel algorithm, since there are only $O(n/\log n)$ intervals. Lemma 3.1 merely states this fact. In section 4.4 there is an extension of the technique described here used in an optimal parallel algorithm for parsing bracket languages.

*Lemma 3.1*

The function $match(i)$ can be computed for all positions $i$ in $O(\log n)$ time using $n/\log n$ processors.                                                                     □

*Figure 3.4.* Partitioning the leaves into left and right intervals

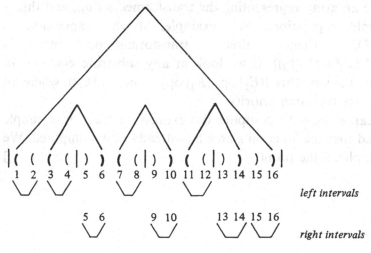

If the input string is a simple expression then, using the function *match*, we have
seen that we can easily construct the expression tree from the string. The
substance of the proof of the following theorem is therefore to show how to
convert the input string into a simple expression.

*Theorem 3.1*
Given a string (stored in a vector) representing an arithmetic expression, the
expression tree can be computed in $O(\log n)$ time using $n/\log n$ processors.

*Proof*
The input is a string representing the arithmetic expression. We assume the
usual priority of operations $*, /, +, -$. Assume also that the whole expression
is enclosed in brackets.
   Perform the following operations.
1.   For each left (right) bracket we insert two additional left (right) brackets
     immediately to the left.
2.   Each symbol + or − is replaced by ')) + ((' or, respectively, ')) − ((' .
3.   Each symbol * or / is replaced by ') * (' or, respectively, ') / (' .
4.   It may happen that many redundant brackets are created. We remove
     redundant brackets as follows. A left bracket is redundant if it is preceded
     by a left bracket and if the matching brackets for these two brackets also
     occur consecutively. In other words there is a situation like: '((. . .))'.
     Analogously a right bracket is redundant if its matching left bracket is
     redundant.

Such a transformation can obviously be achieved in constant time with $n$
processors (which is easily simulated in $O(\log n)$ time using $n/\log n$ processors).
As output we have an array representing the transformed string, and this is
evidently a simple expression. For example, if the expression is
$(a + b - c * d * e * f)$,        then        after        transformation        it        is
$(((a)) + ((b)) + ((c) * (d) * (e) * (f)))$. If we look at any substring enclosed in
brackets then it has the structure $((E_1) \, \mathrm{op}_1 \, (E_2) \, \mathrm{op}_2 \cdots \mathrm{op}_{k-1} \, (E_k))$, where all
the operators, $\mathrm{op}_i$, are the same priority.
   We described earlier how to compute the expression tree for a simple
expression provided that the function *match* has already been computed. We
have therefore completed the proof.                                            □

## 3.2 A parallel pebble game with applications to expression evaluation

We introduce here a parallel pebble game on binary trees. This game forms the basis of the final stage of the first version of the optimal parallel algorithm for expression evaluation described in section 3.3.

Within the game each node $v$ of the tree has associated with it a similar node denoted by $cond(v)$. At the outset of the game $cond(v) = v$, for all $v$. During the game the pairs $(v, cond(v))$ can be thought of as additional edges. Another notion we shall require is that of 'pebbling' a node. At the end of this section we illustrate an application of the pebbling game to arithmetic expression evaluation. Within that application, pebbling a node denotes the fact that in the current state of the game the processor associated with that node has sufficient information to evaluate the subtree rooted there. At the outset of the game only the leaves of the tree are therefore pebbled.

We say that a node $v$ is 'active' if and only if $cond(v) \neq v$.

The three operations *activate*, *square* and *pebble* are components of a 'move' within the game and are defined as follows.

*activate*
 **for** all non-leaf nodes $v$ **in parallel do**
  **if** $v$ is not active and precisely one of its sons is pebbled **then**
                          $cond(v)$ becomes the other son
   **if** $v$ is not active and both sons are pebbled **then**
                          $cond(v)$ becomes one of the sons arbitrarily
*square*
  **for** all nodes $v$ **in parallel do** $cond(v) \leftarrow cond(cond(v))$
*pebble*
  **for** all nodes $v$ **in parallel do if** $cond(v)$ is pebbled **then** pebble $v$

Figure 3.5 shows applications of these operations for the binary tree illustrated there.

Now we define one (composite) move of the pebbling game to be the sequence of individual operations

(*activate*, *square*, *square*, *pebble*)

in that order. Then the following theorem provides a key result.

*Theorem 3.2*
Let $T$ be a binary tree with $n$ leaves. If initially only the leaves are pebbled then after $\log_2 n$ moves of the pebbling game the root of $T$ becomes pebbled.

*Proof*
For simplicity we assume that $n$ is a power of 2. Now we consider a modified
pebbling move consisting of the sequence

(*pebble, activate, square, square*)

It will be enough to prove that after $\log n + 1$ such moves the root will be
pebbled. This is because if a node is pebbled after $k + 1$ of these moves then it
will be pebbled after $k$ of the original moves. The first pebble operation and the
last individual operations *activate, square, square* are redundant in this
context. Let $size(x)$ denote the number of leaves of $T_x$, the binary (sub)tree
rooted at $x$. By $size(x/y)$ we mean $size(x) - size(y)$. We number the modified
moves from 0 to $\log n$.

*Claim*
After the $k$th modified move the following invariants hold.
(I1)   if $size(x) \leqslant 2^k$ then $x$ is pebbled
(I2)       (a) $size(x/cond(x)) \geqslant 2^k$
           or (b) no son of $cond(x)$ is pebbled
           or (c) $cond(x)$ is a leaf.

*Figure 3.5* In (a) we see the initial pebbling of the leaves of the tree, indicated by
darkly coloured nodes, and the bold edges are the $(v, cond(v))$ for those $v$ which are
active after the first execution of the operation *activate*. Now the result of applying
the operation *square* to (a) is shown in (b). Then (c) shows the result of applying
the operation *square* once more. The additional dark nodes in (d) are those which
become pebbled after applying the operation *pebble* to (c).

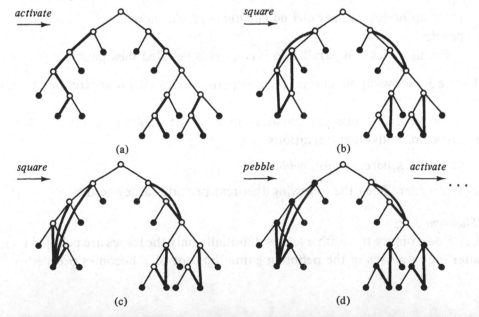

We prove the claim by induction on $k$. After the first move (that is, move 0) I1 holds because the only $x$ for which $size(x) = 1$ are leaves which were pebbled at the outset. I2 holds as follows. If no son of $x$ is a leaf then $x = cond(x)$ and (b) is satisfied. Suppose then that $x$ has a leaf as a son, then $x$ becomes activated. Then, no matter if the *square* operations after $cond(x)$, (a) is satisfied. Thus we have a basis for the induction, and we take as our induction hypothesis that (I1) and (I2) hold after $k - 1$ moves.

First we prove that (I1) holds after $k$ moves. Let $x$ be a node such that $size(x) \leqslant 2^k$. Then each non-leaf node of $T_x$ has a son of size not greater than $2^{k-1}$. From the induction hypothesis, I1 therefore provides that every non-leaf node has a pebbled son after move $k - 1$. Moreover, I2 implies that $cond(x)$ is a leaf or that $size(x/cond(x)) \geqslant 2^{k-1}$. In both cases $cond(x)$ must have been pebbled after move $k - 1$, for (taking the non-trivial case) if $size(x/cond(x)) \geqslant 2^{k-1}$ then $size(cond(x)) \leqslant 2^{k-1}$ and I1 proves the point. In move $k$, the operation *pebble* will pebble $x$. This proves (I1) of the claim.

Next we prove that (I2) holds after move $k$. Let $cond(x) = y$ after move $k - 1$. We know from the induction hypothesis that $y$ is a leaf (in which case it remains so after move $k$ so satisfying (c)) or no son of $y$ is pebbled or $size(x/y) \geqslant 2^{k-1}$. We consider the last two cases in turn.

*Case 1: $size(x/y) \geqslant 2^{k-1}$*

We let $z = cond(y)$ after move $k - 1$ and consider $y$ with respect to I2. If $size(y/z) \geqslant 2^{k-1}$ then after the operation *square*, when $cond(x) = z$, $size(x/cond(x)) = size(x/y) + size(y/z) \geqslant 2^k$ and so (a) is satisfied. Otherwise no son of $z$ was pebbled after move $k - 1$ or $z$ was a leaf. If not then both sons of $z$ were not pebbled after move $k - 1$ or $z$ was a leaf. We need only consider the first case because if $z$ was a leaf $cond(x)$ becomes a leaf after the operation *square* so satisfying (c). If no son of $z$ is pebbled in move $k$ then (b) is satisfied, so consider the case that one of the sons, $z_1$ or $z_2$, of $z$ is pebbled in move $k$. Suppose that $z_1$ is pebbled. We have that $size(z_1) > 2^{k-1}$ because $z_1$ was not pebbled in move $k - 1$. Now the operation *activate* sets $cond(z)$ to $z_2$, hence at this moment $size(z/cond(z)) = size(z_1)$ and after two *square* operations $cond(x) = z_3$ where $z_3$ is a descendant of $z_2$. Both $z_1$ and $z_3$ are descendants of $y$ but not one of the other, thus $size(y) \geqslant size(z_1) + size(z_3)$. It follows that, after move $k$, $size(x/cond(x)) \geqslant size(x/y) + size(z_1) > 2^k$ and so (a) is satisfied.

*Case 2: $y$ is not a leaf and no son of $y$ is pebbled in move $k - 1$*

Let $z_1$ and $z_2$ be the sons of $y$. If no son of $y$ is pebbled in move $k$ then (b) is satisfied. So suppose that $z_1$ is pebbled. The operation *activate* sets

$cond(y) = z_2$. We have from I1 that $size(z_1) > 2^{k-1}$ because $z_1$ was not pebbled in move $k - 1$. Thus $size(x/z_2) > size(y/z_2) = size(z_1) > 2^{k-1}$. Let $cond(z_2) = v$ and $cond(v) = w$ after move $k - 1$. After this move $v$ satisfies I2. Suppose that $size(v/w) \geqslant 2^{k-1}$. In this case, after two *square* moves $cond(x) = w$, so that $size(z_2/w) > size(v/w) \geqslant 2^{k-1}$ and hence $size(x/cond(x)) = size(x/z_2) + size(z_2/w) > 2^{k-1}$ and thus (a) is satisfied.

So we need only consider the cases that no son of $cond(v)$ is pebbled or that $cond(v)$ is a leaf. If $cond(v)$ is a leaf after move $k - 1$ then $cond(x)$ will be the same leaf after move $k$ and thus (c) would be satisfied. The only case left to consider is that no son of $cond(v)$ is pebbled after move $k - 1$. If in move $k$ no son of $cond(v)$ is pebbled then (b) will be satisfied, so suppose that $v_1$ is pebbled where $v_1$ and $v_2$ are sons of $v$. The situation is as illustrated in figure 3.6.

Now $size(z_2/v_2) > size(v/v_2) = size(v_1) > 2^{k-1}$ because $v_1$ was not pebbled after move $k - 1$. After one *square* operation $cond(x) = z_2$ and $cond(z_2) = v_2$. Hence after two *square* operations $cond(x) = v_2$, therefore $size(x/cond(x)) = size(x/z_2) + size(z_2/v_2) > 2^k$ and so (a) is satisfied. Thus we have proved that I2 is preserved and have justified the claim.

Whilst I2 was needed to prove I1, the theorem follows from I1. For we have that $size(\text{root}) = n$ and so after $k$ moves of the pebble game, where $n = 2^k$, the root is pebbled. That concludes the proof of the theorem.   $\square$

The following two examples illustrate applications of the pebbling game.

*Example 3.1*
Consider the arithmetic expression $(((3 + (2 * 3)) * 3) + 5)$ whose tree is shown in figure 3.7(a). We assign a processor to each non-leaf node of the tree (four

*Figure 3.6*

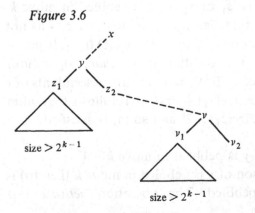

processors in this example). Now we consider first the following naive algorithm.

>    **repeat** 'several' **times**
>        **for** all nodes $v$ **in parallel do**
>            **if** the values of the sons of $v$ are computed **then** compute the value of $v$

In our example 'several' = 4 and, in fact, only one processor is busy at any time. Thus in general this simple algorithm does not necessarily provide any parallel speed-up and, clearly, 'several' = height of the tree = $\Omega(n)$. We refine the algorithm as follows. Suppose that the processor associated with node $v$ is idle

Figure 3.7. After (a), the bold edges represent the pairs $(v, cond(v))$ for which $v$ are active

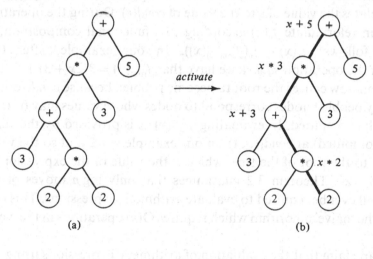

(a)    $\xrightarrow{activate}$    (b)

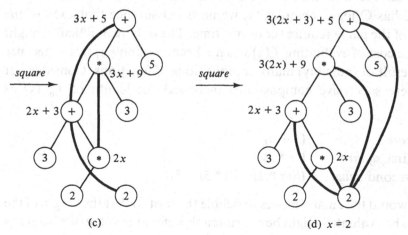

$\xrightarrow{square}$ (c)    $\xrightarrow{square}$    (d) $x = 2$

because not both of its sons, $v_1$ and $v_2$, are computed. However it may be the case that one son (say, $v_2$) has been evaluated. Then the processor associated with $v$, instead of idling, can do some useful work. It can construct the form of the function $f_v(x)$ which relates the value of $v$ to the value at $cond(v)$. Initially $v = cond(v)$, for all $v$, and so we initialise all the $f_v(x)$ to be $x$. During the operation *activate*, $cond(v)$ becomes $v_1$. In this application we add to the operation *activate* a reformulation of $f_v(x)$ according to the functional composition $f_v(x) \leftarrow f_v(x \diamond (\text{value at } v_2))$, where $\diamond$ is the operator at $x$. For example, if $v$ is the root of the tree in figure 3.7 and only the values of the leaves are known, then the value associated with the right son is 5. Then the function $f_v(x)$ becomes $x + 5$ during execution of the *activate* command. We then know that *if* the value of the son $v_1$ is $x$ *then* the value of $v$ is $x + 5$, and this conditional valuation is the motivation for the appellation '*cond*' of $x$. In general $f_v(x)$ relates the value of $v$ to the value of $cond(v)$. During the operation *square* we again reformulate $f_v(x)$ according to a functional composition, in this case as follows: $f_v(x) \leftarrow f_v(f_{cond(v)}(x))$. In our example, after two applications of the operation *square* we have that $f_{\text{root}}(x) = 3(2x + 3) + 5$. The *pebble* operation now causes the root to become pebbled because $cond(\text{root})$ is pebbled. Newly pebbled nodes correspond to nodes whose values may be (and are immediately) computed. In evaluating $f_{\text{root}}(x)$, $x$ is provided by the value (should it be computed) at $cond(\text{root})$. In our example $x = 2$ and so the value corresponding to the root of the tree (which is the value of the expression) is $3(2 * 2 + 3) + 5 = 26$. Theorem 3.2 guarantees that only $\log n$ moves of the pebble game will ever be required to evaluate arithmetic expressions. This is in contrast with the 'naive' algorithm which requires $O(n)$ operations in the worst case.

Before we can claim that the evaluation of arithmetic expressions using the pebble game has $O(\log n)$ complexity, we need reassurance that each of the $\log n$ moves of the game requires constant time. The only real difficulty might arise from the cost of evaluating $f_v(x)$ when $x$ becomes known; this is because $f_v(x)$ is the result of (possibly) many compositions of functions. Consider our example; there successive compositions increased the length of $f_{\text{root}}(x)$ as follows:

| | |
|---|---|
| after *activate* | $(x + 5)$ |
| after the first *square* | $((x * 3) + 5)$ |
| after the second *square* | $((((x * 2) + 3) * 3) + 5)$ |

In general it would take many moves to pebble the root so that the length of the expression to be evaluated might be considerable before the value of $x$ becomes known. However, using the normal rules of algebraic simplification, it is not difficult to see that repeated composition of expressions as required by the algorithm leads to any $f_v(x)$ having at most the general form $f_v(x) = (ax + b)/(cx + d)$, where $a$, $b$, $c$ and $d$ are numerical constants. Initially $a = d = 1$ and $b = c = 0$. Here we assume that the only operations occurring are multiplication, division, addition and subtraction. Thus composing the two functions $f_{v_1}(x) = (a_1 x + b_1)/(c_1 x + d_1)$ and $f_{v_2}(x) = (a_2 x + b_2)/(c_2 x + d_2)$ yields

$$f_{v_1}(x) \leftarrow f_{v_1}(f_{v_2}(x)) = (a_3 x + b_3)/(c_3 x + d_3)$$

where $a_3 = a_1 a_2 + b_1 c_2$, $b_3 = a_1 b_2 + b_1 d_2$, $c_3 = a_2 c_1 + c_2 d_1$ and $d_3 = b_2 c_1 + d_1 d_2$. We can therefore use four constants $a$, $b$, $c$ and $d$ to describe any $f_v(x)$. These can be recomputed in constant time after each functional composition and, when $x$ becomes known, $f_v(x)$ can be calculated also in constant bounded time.

*Example 3.2*
Consider the algebra with carrier $A = \{a, b, c, d\}$ and binary operator $\diamond$:

| $\diamond$ | $a$ | $b$ | $c$ | $d$ |
|---|---|---|---|---|
| $a$ | $b$ | $c$ | $d$ | $a$ |
| $b$ | $c$ | $d$ | $d$ | $b$ |
| $c$ | $d$ | $b$ | $b$ | $c$ |
| $d$ | $a$ | $b$ | $c$ | $d$ |

We wish to evaluate expressions within this algebra and take as an example the expression $E = (((a \diamond (b \diamond c)) \diamond d) \diamond b)$ which, topologically, has the expression tree of figure 3.7(a). If $v_1$ is the root of that tree, then we label the other non-leaf vertices $v_2$, $v_3$ and $v_4$ at increasing distances from $v_1$. We use the pebble game to evaluate $E$ in essentially the same fashion as the arithmetic expression was evaluated in example 3.1. As in that example, in order to claim $O(\log n)$ complexity, we need to show that each of the $\log n$ moves of the augmented pebble game can be achieved at constant-bounded cost. In example 3.1 we stored a representation of an algebraic expression at each internal vertex $v$; here we store the tabular representation of a function $f_v(x)$. The table records the values of $f_v(x)$ for each possible value of the subexpression at $cond(x)$. For example, after the initial *activate* operation, $f_{\text{root}}(x)$ is

| $a$ | $b$ | $c$ | $d$ |
|---|---|---|---|
| $c$ | $d$ | $b$ | $b$ |

Here the first row stores arguments (the possible values of the subexpression at *cond*(root)) while the second row stores the corresponding values of $f_v(x)$. We shall adopt the convention of unambiguously representing such a table by its second row. Thus here $f_{\text{root}}(x) = (c, d, b, b)$. Composing functions in this format is a simple matter. If $f_1 = (c, d, b, b)$ and $f_2 = (c, b, a, d)$ then $f_1(f_2) = (b, d, c, b)$ because $f_2$ maps $a$ to $c$ and $f_1$ maps $c$ to $b$ and so on. Such a composition can clearly be achieved in a time proportional to the table length by a single processor associated with $v_1$. This time is a constant determined by the size of the carrier. Also, when the value at *cond*(x) becomes known, the value of $f_v(x)$ is found in one step by table look-up. Thus for our example expression, utilising similar functional compositions as those described in example 3.1 to augment the component operations of the pebble game, we obtain the successive representations for the $f_v(x)$ shown in figure 3.8. Thus just before the (first) *pebble* operation $f_{\text{root}}(x) = (b, c, c, b)$ and the value at (the leaf) *cond*(root) is $c$. Thus the value of the expression is $c$.

Example 3.2 is obviously generalisable to expressions in any algebra with carrier of constant bounded size, taking this along with example 3.1 we have theorem 3.3.

*Theorem 3.3*
Using the parallel pebble game,
(a)  Arithmetic expressions can be evaluated on a P-RAM in $O(\log n)$ time using $O(n)$ processors,
(b)  Algebraic expressions from an algebra with a carrier of constant bounded size can be evaluated on a P-RAM in $O(\log n)$ time using $O(n)$ processors.                                                                      □

The most important algorithm of this chapter, which is described in the next section, reduces the number of processors required in the evaluations referred to in theorem 3.3 to $n/\log n$.

We complete this section with the following two theorems concerning the

*Figure 3.8*

|                    | $f_{v1}$ | $f_{v2}$ | $f_{v3}$ | $f_{v4}$ |
|--------------------|----------|----------|----------|----------|
| after *activate*      | (cdbb)   | (abcd)   | (bcda)   | (cddb)   |
| after first *square*  | (cdbb)   | (bcda)   | (daac)   | (cddb)   |
| after second *square* | (bccb)   | (daac)   | (daac)   | (cddb)   |

parallel pebble game. Theorem 3.4 shows that, in general, the number of moves required in the game as played on binary trees cannot be decreased.

*Theorem 3.4*

For each $n$ there is a binary tree with $n$ leaves which requires $\log n$ moves to pebble the root.

*Proof*

It is enough to consider only the numbers $n$ which are powers of 2. In this case the regular full binary tree with $n$ leaves satisfies the thesis. □

We could apply the parallel pebble game to directed acyclic graphs (so-called dags). In this situation one can ask if a result analogous to theorem 3.4 holds. In other words, can logarithmic-parallel-time computations be extended to dags? Theorem 3.5 provides a negative answer. In a binary dag each vertex has out-degree of 2, except 'leaves' which have zero out-degree. A root of such a dag has zero in-degree.

*Theorem 3.5*

For $n \geqslant 3$ there is a binary dag which requires $(n-2)/2$ moves to pebble the root, where $n$ is the number of nodes.

*Proof*

We construct the required graphs, $G_n$, recursively. $G_3$ has three nodes: nodes 1 and 2 are sons of node 3. $G_{n+1}$ is constructed from $G_n$ by adding node $n + 1$. This becomes the root and has sons $n$ and $n - 1$. After the first move of the pebble game nodes 3 and 4 become pebbled. After the second, nodes 5 and 6 are pebbled and so on. In general the root of $G_n$ is pebbled after $(n-2)/2$ moves. □

## 3.3 An optimal parallel algorithm for expression evaluation

In this section we describe the main algorithm to be presented in this chapter. The algorithm takes, as input, the evaluation tree of an expression and in $O(\log n)$ time using $n/\log n$ processors evaluates the expression. Thus the algorithm we describe is an optimal parallel algorithm. Given the expression in the form of a string of symbols, then the optimum algorithm described in section 3.1 may be employed to produce the corresponding expression tree.

We describe the algorithm as applied to arithmetic expressions. In this exposition we shall only consider the arithmetic operations of addition, subtraction, multiplication and division. We assume that the cost of each of these operations is $O(1)$. In a manner similar to that employed at the end of section 3.2 for the pebble game algorithm, it is an easy matter to see that the present algorithm also works for expression evaluation in algebras with carriers of constant bounded size.

The first step of the algorithm described below requires that the leaves of the expression tree are numbered consecutively from left to right. The input to the algorithm of section 3.1, which produces the tree, is an array storing the expression. We can associate the number 1 with operands in this array and 0 with all other elements. Then the optimal partial-sums algorithm, described in chapter 1, can be employed on the array to number the operands. Each operand retains its numbering through the course of constructing the expression tree and so the leaves acquire their consecutive numbering. In some contexts it may be the case that an expression is provided directly in the form of its corresponding tree and without the leaves being consecutively numbered. We note here that we could then number the leaves by applying an optimal list-ranking algorithm, due to Cole and Vishkin,[4] to the traversal list of the expression tree. The details of the (optimal) list-ranking algorithm are rather sophisticated and beyond the scope of this text.

We assume (for ease of exposition) that $\log n$ is an integer and that $n$ is divisible by $\log n$. In general we can add dummy locations to the end of the expression to ensure that this is the case, and this can be done without detriment to the complexity of the algorithm. The example of figure 3.9, where $n = 16$, satisfies this assumption. The example of this figure will be used to illustrate the algorithm whilst at the same time we indicate how the algorithm works for the general case.

We describe two versions of the algorithm. Within the first we introduce the ideas which make theorem 3.6 possible. The second version is a considerable simplification and has the advantage that proof of its validity is obvious compared with the pebble game (section 3.2) which is used in the final step of the first version of the algorithm.

*Algorithm 3.1 (first version)*

*Step 1*
The input to this initial stage of the algorithm is an expression tree with the leaves (corresponding to operands of the expression) numbered from left to

right. The leaves are then grouped into $n/\log n$ consecutive segments, each segment of length $\log n$. For our example we obtain four segments each of length 4 as indicated in figure 3.9.

A processor is assigned to each segment of leaves and conducts a partial evaluation of the expression as follows. Every subexpression which corresponds to a maximal subtree for which every leaf is contained within the same segment is evaluated, and the tree is modified by reducing this subtree to a single leaf vertex to which the value of the subexpression is assigned. In our example each segment contains just one subtree (generally of course it can be any number) and these are indicated in figure 3.9 and the modified tree is shown in figure 3.10. This step can be achieved in $O(\log n)$ parallel time as follows. A vertex is called a vertex of type '/' if it is a left son of some vertex; similarly a right son is called a vertex of type '\'. If each vertex in the representation of the tree has a record of its type, then we can use a simple stack and a single pass of the $\log n$ leaves in a segment to achieve our aim. The type of each leaf simply plays the part of the bracket, so that the subtrees can be reduced in an obvious way.

*Figure 3.9*

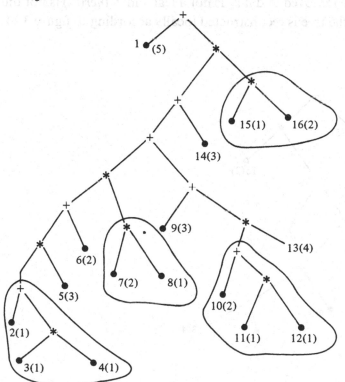

It is easy to see that, after reduction of these subtrees, the resulting leaves in any segment (if we represent the leaves by their types) can form strings only of the kind $\backslash\backslash \ldots \backslash //\ldots / = \backslash^i /^j$, where it is possible that one of $i$ and $j$ is zero. For step 2 of the algorithm we call the first leaf of type "$\backslash$' and the last leaf of the type '$/$' in this sequence *irreducible*. All other leaves are called *reducible*. Observe that in general there are at most $O(n/\log n))$ irreducible leaves.

### Step 2
This step of the algorithm reduces the tree further by removing all reducible leaves. We describe a parallel means of doing this, but essentially such a leaf is removed by local reconstruction of the tree.

A functional form (an algebraic expression) $f_i(x)$ is associated with each *internal* vertex $v_i$. Initially $f_i(x) = x$. When computing the value associated with $v_i$ the functional form $f_i(x)$ is used in the following way. If $\diamond$ is the operator associated with $v_i$ and the sons of $v_i$ have associated values $c_1$ and $c_2$, then the value of $v_i$ is given by substituting $(c_1 \diamond c_2)$ for $x$ in $f_i(x)$.

Consider removing a single reducible leaf and imagine for the moment that no other such leaves have been removed. If $v_2$ is the leaf (with an associated constant value $c$) to be removed and if $v_1$ is not a leaf and $father(v_2)$ is not the root of the tree, then the tree is reconstructed locally according to figure 3.11.

*Figure 3.10*

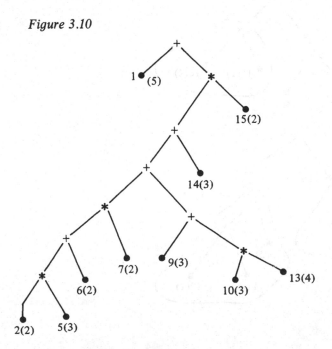

The value of the subtree rooted at $v_1$ is represented by $x$, so that, after reconstruction, the vertex $v_1$ requires a means of storing the functional form $(x \diamond c)$. Here $\diamond$ is the operator associated with $v_3$. The value of the function stored at $v_1$ is of course the value of the subtree originally rooted at $v_3$ and so the new tree computes the same expression as the original tree.

If the operator at $v_3$ is non-commutative, the functional form stored at $v_1$, after reconstruction, properly reflects this. This is shown in figure 3.12. If *father*$(v_2)$ is the root of the tree then, in figures 3.11 and 3.12, $v_4$ is removed.

Thus we have described the removal of a first and just one reducible leaf. If $x$ represents the value of the subtree rooted at $v_i$ in the original tree, then in general we wish to store at $v_i$ the functional form $f_i(x)$ resulting from possibly many such reductions. After the single first reduction just described $f_i(x)$ is set to the expression $(x \diamond c)$; however, we need to describe the general removal of a reducible leaf after the tree has already been subjected to many reductions. We do this schematically according to figure 3.13, where again, without loss of

*Figure 3.11.* The functional forms $f_v(x)$ are shown in brackets for $v_1$ and $v_2$

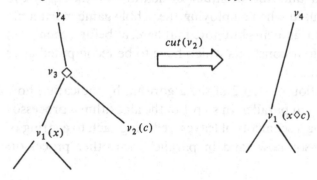

*Figure 3.12*

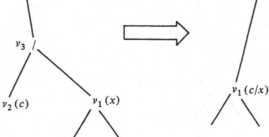

generality, *father*($v_2$) is presumed not to be the root of the tree and $v_1$ is assumed not to be a leaf.

If $v_1$ is a leaf then instead of storing at $v_1$ a functional form we store a value which results from evaluating (in this case) a subtree with leaves $v_1$ and $v_2$.

Let *cut*($v_2$) be the operation of removing the leaf $v_2$ and re-specifying the functional form associated with $v_1$; see figure 3.13. In this operation $v_1$ becomes the son of $v_4$. Define *involved*($v_2$) = $\{v_1, v_2, v_3\}$. We say that two operations *cut*($v$) and *cut*($v'$) are independent if and only if *involved*($v$) $\cap$ *involved*($v'$) = $\emptyset$.

The crucial property of the operation *cut* is that a set of mutually independent operations *cut* can be performed in parallel without read and write conflicts. Moreover the operations *cut*($v$) and *cut*($v'$) are independent whenever $v$ and $v'$ are two non-consecutive leaves of the same type (both left sons or both right sons).

A crucial observation concerning the removal of a reducible leaf is that it can be achieved in constant bounded time (as can the eventual evaluation of the $f_v(x)$). Such a removal involves a composition of two arithmetic functions and local tree reconstruction. The tree reconstruction merely involves the movement (of a constant number) of father and son pointers. The arguments for functional composition and the eventual evaluation of the $f_v(x)$ are essentially similar to those used when employing the pebble game in example 3.1. We need not repeat the arguments but note that here, as before, each $f_v(x)$ can be represented by just four constants which have to be recomputed after each functional composition.

We complete the description of step 2 of the algorithm by indicating how reducible leaves are removed in parallel. In step 1 of the algorithm a processor was assigned to each of $n/\log n$ segments of leaves, reducing each to a string of the form $/^i\backslash^j$. Each processor now (and in parallel with other processors

*Figure 3.13*

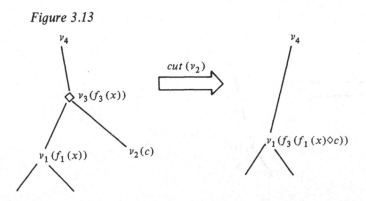

working on their respective segment) first removes reducible leaves of the type '/'. It does this in a single left-to-right pass of the leaves in this segment. On completion of that parallel operation the processors now in parallel remove reducible leaves of type '\' in a single right-to-left pass of their segments. Since individual reductions can be achieved in constant time and segments are of length at most $\log n$, this step of the algorithm requires $O(\log n)$ time. Notice that the order of leaf removal described ensures that removals are carried out independently. Figure 3.14 illustrates these reduction steps for our example.

### Step 3

The output from step 2 of the algorithm is a binary (reduced) tree, denoted by $RT$, with $O(n/\log n)$ leaves. Hence the number of internal (that is, non-leaf) vertices of $RT$ is also $O(n/\log n)$. Each internal vertex $v_i$ has an associated functional form $f_i(x)$ and an arithmetic operator. This final stage of the algorithm subjects $RT$ to the pebble game application as described in example 3.1. In this case however the initial form of the $f_v(x)$ which relate the values of $v$ to the values of $cond(v)$ are (instead of being the identity functions $f_v(x) = x$ just before the first application of the operation *activate*) the forms $f_i(x)$ output from step 2 of this algorithm. Otherwise the pebble game application proceeds as before. The number of processors used is proportional to the number of internal nodes of the tree. Since our tree $RT$ has $O(n/\log n)$ nodes, the required number of processors for this step is also $O(n/\log n)$. According to theorem 3.2, after $\log$(number of internal nodes) $= \log n$ pebbling moves the value corresponding to the root will be evaluated.
**end** of algorithm 3.1

Just as was the case for the pebble game in example 3.2, the current algorithm can clearly be applied to algebraic expressions in an algebra with a carrier of constant-bounded size. As before, instead of a functional form at each vertex we use a function. This describes the value (an element of the carrier) at the vertex for each possible value (also an element of the carrier) of the argument $x$. Such functions reflect the dependence of the value associated with one node upon the value associated with another node. The description of these functions, and their evaluation when $x$ becomes known, is of constant size because the number of values and arguments is constant. Essentially the whole algorithm works in the same way. The time complexity and the number of processors used are not affected. Taking this, along with the example used to illustrate the algorithm, we have theorem 3.6.

*Figure 3.14*

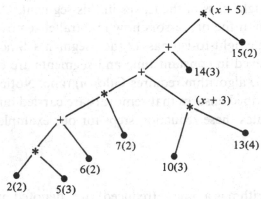

(a)   After leaves 1 and 9 have been simultaneously removed.

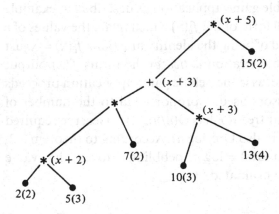

(b)   After leaves 6 and 14 have been simultaneously removed.

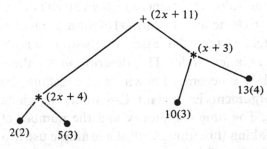

(c)   After simultaneously removing leaves 7 and 15.

*Theorem 3.6*

(a)   Arithmetic expressions can be evaluated on a P-RAM in $O(\log n)$ time using $n/\log n$ processors.

(b)   Algebraic expressions from an algebra with a carrier of constant bounded size can be evaluated on a P-RAM in $O(\log n)$ time using $n/\log n$ processors.                                                                                       □

*Algorithm 3.1 (second and simplified version)*

Utilising details from our account of the first version of this algorithm we now present a much simpler version. First we recall, from step 2 of the original, that two operations $cut(v)$ and $cut(v')$ are independent whenever $v$ and $v'$ are two non-consecutive leaves of the same type. This enables us to define a parallel operation which we call *leaves-cutting*.

A single operation of leaves-cutting is as follows. Every second leaf (from left to right) is marked starting with the first leaf. Then for all marked leaves $v$ which are left sons we perform in parallel the operation $cut(v)$. Next for all marked leaves $v$ which are right sons perform in parallel $cut(v)$. In this way the new number of leaves does not exceed $n/2$.

For each of a number of consecutive applications of the leaves-cutting operation we need a consecutive numbering of leaves from left to right (to associate processors with operations $cut(v)$ in $O(1)$ time). However such a numbering can be easily computed on an ERLW P-RAM in $O(1)$ time from the previous numbering, because we know that precisely every second leaf was cut.

Starting with the same input as that for step 1 of the first version of the algorithm (namely, the parse tree of the expression with its leaves numbered from left to right) our simplified version of the algorithm merely consists of repeatedly applying the leaves-cutting operation. After one stage the number of leaves is reduced by a factor of $\frac{1}{2}$. Only the root of the tree remains after $\log n$ operations and the whole expression is computed. At this time, the values of all nodes are also computed. There are no read conflicts (as well as no write conflicts) in the leaves-cutting operation.

Our description would imply that the algorithm runs in $O(\log n)$ time using $n/2$ processors. Here $n/2$ is the number of leaves cut in the first application of leaves-cutting. However, without detriment to the parallel-time complexity, the number of processors can be reduced to $n/\log n$ by a straightforward application of Brent's theorem. We leave the details to the reader.

**end** of algorithm 3.1

## 3.4 The optimal parallel transformation of regular expressions to non-deterministic finite automata

We show that the transformation of an arbitrary regular expression to a corresponding non-deterministic finite automaton (ndfa) can be achieved in $O(\log n)$ time using $n/\log n$ processors on a P-RAM. The well-known and basic concepts of regular expression and ndfa may be found in any standard text in the field of languages and automata. For example, the reader might refer to Hopcroft and Ullman[6] or to Sedgewick.[15] In fact both these texts describe transformations from regular expressions to ndfa. The construction explained in Sedgewick is more economical, in the sense of producing an ndfa with fewer states, than the classical construction described in Hopcroft and Ullman. We shall describe parallelisations of both methods. It is not difficult in fact to parallelise the transformation of Hopcroft and Ullman. Parallelisation of Sedgewick's transformation is more interesting and it is obtained by applying (in two stages) a homomorphism which relates the automaton obtained through the transformation from [6] to the one obtained through the transformation from [15]. The virtue in describing a parallelisation of the Hopcroft and Ullman construction is that this provides an easy starting point for parallelisation of the more economical method of Sedgewick.

Interest in this section is not narrowly confined to the specific transformations described here. The techniques employed are interesting methodologically. They can clearly be used for the very efficient parallelisation of known sequential algorithms of the same (and common) form as that typified by the regular expression to ndfa transformations. The sequential transformations referred to employ a recursive technique for the construction of the ndfa. The following technique is used to parallelise this. We construct the tree of the recursion and certain parameters associated with the nodes of this tree (pairs of states of the corresponding ndfa) are computed. This is the main step. Then, instead of simulating the recursion bottom up or top down,

*Figure 3.15.* The ndfa corresponding to the expression $a^* \cdot b \cdot (a+c)^*$ obtained through Hopcroft and Ullman transformation

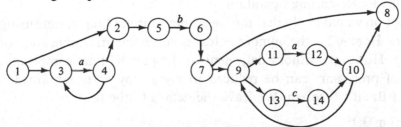

appropriate constructing actions are executed for each node of the recursion tree in parallel. The parameters associated with the nodes are such that the action for a given node is, at this stage, independent of the action for any other node.

The representation of ndfas chosen here is the same as that used by Sedgewick. Any ndfa has a number of states, which are denoted by the consecutive integers 1 to $m$. The automaton can be described by a directed graph with the vertices representing states. The edges of the graph define state transitions and each either is labelled with an individual letter (whose input causes the transition) or is unlabelled and such an edge corresponds to a spontaneous state change. An example of this representation is shown in figure 3.15. In figure 3.16(b) we see a tabular representation of the same automaton. The automata we construct are such that the maximum out-degree of any vertex in the graph is 2. Moreover, if an edge $(u, v)$ is labelled, then this is the only edge directed from $u$. Thus the table describing an automaton requires no more than four columns. The third and fourth columns contain the states (called *next1* and *next2*) to which the automaton may move after the state specified in column 1. If there is just one such state, then column 4 is empty. Where appropriate, the second column (headed 'symbol') stores the input letter causing a transition.

The input to our algorithms is a regular expression which we take to be stored in an array of length $n$. This representation was adopted for arithmetic

**Figure 3.16.** The parsing tree of the expression $a* \cdot b \cdot (a + c)*$ and the corresponding ndfa

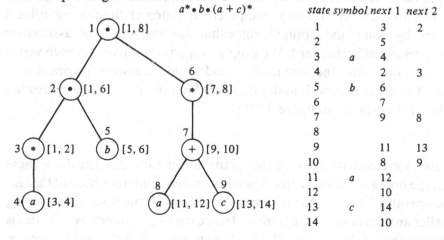

$a* \cdot b \cdot (a + c)*$

| state | symbol | next 1 | next 2 |
|---|---|---|---|
| 1 | | 3 | 2 |
| 2 | | 5 | |
| 3 | a | 4 | |
| 4 | | 2 | 3 |
| 5 | b | 6 | |
| 6 | | 7 | |
| 7 | | 9 | 8 |
| 8 | | | |
| 9 | | 11 | 13 |
| 10 | | 8 | 9 |
| 11 | a | 12 | |
| 12 | | 10 | |
| 13 | c | 14 | |
| 14 | | 10 | |

(a)                                  (b)

expressions in section 3.1. Given a regular expression our algorithms construct the array representation of the corresponding automaton.

### 3.4.1 PARALLELISING THE HOPCROFT AND ULLMAN TRANSFORMATION

The sequential construction of the ndfa is recursive. Given automata for the subexpressions $p$ and $q$, then the automaton for $p + q$ or for $p \cdot q$ or for $p^*$ is constructed according to whichever operator is used in the composition. Here 'or' is denoted by $+$, concatenation by $\cdot$ and Kleene closure by $*$. The rules of composition are implied (with greater clarity later) in figure 3.16(a). If these rules are applied to the expression $a^* \cdot b \cdot (a + c)^*$ then, to within a renaming of states, we obtain the automaton of figure 3.15. Our algorithm is described informally using this example.

The parallel algorithm we describe constructs the ndfa using the parse tree of the regular expression. With every node of this tree we shall associate the pair $[p_1, p_2]$ of initial and terminal states of an ndfa corresponding to the subexpression rooted at this node.

*Algorithm 3.2*
{parallel version of the Hopcroft and Ullman transformation}

*Step 1*
We construct the parse tree from the regular expression. This can be done using the optimal parallel algorithm of Bar-On and Vishkin described in section 3.1. Then the nodes of the tree are numbered in preorder using the optimal parallel algorithm described in chapter 2. The nodes are numbered from 1 to $r$, where $r = O(n)$. This number is easily computed in $O(\log n)$ time using $n/\log n$ processors by using the optimal algorithm for evaluation of associative functions described in chapter 1. We simply assign the number 2 to each vertex giving rise to two states and zero to other nodes and the associative operator is addition. The parse tree, with nodes numbered in preorder, for the expression $a^* \cdot b \cdot (a + c)^*$ is shown in figure 3.16(a).

*Step 2*
In this step we create the set of states of the automaton and distribute these amongst the nodes of the parse tree. Each leaf and each internal node of the tree with the operator $*$ or $+$ needs two states (according to the rules of combining two smaller automata into a larger one). Hence the total number, $m$, of states is twice the number of these nodes. Within the preordering of the vertices we can

rank those nodes requiring two new states. This corresponds to the ranking of marked entries in a vector and can be done by the optimal parallel algorithm for this described in chapter 1. Then the node ranked $k$ receives the pair of states $[2k - 1, 2k]$. In our example the ranked nodes are 3, 4, 5, 6, 7, 8 and 9. Node 3 is ranked first and receives the pair of states $[1, 2]$, 4 is second and receives $[3, 4]$ and so on. The pair of states associated with a given node correspond respectively to the initial and final state of the ndfa associated with the subexpressions of the parse (sub)tree rooted at that node. Now we compute the pairs $[p, q]$ associated with nodes containing the operator $\cdot$. We call such nodes non-marked nodes and all other nodes marked nodes. Let $left(v)$ be the left son and $right(v)$ be the right son of the non-marked node $v$. Let $leftmarked(v) = left^k(v)$, where $k$ is the smallest number such that $left^k(v)$ is marked. We define $rightmarked(v)$ analogously. We associate with each non-marked node $v$ the pair of states $[p, q]$, where $p = leftmarked(v)$ and $q = rightmarked(v)$. In our example the states associated with node 1 are $[1, 8]$, because $leftmarked(1) = 3$ and $rightmarked(1) = 6$.

If the functions $leftmarked$ and $rightmarked$ are computed then the computation of the pairs of states associated with non-marked nodes can be easily achieved in $O(1)$ time with $n$ processors (which is easily simulated in $\log n$ time with $n/\log n$ processors). We now show how to compute these functions in $\log n$ time with $n/\log n$ processors. Consider the vector of nodes of the parse tree in preorder. For each non-marked element $v$, $leftmarked(v)$ is the first marked element to the right of $v$ within this vector. Notice that such an element always exists, because leaves are marked. For our example the vector is $[1, 2, 3, 4, 5, 6, 7, 8, 9]$ where the only non-marked nodes are 1 and 2. We now take the corresponding vector of 0s and 1s where a 1 replaces a non-marked entry and a 0 a marked entry. Thus for our example this vector is $[1, 1, 0, 0, 0, 0, 0, 0, 0]$. We need to compute, for each position $v$ containing 1, the number $d(v)$ of consecutive 1s from (and including) this position to the right, because then $leftmarked(v) = v + d(v)$. We now show how to compute $d(v)$ in $\log n$ time with $n/\log n$ processors.

In fact we shall show how to compute, for each position $v$, a function $f(v)$ whose value depends on the string stored in locations $v$ to the end of the vector. We can define this function for any string $s$ consisting of 1s and 0s, and in this context we take the argument to be $s$. Let $s$ be of length $p > 0$, and suppose that it begins with a substring consisting entirely of 1s of (maximal) length $q \geqslant 0$. Then $f(s)$ is defined as follows: $f(s) = (\textbf{if } p = q \textbf{ then } q \textbf{ else } -q)$.

We see that $f(s)$ is negative iff $s$ contains at least one 0. Thus for the vector of 0s and 1s, $d(v) = |f(v)|$ for all positions $v$. Suppose that $s$ is formed by concatenating two strings $t$ and $u$, that is $s = t \cdot u$, then in a natural way we define the operation $\copyright$ as follows.

$$f(s) = f(t) \copyright f(u) = \textbf{if } (f(t) > 0 \textbf{ and } f(u) > 0) \textbf{ then } f(t) + f(u)$$
$$\textbf{else } (\textbf{if } f(t) \leqslant 0 \textbf{ then } f(t) \textbf{ else } -(f(t) + |f(u)|))$$

If we have a vector of length $r$, consisting of 0s and 1s with $x_i$ in position $i$, then

$$f(v) = x_v \copyright x_{v-1} \copyright \cdots \copyright x_r$$

as can be seen by a simple inductive argument on the length $r - v$. There are no brackets in this expression because $\copyright$ is associative. Hence we can compute $f(v)$, for all positions $v$, in $\log n$ time with $n/\log n$ processors using a standard prefix computation such as that used for partial sums in chapter 1.

Thus we have seen that the function *leftmarked* can be found in $\log n$ time with $n/\log n$ processors. Notice that, if in the parse tree of the regular expression we temporarily interchange left and right sons, then the same algorithm as that used to find *leftmarked(v)* will find *rightmarked(v)*.

*Step 3*
We make use of the following procedure.

```
procedure gen(s, sym, s₁, s₂)
begin
if sym is a letter then symbol[s] ← sym
next[s] ← s₁
if s₂ is defined then next2[s] ← s₂
end
```

A call of this procedure 'creates' an edge (in the tabular description of the ndfa to be constructed) from $s$ to $s_1$ and (if the actual parameter for $s_2$ is not blank) an edge from $s$ to $s_2$. If the actual parameter for *sym* is a letter (as opposed to being the empty string) then this labels the edge from $s$ to $s_1$ and no procedure call in this case creates an edge from $s$ to $s_2$.

Calls of the above procedure are made in the following statement which constitutes this step of the algorithm.

**for** all nodes $v$ of the parse tree **in parallel do**
  perform actions according to the nature of $v$ as
    prescribed in the column headed 'Action' in figure 3.17

This requires constant time with $n$ processors and is easily simulated in $\log n$

time using $n/\log n$ processors. In figure 3.17 the missing parameters in various procedure calls correspond to empty spaces in either the '*symbol*' column or the '*next2*' column of the table of the ndfa. It is self-evident that the various actions employed in this step of the algorithm will correctly construct a tabular representation of the automaton.

**end** of algorithm 3.2

We have seen that algorithm 3.2 simulates the Hopcroft and Ullman transformation in $\log n$ parallel time using $n/\log n$ processors. Thus we have an optimal parallel algorithm which transforms any regular expression to a corresponding non-deterministic finite automaton. The algorithm we have described is not as economical in terms of the number of states of the ndfa that are generated as might be the case. In the next section we see an improvement in this regard.

### 3.4.2 A PARALLELISATION OF SEDGEWICK'S TRANSFORMATION

The sequential construction of the ndfa is recursive. Given automata for the subexpressions $p$ and $q$, then the automaton for $p + q$ or for $p \cdot q$ or for $p*$ is

*Figure 3.17.* Composition rules in Hopcroft and Ullman transformation

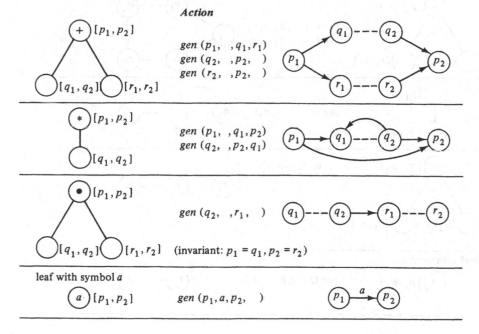

constructed according to whichever operator is used in the composition. The rules of composition are presented in the last column of figure 3.19. Applying these rules to our example expression $a^* \cdot b \cdot (a + c)^*$ we obtain the ndfa shown in figure 3.18.

The input to the following algorithm is the output from step 2 of algorithm 3.2. For our example expression this would be the tree of figure 3.16(a) which includes for each node of the parse tree a pair of states. The central task of the present algorithm is to modify these state pairs.

*Figure 3.18.* The ndfa corresponding to the expression $a^* \cdot b \cdot (a + c)^*$ obtained through Sedgewick's transformation

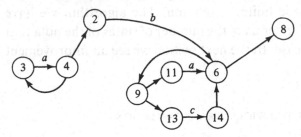

*Figure 3.19.* Composition rules in Sedgewick's transformation

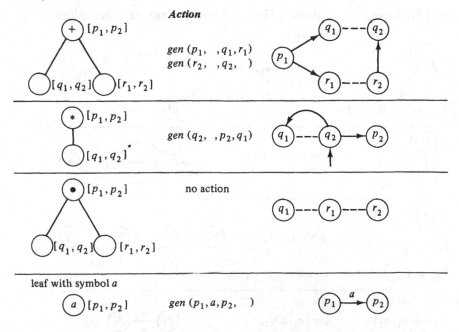

*Algorithm 3.3*
{a parallel version of the Sedgewick transformation}

*Step 1*
This step essentially consists of merging certain states of the ndfa encoded in the input to the algorithm. This particular merging involves the excessive number of states in the ndfa due to the different composition rules for the operators + and * in the Hopcroft and Ullman transformation as opposed to the transformation of Sedgewick. We deal with the case involving the operator · in step 2. We make use of an array called *contract* for which initially *contract*$[s] = s$ for each state $s$ of the ndfa. Then for each node $v$ of the parse tree containing the operator + or * we change an entry in the array according to the following assignments (where $p_1$, $p_2$ and $q_2$ are defined for + and for * separately in figure 3.19).

**if** the operator is + **then** *contract*$[p_2] \leftarrow q_2$
**if** the operator is * **then** *contract*$[p_1] \leftarrow q_2$

The implication of these assignments is that, for +, state $p_2$ should be identified with state $q_2$, and, for *, state $p_1$ should be identified with state $q_2$. These assignments alone do not solve the problem however. In our example they imply that state 7 has to be identified with state 10 and that state 10 has to be identified with state 12. Clearly we have yet to ensure that state 7 is identified with state 12. We need to compute the transitive closure of this identification process. Putting aside complexity considerations for a moment, the problem can be completely solved by treating the array *contract* as a function and iterating it. Thus we could compute the array *contract\**$[s] = $ *contract*$^k[s]$, where $k$ is the smallest integer such that, for all $s$, *contract*$^k[s] = $ *contract*$^{k+1}[s]$. Then, denoting the pair of states associated with node $v$ by $[p_1, p_2]$ we can execute the following –

**for** all nodes $v$ **in parallel do** $[p_1, p_2] \leftarrow [$ *contract\**$[p_1]$, *contract\**$[p_2]]$

to ensure complete state contraction in connection with the operators + and *. This requires constant time with $n$ processors and is easily simulated in $\log n$ time using $n/\log n$ processors. For our example expression we obtain *contract*$[7] = 10$, *contract*$[11] = 12$, and *contract*$[1] = 4$ and then subsequently we obtain *contract\**$[7] = 12$, *contract\**$[11] = 12$, and *contract\**$[1] = 4$. For all other entries $s$ we have *contract\**$[s] = s$. The tree with corresponding modified pairs of states is that shown in figure 3.20(a).

Before completing this step we need to indicate how *contract\** can be computed in log *n* time with *n*/log *n* processors. It is an easy matter to compute *contract\** in log *n* time using *n* processors by assigning a processor to each element of the array *contract* and then using the standard doubling technique. In order to reduce the number of processors we choose an alternative method of computation. We make use of the observation that all those states that have to be merged into a single state lie on a common path in the parse tree. In general there are several such (vertex-disjoint) paths. This observation follows immediately from the details of the initial assignments (associated with the operators + and \*) to elements of the array *contract*. Now the parse tree can be 'reduced' in log *n* time with *n*/log *n* processors using (essentially) algorithm 3.1. During the reduction the function *contract\** may be computed. It is an interesting but straightforward business to formulate the details of this evaluation. We associate a function with each node of the tree, much in the style of example 3.2. In this case the function is from *S* to *S*, where *S* is the set of states of the ndfa. Initially this would be the identity function, then when the subtree associated with a node has been evaluated the corresponding function will reflect the merging of states implied in the subtree. Thus the (evaluated) function associated with the root will be *contract\**. Whilst algorithm 3.1 provides a perfectly adequate means of evaluating *contract\**, a perhaps more appropriate form of parallel tree reduction (which is again optimal) can be found for this application in section 4.4.

*Figure 3.20*

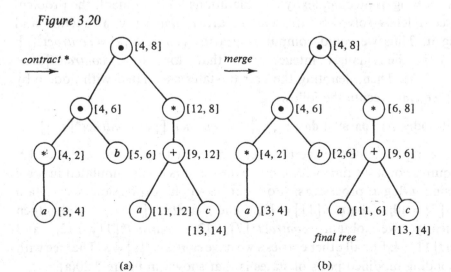

(a)                                         (b)

*Step 2*

This step again consists of merging certain states. This particular merging involves the excessive number of states of the ndfa due to the different composition rule for the operator · in the Hopcroft and Ullman transformation as opposed to the transformation of Sedgewick. We make use of an array called *merge* and initially (for each state $s$) we set $merge[s] = s$. If $r_1, q_2, p_1$ and $p_2$ are as defined for the operator · in figure 3.19, we then execute

**for** all nodes $v$ with operator · **in parallel do** $merge[r_1] \leftarrow q_2$
**for** all nodes $v$ **in parallel do** $[p_1, p_2] \leftarrow [merge[p_1], merge[p_2]]$

In our example the first statement sets $merge[5] = 2$ and $merge[13] = 6$ whilst the second statement causes states 5 and 12 to be replaced everywhere by 2 and 6, respectively. The tree with final association of pairs of states with each vertex is shown in figure 3.20(b). This all requires constant time with $n$ processors which is easily simulated in $\log n$ time using $n/\log n$ processors. Notice that, in this step of the algorithm, merged states are linked not by tree edges but by cross edges between sons of the same vertex. The binary nature of the tree then precludes having to deal with longer chains of merging as was the case in the previous step of the algorithm.

*Step 3*

This step constructs the tabular description of the ndfa from the parse tree with state pairs associated with its vertices as output from step 4. It does this using the procedure named gen whose declaration appeared in step 3 of algorithm 3.2. Calls of the procedure then play a part in execution of the following:

**for** each node $v$ of the parse tree **in parallel do**
    perform actions according to the nature of $v$ as
        prescribed in the column headed *Action* in figure 3.19

This requires constant time with $n$ processors and is easily simulated in $\log n$ time using $n/\log n$ processors. For our example regular expression the tabular representation we have at this point corresponds to (including the numbering of states) the ndfa of figure 3.18. Should we wish to number the states consecutively, we first mark each state $s$ such that $contract^*[s] \neq s$ or $merge[s] \neq s$. We then number non-marked states consecutively from 1 to $m$ (say) and modify the array representation in such a way that only the entries for non-marked states remain. This is easily done in $\log n$ time using $n/\log n$ processors.

**end** of algorithm 3.3

We have seen that algorithm 3.3 simulates the transformation of Sedgewick in $O(\log n)$ parallel time using $n/\log n$ processors. Thus we have an optimal parallel algorithm which transforms any regular expression to a corresponding non-deterministic finite automaton with greater economy (in terms of the number of states that are generated) than the Hopcroft and Ullman transformation.

## 3.5 Evaluation of generalised expressions: straight-line programs

Assume that we have a vector of $m$ input values $x = (x_1, \ldots, x_m)$ and the set of $r$ variables $(v_1, v_2, \ldots, v_r)$. A straight-line program $P$ is a sequence of assignment statements; the $i$th statement is of the form $v_i \leftarrow a \cdot b$, where $\cdot$ is a binary operation while $a$ and $b$ are input values or variables. We require that if one of $a$ and $b$ is a variable with index $k$ then $k < i$.

For given input values of the vector of input variables $x = (x_1, x_2, \ldots, x_m)$, the program computes the output value $P(x)$ equal to the last value of the variable $v_r$ (if it is determined). Such programs are straightforward generalisation of expressions.

For example, the expression $((x_1 + x_2) * (x_2 + x_3) + (x_1 + x_2)) * (x_1 + x_2) * (x_2 + x_3)$ can be represented by the tree of figure 3.21. Then we can treat node $v_i$

*Figure 3.21.* The parsing tree $T$ of the expression $((x_1 + x_2) + (x_1 + x_2) * (x_2 + x_3)) * (x_1 + x_2) * (x_2 + x_3)$ and its compact representation as a directed acyclic graph $G$ (straight-line program)

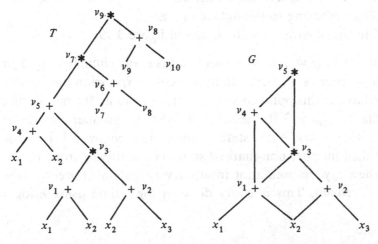

of the tree as a variable whose value has to be computed. If node $v_i$ has sons $v_j$ and $v_k$, and its operator is $\cdot$, then the $i$th statement is $v_i \leftarrow v_j \cdot v_k$. The straight-line program corresponding to the tree $T$ of figure 3.21 is

$$v_1 \leftarrow x_1 + x_2$$
$$v_2 \leftarrow x_2 + x_3$$
$$v_3 \leftarrow v_1 * v_2$$
$$v_4 \leftarrow x_1 + x_2$$
$$\cdots$$
$$v_9 \leftarrow v_7 * v_8$$

However, such a program has many redundancies. Some calculations are repeated. For example $v_1$ and $v_4$ compute the same value. A more economical program computing the same expression corresponding to the directed acyclic graph (a so-called dag) $G$ of figure 3.21 is

$$v_1 \leftarrow x_1 + x_2$$
$$v_2 \leftarrow x_2 + x_3$$
$$v_3 \leftarrow v_1 * v_2$$
$$v_4 \leftarrow v_1 * v_3$$
$$v_5 \leftarrow v_4 * v_3$$

In general every straight-line program can be represented by such a dag. We assume later that whenever we consider straight-line programs they are represented as dags. The aim of this section is to investigate the parallelisation of computing straight-line programs and their corresponding dags. However, the problem is hopeless in general. From the point of view of parallel computations, as we shall see in chapter 7, computing the value of a dag is one of the hardest problems in the class $P$. By $P$ we refer to the class of problems that are sequentially computable in polynomial time. In chapter 7 we shall see that if the operations are boolean operations and input variables are boolean values then the problem is called the circuit value problem. This is $P$-complete even if the dag is planar.

In this section we only consider the operations of addition and multiplication of integers. The input–output function of the program is a polynomial with variables $x_1, \ldots, x_m$. From the point of view of parallel computations the critical parameter of such a polynomial is its degree. This is best seen when we have only one input variable. The polynomial is of the form $ax^h$. We can compute this easily in $O(\log h)$ parallel time. However, if the straight-line program is $v_1 \leftarrow x * x$ and $v_{i+1} \leftarrow v_i * v_i$ for $i = 1, \ldots, n$, then the degree $h$ is exponential and we cannot expect the problem of computing $x^h$ to be in $NC$. Surprisingly, if the degree of the straight-line program is polynomial then it can always be computed in $O(\log^2 n)$ time with a polynomial number of processors. However, the general case of straight-line programs with degree bounded by a polynomial is much more difficult than computing $x^h$ with $h$ bounded by a polynomial.

If the program is given by a dag then the degree can be defined more formally as follows. The degree of each leaf is 1, the degree of a node with the operator $+$ is equal to the maximum of degree of its sons and the degree of a multiplication node is equal to the sum of degrees of its sons. The degree of the whole dag is the maximum degree of its nodes. For example the degree of the dag $G$ from figure 3.21 is 4.

First we shall consider two special cases of dags with polynomial degree. These dags will have nodes all of the same type, either multiplication or addition.

When all the nodes are of the multiplication variety, the degree of the dag $G$ is equal to the number of leaves of the tree version $T\ (=T(G))$ of $G$. Here $T(G)$ is a tree such that the set of paths from the root to the leaves in $G$ and $T$ is the same. See for example figure 3.22. The number of leaves of $T(G)$ is also called the tree-size of $G$. In this case, if the tree-size of $G$ is polynomial then our parallel pebble game can be successfully applied to $G$. The time required to pebble the root of $T(G)$ is exactly the same as the time required to pebble the root of $G$ because of the correspondence between $G$ and $T(G)$. Thus, if the degree is small and all nodes are multiplication nodes then the computation can be performed by an efficient algorithm using the same methods as we employed for expressions and their trees.

*Figure 3.22.* The dag $G$ all nodes of which are multiplication nodes and its tree version $T$. The degree of $G$ equals the number of leaves of $T$

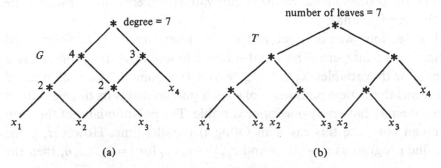

(a)                                                    (b)

In the second case, when all the nodes are plus nodes, the degree of $G$ is 1; however, the tree-size can be exponential. Fortunately the exponentiality of the tree-size does not cause any problems in this case. We can compute (we see how in a moment) the number $\Delta_i$ of paths from the root to the leaf $x_i$. Then in one parallel step we can compute the values $\Delta_i x_i$ and then we can sum these values in $\log n$ parallel time. For example, in figure 3.23 $\Delta_1 = 3$, $\Delta_2 = 5$ and $\Delta_3 = 2$. Hence the value at the root is $3x_1 + 5x_2 + 2x_3$.

As is well known, the number of paths of length $k$ in graph from a node $i$ to a node $j$ is given by $A^k(i, j)$, the $(i, j)$th element of the $k$th matricial product of the adjacency matrix $A$, defined inductively as follows.

$$A^k(i, j) = \sum_s A^{k-1}(i, s) A(s, j), \quad \text{where } A^1(i, j) = A(i, j)$$

In general this computation gives the number of distinct non-simple (as well as simple) paths. However, for dags all paths are simple and so $A^k$ counts all the proper paths (of length $k$). We use this fact in the following computation of the multiplicities $\Delta_i$. The required result can be achieved within a logarithmic number of matrix multiplications. We associate, with each pair of nodes $[i, j]$ of the dag, a non-negative number $M(i, j)$, called its weight or multiplicity. In the course of the computation $M(i, j)$ will correspond to the number of paths up to a certain length from $i$ to $j$ in the dag. Initially $M$ is the adjacency matrix of the input dag. Thus $M(i, j) = 1$ if $A(i, j) = 1$, otherwise $M(i, j) = 0$.

Let $M_{\text{sink}}(i, j) = \textbf{if } j$ has out-degree 0 **then** the current $M(i, j)$ **else** 0. $M_{\text{sink}}$ is that part of $M$ corresponding to edges leading to a sink (nodes with out-degree

Figure 3.23. Computing the multiplicities by applying the operation *square"* three times. For clarity only the nodes and edges relevant to the final multiplicities of the root are displayed. The nodes $v_2, v_4$ are omitted in the second graph, and all nodes except the root and leaves are omitted in the third graph. Observe that $val(v_5) = 3x_1 + 5x_2 + 2x_3$

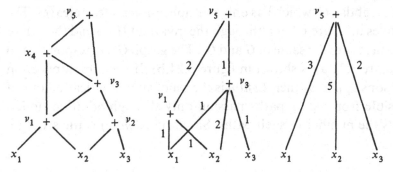

0). Thus initially $M_{sink}$ corresponds only to edges of the dag which are incident to leaves.

We define the following operation *square"* to be $M \leftarrow M * M + M_{sink}$. As is readily seen, after executing the operation *square'* $\log n$ times, the matrix $M$ gives for each node $i$ and a leaf $j$ the number $M(i, j)$ of paths from $i$ to $j$. An example of such a computation is graphically shown in figure 3.23. On the left of the figure is the dag and to the right are those dags successively described by the matrix $M$ in the course of two applications of *square"*. The edge labels are the current values of the $M(i, j)$.

Binary dags are generalisations of trees. The concepts of left and right sons and of father are well defined. We introduce the concept of a generalised binary dag (gbdag). A gbdag $G$ is a dag with the notions of father, root and leaves all well defined. For each non-leaf node $v$ we define the set $Left(v)$ of left sons of $v$ and the set $Right(v)$ of right sons of $v$. These sets can be non-disjoint. Hence such a graph is a multigraph. We can have at most two edges between the same pair of nodes, one corresponding to the link father–(left son) and the other to father–(right son). Within a gbdag the same node can simultaneously be the left and right son of the same node. An integer is associated with each edge, called the weight of this edge. $LW(v, w)$ is the weight of the edge from $v$ to its left son $w$, and $RW(v, w)$ is the weight from $v$ to its right son $w$.

Initially the operation associated with each node of $G$ is multiplication. In the course of the computation some of the nodes become activated and their values are computed according to an invariant (In2) to be described later.

If $v$ is a multiplication node which is not activated with $Left(v) = \{l_1, l_2, \ldots, l_k\}$ and $Right(v) = \{r_1, r_2, \ldots, r_j\}$ then the following invariant holds:

$$(In1): \quad val(v) = (LW(v, l_1) * val(l_1) + \cdots + LW(v, l_k) * val(l_k)) * \\ (RW(v, r_1) * val(r_1) + \cdots + RW(v, r_j) * val(r_j))$$

If we have a dag $G$ with multiplication and addition nodes then we can transform it into a gbdag $G'$ which has only multiplication nodes or leaves. The values of the nodes in $G'$ are related through the invariant (In1) and the values of the root and leaves are the same in $G$ and $G'$. The graph $G'$ corresponding to the dag from figure 3.24(a) is shown in figure 3.24(b). If $v$ is a multiplication node in $G$ with sons $v_1$ and $v_2$ then $Left(v)$ is the set of all multiplication or leaf nodes $w$ accessible from $v_1$ by paths passing only through addition nodes. $LW(v, w)$ equals the number of such paths. Similarly $Right(v)$ is the set of all multiplication or leaf nodes $w$ accessible from $v_2$ by paths passing only through addition nodes. $RW(v, w)$ equals the number of such paths. The transformation can be easily done in $O(\log n)$ time with $n^3$ processors using the operation *square"* $\log n$ times. In the computation the matrices $RW$ and $LW$ should be used instead of $M$. In the context of this transformation, the multiplication nodes are treated as though they were sinks.

We can from now on assume that the computation of a straight-line program is reduced to the computation of the root value of a gbdag.

We describe a variant of the parallel pebble game on generalised binary dags. We disregard (for a moment) the weights of the edges. Let us introduce the boolean matrix $H$, which is an adjacency matrix of the graph of activated edges. $H$ will in general reflect the fact that a node has many sons but there is no encoding of which are left and which are right sons. $H_{\text{sink}}$ is the part of $H$ corresponding to all edges leading to sinks. Assume initially that the matrix $H$ contains only values false and the corresponding graph (of activated edges) has no edges. A node is non-active iff it is a sink (has out-degree 0) in the dag

*Figure 3.24.* The arithmetic dag and its corresponding gbdag. $Left(v_1) = Right(v_1) = \{x_1, x_2\}$, $Left(v_2) = \{x_1\}$, $Right(v_2) = \{x_1, x_2\}$, $Left(v_3) = \{x_2\}$, $Right(v_3) = \{x_3, x_4\}$, $Left(v_5) = \{x_3\}$, $Right(v_5) = \{v_4\}$, $Left(v_6) = \{v_1, v_2, v_3, v_5\}$, $Right(v_6) = \{v_3, v_5\}$, $degree(v_6) = 5$. Bold edges go down from the node to its right sons. Light edges go to left sons. The values $LW, RW$ are placed at the edges. $val(v_6) = (1 * val(v_1) + 2 * val(v_2) + 2 * val(v_3)) * (2 * val(v_3) + 1 * val(v_5))$

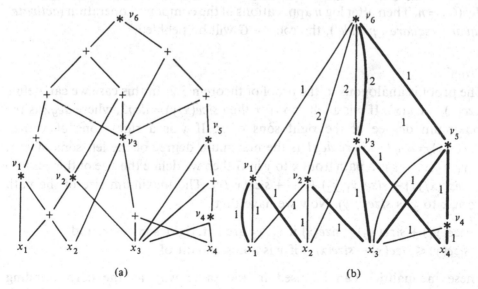

(a)            (b)

represented by $H$. We define the operations

activate'
    **for** all non-active nodes $v$ **in parallel do**
        **if** all left sons are pebbled **then**
            **for** all right sons $r$ **in parallel do** $H(v,r) \leftarrow$ **true else**
            **if** all right sons are pebbled **then for** all left sons $l$
                                  **in parallel do** $H(v,l) \leftarrow$ **true**

square'
    $H := H * H \vee H_{\text{sink}}$

pebble'
    **for** all active non-leaf nodes $v$ **in parallel do**
        **if** the node $w$ is pebbled for every $w$ satisfying $H(v,w)$ **then**
                                    pebble the node $v$

The main difference between these operations and the operations *activate*, *square*, *pebble* is that now we have many left and many right sons. A node can be activated if *all* its left, or *all* its right sons are pebbled.

Let $deg(v) = 1$ for each leaf $v$, and $deg(v) = deg1 + deg2$. Here, if $v$ is an internal node, then $deg1$ is the maximum degree of the left sons, and $deg2$ is the maximum degree of the right sons.

### Theorem 3.7

Let $G$ be a generalised binary dag with all leaves initially pebbled and $deg(G) = n$. Then after $\log n$ applications of the compound operation (*activate'*, *square'*, *square'*, *pebble'*), the root of $G$ will be pebbled.

### Proof

The proof is analogous to the proof of theorem 3.2. In this case we can define $size(x) = deg(x)$. If $y$ is a left son of $x$ then $size(x/y) = deg2$, where $deg2$ is the maximum degree of the right sons of $x$. If $y$ is a right sons of $x$ then $size(x/y) = deg1$, where $deg1$ is the maximum degree of the left sons of $x$. If $x, y_1, y_2, \ldots, y$ is a path from $x$ to $y$ in $G$ then we define the size of this path to be $size(x/y_1) + size(y_1/y_2) + \cdots + size(y_k/y)$. The maximum size of the path from $x$ to $y$ is $size(x/y)$. Now we have that

$size(y_1) + size(y_2) \leqslant size(x)$ if $y_1, y_2$ are left, right sons of $x$, and
$size(y) \leqslant size(x) - size(x/y)$ if $y$ is a descendant of $x$

These inequalities can be used in the same way as the corresponding inequalities (in the proof of theorem 3.2) in order to prove the analogous invariants.

After the $k$th modified move

(I1′)  if $size(x) \leqslant 2^k$ then $x$ is pebbled
(I2′)  if $H(x, y) = \mathbf{true}$ then $\{y$ plays the role of $cond(x)\}$
        (a) $size(x/y) \geqslant 2^k$
        or (b) not all left sons of $y$, or not all right sons of $y$ are pebbled
        or (c) $y$ is a leaf

Here (I1′) and (I2′) are analogies of (I1) and (I2) used in theorem 3.2 for the original pebble game. The $k$th modified move is defined as in theorem 3.2 to be $(pebble', activate', square', square')$. When we verified invariant (I1), the crucial point was that if $size(x) \leqslant 2^k$ and the invariant held before then for each descendant $y$ of $x$, then all of its left sons are pebbled or all its right sons are pebbled. This follows from the fact that if $size(y) \leqslant 2^k$ then $size(y_1) \leqslant 2^{k-1}$ for all left sons of $y$, or $size(y_2) \leqslant 2^{k-1}$ for all right sons $y_2$ of $y$. Hence case (b) in (I2′) is not possible if $size(x) \leqslant 2^k$. If $y$ is a leaf then it is pebbled, otherwise $size(x/y) \leqslant 2^{k-1}$ holds and $size(y) \leqslant 2^{k-1}$. Hence all sons (in $M'$) of $x$ are pebbled and $x$ is pebbled in the $k$th move if the invariant held after the $(k-1)$th move. This proves (I1′). Verification of (I2′) is proved in a similar fashion to the proof of (I2) in theorem 3.2. We leave the details to the reader. □

### Theorem 3.8
Every straight-line arithmetic program with $m$ operations $+$ or $*$ and maximum degree $d$ can be computed in $O(\log^2 n + \log n \cdot \log d)$ parallel time using $O(m^3)$ processors on a **P-RAM**.

### Proof
We introduce the matrix $M$ of weights, which is initially a matrix with zero elements. The matrix $M$ contains weights of edges of the dag represented by the matrix $H$. Remember that a node $v$ is said to be non-active if and only if $v$ is a sink in this dag. This means that the operation $activate'$ was not really applied to the node $v$. Initially the dag $H$ has no edges. Then edges will be created by an operation analogous to the $activate$ operation in our parallel pebble game. The active node will play the role of the addition node. The following invariant will be satisfied.

(In2): if $v$ is an active node with sons $s_1, \ldots, s_k$ (in the graph represented by $H$)
        with multiplicities $M(v, s_i) = m_i$, then $val(v) = m_1 val(s_1) + m_2 val(s_2) + \cdots + m_k val(s_k)$

Hence if the values of sons of an active node are computed then the value of $v$ can be computed in $O(\log n)$ parallel time.

The algorithm is pebble-driven. The pebble game is played on a gbdag and simultaneously some additional computations are performed. We extend the operations *square'*, *pebble'* and *activate'*. In the extended operation *pebble'* whenever a node is pebbled then its value is computed according to the invariant (In2).

Also, in the operation *activate'* if all the left sons $\{l_1, \ldots, l_k\}$ of $v$ are pebbled then we set, for each right son $r_i$, $M(v, r_i) \leftarrow u * RW(v, r_i)$ where $u = LW(v, l_1) * val(l_1) + \cdots + LW(v, l_k) * val(l_k)$. An analogous operation is performed if all the right sons are pebbled and all the edges to left sons are activated. Moreover whenever the operation *square'* is performed then we perform also *square''*. The main invariant is now as follows. If a node $v$ is pebbled then its value $val(v)$ is correctly computed. This follows from the invariants (In1) and (In2). According to theorem 3.7, after applying $\log d$ operations (*activate'*, *square'*, *square'*, *pebble'*), with our extended versions of *pebble'* and *activate'*, the value of the root will be correctly computed. $O(\log m)$ time is required to transform an initial dag to a gbdag which has only multiplication and leaf nodes. $O(m^3)$ processors are used to perform the operation *square'*. This completes the proof.                                                                                          □

As an example we consider the binary dag of figure 3.24. Let $val(x_1) = 1$, $val(x_2) = 2$, $val(x_3) = 2$ and $val(x_4) = 3$. The graph $M'$ after performing *activate'* is shown in figure 3.25. Then the graph obtained after additionally performing the operations *square*, *pebble* and *activate* is shown in figure 3.26.

We now describe some applications of theorem 3.8 to dynamic programming problems. Dynamic programming is a method of computing the cost of obtaining an optimal solution to a problem by reducing the computation to smaller subproblems. The essential property is that optimality of the whole problem implies the optimality of subproblems. We provide three examples to illustrate the method.

*Figure 3.25.* The graph $M'$ after performing the extended operation *activate'*. The multiplicity of $(v_2, x_3)$ is $(LW(v_2, x_1) * val(x_1) + LW(v_2, x_2) * val(x_2)) * RW(v_2, x_3) = (1 * 1 + 1 * 2) * 1 = 3$

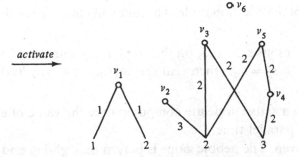

*Example* (minimum cost to evaluate the product of $n$ matrices)

We consider the evaluation of the product of $n$ matrices $M = M_1 \otimes M_2 \otimes \cdots \otimes M_n$, where $M_i$ is a matrix with $r_{i-1}$ rows and $r_i$ columns. We take the cost of multiplying a $k * l$ matrix by an $l * j$ matrix to be the product $klj$. The order in which the matrices are multiplied together can greatly affect the total cost (which for any order of evaluation is a sum of $n-1$ such products) of the evaluation. Let $m_{i,j}$ be the minimum cost of computing $M_{i+1} \otimes M_{i+2} \otimes \cdots \otimes M_j$. We have that

$$m_{i,i+1} = 0, \quad \text{for } i = 0, \ldots, n-1$$
$$m_{i,j} = \min\{m_{i,k} + m_{k,j} + r_i r_k r_j \mid i < k < j\}$$

We can compute all the products $r_{i-1} r_k r_j$ in $O(1)$ time with $n^3$ processors and assume later than these values are available. Then each of the equations for the $m_{i,j}$ ($j \neq i + 1$) can be rewritten as a part of a straight-line program with $O(n)$ statements. The variables $m_{i,k,j}$ can be introduced to compute $m_{i,k} + m_{k,j} + r_{i-1} r_k r_j$. Now we have a straight-line program to compute $m_{0,n}$, which is the minimum cost of evaluating the product of all the matrices. Here the operation min plays the role of $+$, and the operation $*$ is replaced by '$+$'. It is easy to see that the degree of the program is $O(n)$. The length is $O(n^3)$. The operations min and '$+$' satisfy all the rules of the operations '$+$' and '$*$' that are required in the proof of theorem 3.8. From theorem 3.8 we obtain the following.

*Corollary*

The minimum cost of evaluating the product of $n$ matrices can be computed in $O(\log^2 n)$ time using $n^9$ processors.

*Figure 3.26.* The graph $M'$ after executing the sequence of extended operations *square'*, *pebble'*, *activate'*. Now $val(v_6)$ can be computed as $M(v_6, v_3) * val(v_3) + M(v_6, v_5) * val(v_5) = 70 * 10 + 35 * 16$

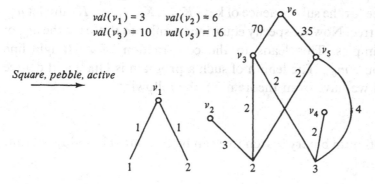

$val(v_1) = 3 \quad val(v_2) = 6$
$val(v_3) = 10 \quad val(v_5) = 16$

Square, pebble, active

However, the problem of computing the optimal order of the evaluation still remains. This can be found within the same time and processor bounds using a method similar to that used in the construction of a parsing tree from a parsing matrix. This is described in chapter 4. In fact the bound of $n^9$ on the number of processors can be lowered to $n^6$ using methods similar to that for the recognition of context-free languages.

*Example* (the triangulation problem)
Given the nodes of a polygon and a distance between each pair of nodes, the problem is to select a set of diagonals (lines between non-adjacent nodes) such that no two diagonals cross each other and such that the entire polygon is divided into triangles. The cost is the minimum total length of the diagonals. Let the polygon be given by its nodes (in clockwise order) $v_0, v_1, \ldots, v_n$. The subproblem with parameters $(i, j)$ is the computation of the minimal triangulation of the polygon given by the contiguous subset of nodes (in clockwise order) $v_i, v_{i+1}, \ldots, v_j$. Let $m_{i,j}$ be the cost of this subproblem. Equations similar to those for the $m_{i,j}$ of the previous example can then be employed in a straight-line program of length $O(n^3)$ and degree $O(n)$. Applying theorem 3.8 we obtain the following.

*Corollary*
The triangulation problem can be solved in $O(\log^2 n)$ time using $O(n^9)$ processors.

*Example* (optimum binary search trees)
Let $K_1, K_2, \ldots, K_n$ be some keys in increasing order. Let $p_i$ be the frequency of access to key $K_i$. The problem is to construct a binary tree $T$ with leaves $K_1, K_2, \ldots, K_n$ which has the property that $\sum_{i=1}^{n} l_i p_i$ is a minimum. Here $l_i$ is the length of the path from the root to $K_i$. For $0 \leqslant i < j \leqslant n$ let $T_{i,j}$ be the minimum-cost tree for the subsequence of keys $K_{i+1}, K_{i+2}, \ldots, K_j$ and let $m_{i,j}$ be the cost of this tree. Now we specify equations similar to those for the $m_{i,j}$ of the previous examples. This leads to the construction of a straight-line program to compute $m_{0,n}$. The length of such a program is $O(n^3)$ and degree $O(n)$. Once again we have from theorem 3.8 the following.

*Corollary*
The cost of an optimum binary search tree can be computed in $O(\log^2 n)$ time using $n^9$ processors.

Notice that, in these three examples, not only are the minimum costs of interest but also are certain optimal trees. In the first example this tree describes the optimal order of matrix multiplication (that is, the imposition of a bracket structure). In the second example such a tree corresponds to the structure of diagonalisation. The problem of recognising context-free languages can be also formulated as a dynamic programming problem. In this case we have to compute the boolean value which is **true** if and only if the string in question is generated by the given grammar. The parsing problem for context-free languages is to find a parse tree if one exists. The determination of optimal trees for the last three examples can be thought of as a generalisation of the parsing problem.

## 3.6 More efficient algorithms for dynamic programming

Dynamic programming problems can be reformulated as straight-line programs. However, they have very special structures and more specific algorithms can be constructed instead of applying the very general method of parallelisation of straight-line programs. The number of processors can thereby often be considerably reduced.

Many dynamic programming problems can be reduced to the computation of recurrences of the form

$$cost(i, j)$$
$$= \min\{cost(i, k) + cost(k, j) + f(i, k, j) \mid i < k < j, \text{ for } 0 \leqslant i \leqslant j - 2 \leqslant n - 2\}$$
$$cost(i, i + 1) = init(i), \quad \text{for } i = 0, \ldots, n$$

where the values of $f(i, k, j)$ and $init(i)$ are known in advance. The value of $cost(0, n)$ and a tree $T$ realising this value are to be found. We shall reformulate the problem later and will then specify what we mean by such a tree $T$.

For example, in the last section we considered the problem of finding the minimum cost to evaluate the product of $n$ matrices. There we presented recurrences for the $m_{i,j}$. In this case $init(i) = 0$ and $f(i, k, j) = r_i r_k r_j$.

Intuitively, a dynamic programming problem can be thought of as an instance of the following parenthesisation problem. Given a string $a_1 a_2 \ldots a_n$ of $n$ objects, find a minimum (in some sense) bracketing of the string. Then the optimal tree $T$ is the tree corresponding to the optimal parenthesisation. Also, $cost(i, j)$ is the minimum cost of bracketing the substring $a_{i+1} \ldots a_j$.

We denote by $S$ the set of all trees $T$ with weighted nodes such that

(i)   the nodes of $T$ are pairs $(i, j)$, $0 \leqslant i < j \leqslant n$,

(ii)   if $(i, j)$ is an internal node then its sons are of the form $(i, k), (k, j)$, for $i < k < j$, and $weight(i, j) = f(i, k, j)$, the weights are non-negative numbers,

(iii)  the leaves of $T$ are $(i, i + 1)$, for $0 \leqslant i < n$, and $weight(i, i + 1) = init(i)$.

Now we define the weight $W(T)$ of a tree $T$ as a sum of the weights of the nodes of $T$. Let

$$w(i, j) = \min\{W(T) \mid T \in S, \text{ the root of } T \text{ is } (i, j)\}$$

Here, the tree $T$ which realises the minimal weight also realises the minimum $cost(i, j)$. It is easy to see that $w(i, j) = cost(i, j)$. Let $S'$ be the set of trees from $S$ whose root is $(0, n)$.

Now the dynamic programming problem can be simply reformulated as the problem of finding the minimum weight of a tree $T \in S'$.

A crucial concept in parallel computations related to such trees is the concept of a partial tree, or a tree with a gap. This is a tree $T$ from the set $S$ rooted at some vertex $(i, j)$ with one of its non-leaf nodes $(p, q)$ treated as a leaf. In other words it is a tree $T$ with the subtree $T'$ rooted at $(p, q)$ deleted. In the deletion, $(p, q)$ becomes a leaf of $T$. $T'$ can be treated as a gap. More formally, we say that the node $(p, q)$ is the gap of $T$. For a given $(i, j)$ and $(p, q)$, we denote the set of such partial trees rooted at $(i, j)$ and with the gap $(p, q)$ by $PT(i, j, p, q)$.

The (partial) weight $PW(T)$ of a partial tree $T \in PT(i, j, p, q)$ is the sum of the weights of all its nodes except the node $(p, q)$. Let

$$pw(i, j, p, q) = \min\{PW(T) \mid T \in PT(i, j, p, q)\}$$

Observe that $pw(i, j, i, j) = 0$.

Let $T$ be a tree rooted at $(i, j)$, where the sons of $(i, j)$ are $(i, k), (k, j)$. Also, let $T_1$ be the tree rooted at $(k, j)$ and $T'$ be the partial tree rooted at $(i, j)$ with the node $(i, k)$ treated as a leaf $((i, k)$ is the gap). Then

(1′)   $PW(T') = f(i, k, j) + W(T_1)$

This implies the following equality.

(1a)   $pw(i, j, i, k) = f(i, j, k) + w(k, j)$, where $(k, j)$ is the right sone of $(i, j)$ in the tree realising the minimum of $cost(i, j)$.

Similarly one can derive the equality

(1b)   $pw(i, j, k, j) = f(i, j, k) + w(i, k)$, where $(i, k)$ is the left son of $(i, j)$ in the tree realising the minimum of $cost(i, j)$.

Let $T$ be a partial tree with the root $(i, j)$ and the gap $(p, q)$. Also, let $(r, s)$ be an intermediate node on the path from $(i, j)$ to $(p, q)$. We denote by $T_1$ the subtree of $T$ rooted at $(i, j)$ with the gap $(r, s)$, and by $T_2$ the subtree of $T$ rooted at $(r, s)$ with the gap $(p, q)$. Then

$$(2') \quad PW(T) = PW(T_1) + PW(T_2)$$

and the following equality follows.

$$(2) \qquad pw(i, j, p, q) = \min\{pw(i, j, r, s) + pw(r, s, p, q) \mid i \leqslant r \leqslant p \text{ and } q \leqslant s \leqslant j\}$$

If $T$ is a tree rooted at $(i, j)$, $T_1$ is a subtree of $T$ rooted at an internal vertex $(p, q) \neq (i, j)$ and $T_2$ is a partial subtree rooted at $(i, j)$ with gap $(p, q)$, then

$$(3') \quad W(T) = W(T_1) + PW(T_2)$$

This implies the equality

$$(3) \qquad w(i, j) = \min\{pw(i, j, p, q) + w(p, q) \mid i \leqslant p < q \leqslant j, (p, q) \neq (i, j)\}$$

We introduce the auxiliary arrays $w'(i, j)$ and $pw'(i, j, p, q)$. At the end of the algorithm we want $w' = w$ and $pw' = pw$. Initially all entries of the arrays $w'$ and $pw'$ contain the value $+\infty$, except for the entries $w'(i, i + 1) = init(i)$. Then in the course of the algorithm some of the values will decrease. We also introduce three parallel operations called *activate1*, *square1* and *pebble1*. These correspond respectively to the equalities ((1a) and (1b)), (2) and (3).

> *activate1*
> **for all** $i, j, k,\ 0 \leqslant i < k < j \leqslant n$, **in parallel do**
> $\quad pw'(i, j, i, k) \leftarrow \min\{pw'(i, j, i, k), f(i, j, k) + w'(k, j)\}$
> $\quad pw'(i, j, k, j) \leftarrow \min\{pw'(i, j, k, j), f(i, j, k) + w'(i, k)\}$
> *square1*
> **for all** $i, p, q, j,\ 0 \leqslant i < p < q < j \leqslant n,\ j - i \geqslant 2$, **in parallel do**
> $\quad pw'(i, j, p, q) \leftarrow \min\{pw'(i, j, r, s) + pw'(r, s, p, q) \mid i \leqslant r \leqslant p, q \leqslant s \leqslant j\}$
> *pebble1*
> **for all** $i, p, q, j,\ 0 \leqslant i \leqslant p < q \leqslant j \leqslant n,\ j - i \geqslant 2$, **in parallel do**
> $\quad w'(i, j) \leftarrow \min\{pw'(i, j, p, q) + w'(p, q) \mid i \leqslant p < q \leqslant j\}$

The whole algorithm is now briefly described as follows.

> **Algorithm** *Evaluate*
> **repeat** $\log_2 n$ **times**
> $\quad$ **begin**
> $\quad$ *activate1, square1, square1, pebble1*
> $\quad$ **end**

*Theorem 3.9*

After termination of the algorithm *Evaluate*, $w'(i, j) = w(i, j)$ for each $0 \leqslant i < j \leqslant n$. The recurrences for the $cost(i, j)$ can be computed in $\log^2 n$ time using $n^6/\log n$ processors on a P-RAM.

*Proof*

It is easy to see that $w'(i, j) \geqslant w(i, j)$ and that $pw'(i, j, p, q) \geqslant pw(i, j, p, q)$ for every $i, j, p, q$ in the course of the algorithm. It is enough to show that at some stage in the computation the equalities can be obtained. The essential point is to prove that $\log_2 n$ repetitions are sufficient. We do this using a relationship between the operations *activate1*, *square1* and *pebble1* and the operations *activate*, *square*, *pebble* as defined for the original parallel pebble game.

Consider a pair $(i, j)$, $0 \leqslant i < j - 1 < n$. Also consider a particular tree $T \in S$ (one of possibly many) with minimal weight and with the root $(i, j)$. Now $w(i, j)$ equals the weight of this tree and, for each node $(p, q)$ of $T$, $w(p, q)$ equals the weight of the subtree of $T$ rooted at $(p, q)$. Moreover $pw(i, j, p, q)$ is the weight $PW(T')$ of the partial tree $T'$ which is a subtree of $T$ with root $(i, j)$ and gap $(p, q)$. Hence, as far as nodes of $T$ only are concerned, the weights $pw'$ and $w'$ reach their minimal values in computations involving only nodes of $T$. Therefore in considering the final value of $w'(i, j)$ we can ignore all pairs $(k, l)$ which are not nodes of $T$.

Now we play the parallel pebble game on $T$ in the course of the algorithm *Evaluate*. We consider an extended version of the algorithm *Evaluate* which we call *Evaluate1*. Assume that initially all the leaves of $T$ are pebbled.

**Algorithm** *Evaluate1*
**repeat** $\log_2 n$ **times**
  **begin**
  *activate, activate1*
  *square, square1*
  *square, square1*
  *pebble, pebble1*
  **end**

It is easy to see that the following two invariants hold after each of the operations *activate1*, *square1*, *pebble1*:

  **if** $(p, q)$ is pebbled **then** $w(i, j) = w'(p, q))$
and
  **if** $cond(p, q) = (r, s)$ **then** $pw(p, q, r, s) = pw'(p, q, r, s)$

for every pair of nodes $(p, q)$ and $(r, s)$ of the tree $T$. In other words, if the node is pebbled then its weight $w'$ reaches its minimal value. Similar statements hold for pairs of nodes related through the function *cond* and partial weights $pw'$.

Initially only the leaves of $T$ are pebbled, but all of them are of the form $(i, i + 1)$ and their values $w'(i, i + 1) = w(i, i + 1)$ are correctly computed and set to *init(i)*. Then the equalities (1′), (2′), (3′) and (1a), (1b), (2) and (3) can be used to show that in the course of the algorithm *Evaluate1* the invariants are preserved.

Hence at the moment of pebbling the node $(i, j)$, the value of $w'(i, j)$ is correctly computed. This node will be ultimately pebbled. Observe now that the pebble game performed on the tree $T$ can be ignored and the operations *activate*, *square* and *pebble* removed. They were introduced only to show correctness. Then algorithm *Evaluate1* becomes our initial algorithm *Evaluate*. Hence $w'(i, j)$ is correctly computed in the algorithm *Evaluate*. The same argument applies to every pair $(i, j)$ by taking a suitable optimal tree $T$ with the root $(i, j)$. This completes the proof. $\qquad\square$

### Corollary

The minimum cost of the evaluation of the product of $n$ matrices can be computed in $O(\log^2 n)$ time using $n^6/\log n$ processors. $\qquad\square$

### Corollary

The triangulation problem can be solved in $O(\log^2 n)$ time using $O(n^6/\log n)$ processors. $\qquad\square$

### Corollary

The cost of an optimum binary search tree can be computed in $O(\log^2 n)$ time using $O(n^6/\log n)$ processors. $\qquad\square$

As we observed at the end of the previous section, the computation of optimal trees for the last three examples can be thought as a generalised parsing problem. It is shown in chapter 4, which is about context-free languages, that if we have computed the parsing matrix then the parsing tree can be found using an efficient parallel algorithm. The matrix *cost(i, j)* plays the same role in dynamic programming problems as the parsing matrix in the case of context-free languages. The next theorem follows by using the same method as that used in chapter 4 for the computation of parse trees from parsing matrices. We refer the reader to that chapter for the details.

*Theorem 3.10*

The optimal tree $T$ realising the minimal value of $cost(0, n)$ from the recurrence relations for the $cost(i, j)$ can be computed in $O(\log^2 n)$ time using $n^6$ processors on a P-RAM.                                                    □

Theorem 3.10 implies (for example) that not just the cost of the optimal binary search tree can be efficiently found using a parallel algorithm. We can actually find such a tree in a similarly efficient manner. The same observation applies to the other two dynamic programming problems which we used as examples.

## 3.7 A more algebraic point of view: a method of simultaneous substitutions

In this section we look briefly at the parallel evaluation of expressions and straight-line programs from a more algebraic point of view. An alternative and more algebraic way to design algorithms for parallel evaluation of expressions and straight-line programs consists of manipulating many algebraic expressions in parallel by making suitable substitutions. We shall call such a method the simultaneous-substitutions method. In fact this will be a reformulation of previously described methods which used our parallel pebble game. The simultaneous-substitutions method is a generalisation of the parallel execution of assignment statements:

$$(x_1, x_2, \ldots, x_n) \leftarrow (val_1, val_2, \ldots, val_n)$$

We compute here the values of $n$ variables in one parallel step. Instead of the values $val_j$ we could let some terms on the right-hand side be algebraic formulas, $f_j$, involving the variables $x_i$. Thus we would have a version of some straight-line program. Then we could replace any variable $x_j$, in formulas in which it appears on the right side, by $f_j$ without changing the final values of the variables.

Assume that we have a straight-line program $P: x_n = f_1, x_{n-1} = f_{n-1}, \ldots, x_1 = f_1$, where $f_i$ are terms involving the variables $x_j$. All variables occurring in $f_i$ have a lower index than $i$. Thus $f_1$ contains no variables.

Let $subst(i, j)$ be the operation of replacing $x_j$ in $f_i$ (if $x_j$ appears in $f_i$) by the expression for $f_j$ and making a suitable reduction of the formula obtained. For example if $f_5 = x_3 + x_2$ and $f_3 = x_2 + 5$ then after performing $subst(5, 3)$ we obtain $f_5 = 2 \times 2 + 5$. If we have several operations $subst(i, j_1), subst(i, j_2), \ldots, subst(i, j_k)$ involving variables $x_j$ appearing in $f_i$ (each variable at most once) then all the substitutions can be performed simultaneously. The bottleneck of the method is the size of formulas $f_j$. If we replace some variables by formulas without making suitable reductions then the size of the affected formula can become very long. This would be problematic after a series of such replacements. The size of the formulas will not be kept within constant bounds.

Fortunately we can keep the sizes of formulas within constant bounds when the operations are only + and *. We define the substitution *subst(i, j)* to be safe if *degree*$(f_j) \leqslant 1$. Then one step of the algorithm consists of the simultaneous execution of all safe substitutions together with the subsequent reduction of the formulas obtained. After $O(\log n + \log d)$ such steps the formula $f_n$ is the required output value.

Suppose that the formula corresponds to a previously stated invariant, namely

$$v = (LW(v, l_1) * l_1 + \cdots + LW(v, l_k) * l_k) * (RW(v, r_1 + \cdots + RW(v, r_j) * r_j)$$

where $v$, $l_i$ and $r_i$ are variables, and $LW(v, l_i)$ and $RW(v, r_i)$ are constant coefficients. Then the replacement of all the $l_i$ by their constant values, or all the $r_i$ by their computed constant values, corresponds to the operation *activate'*. Here some variables are replaced by formulas of degree 0. Hence the main effect of such substitutions is to decrease the degree of the formula for $v$ by 1. The operation *square'* corresponds to replacing some variables in formulas of degree 1 by formulas of degree 1. The operation *pebble'* corresponds to replacing all variables in a given formula of degree 1 by constant values and this decreases the degree to zero.

We can treat the operations *pebble*, *square* and *activate* (together with the manipulation of associated values and conditional functions) in a similar fashion.

### Bibliographic notes

The parallel evaluation of arithmetic expressions was considered in [2]; however, the cost of preprocessing was not counted. Miller and Reif[9] defined dynamic expression evaluation as the problem of expression evaluation when the preprocessing is not free. They presented an (almost optimal) deterministic algorithm with parameters time $= \log n$, number of processors $= n$, and they also described an optimal parallel randomised algorithm. Their algorithm was based on a special technique called tree contraction. A similar technique was independently invented earlier by Rytter and presented in [10], where it was called a parallel pebble game. It was used in [10] to construct efficient parallel algorithms for recursive programs with independent calls. Expression evaluation is a special case of recursive programs with independent calls. The parallel pebble game was redefined in [11], where the upper complexity bound of exactly $\log_2 n$ was proved for the number of parallel steps. That is, the coefficient of $\log n$ in the $O(\log n)$ number of steps was shown to be 1. The coefficient of $\log n$ in the number of stages of the Miller and Reif tree contraction technique is much more complicated.

The optimal deterministic algorithm for dynamic expression evaluation was given by Gibbons and Rytter[5] using a new simple method of tree compression. The optimal parallel algorithm for parsing expressions was described by Bar-On and Vishkin.[1] The problem of parsing bracket languages can be thought of as a generalisation of parsing expressions. The optimal parallel algorithm for this problem follows from the optimality of parallel evaluation of expressions for algebras with $O(1)$ bounded carrier. Application of expression evaluation to the construction of finite automata is from [12]. Recently a new method for expression evaluation was proposed in [3]. The form of the input in this chapter was a vector storing the expression as a string. Such an input guarantees an optimal algorithm for consecutive numbering of the leaves (from left to right) of the expression tree. If the input is the expression tree without the leaves being consecutively numbered, then the optimal parallel algorithm for list ranking [4] (numbering consecutively elements of a given list) could be easily applied to number leaves consecutively from left to right in $O(\log n)$ time with $n/\log n$ processors. The Euler tour technique for trees gives easily the list of leaves. Then the algorithms from this chapter can be applied. However, the advanced optimal algorithm for list ranking is beyond the scope of this text.

The extension of parallel computation of arithmetic trees to arithmetic directed acyclic graphs with small degree was initially described in [17] and then modified in [8]. However, our exposition differs slightly from both of them. It uses a natural extension of the parallel pebble game to dags with many left and many right sons. The parallel computation of dynamic programming problems is from [13].

**Bibliography**

[1] I. Bar-On and U. Vishkin. Optimal parallel generation of a computation tree form. *ACM Transactions on Programming Languages and Systems* 7, 2 (1985), 348–57.

[2] R. P. Brent. The parallel evaluation of general arithmetic expressions. *Journal of the ACM* **21**, 2 (1974), 201–8.

[3] R. Cole and U. Vishkin. Accelerated centroid decomposition technique for optimal parallel tree evaluation in logarithmic time. Manuscript, autumn 1986.

[4] R. Cole and U. Vishkin. Approximate and exact parallel scheduling with applications to list, tree and graph problems. *27th IEEE Symposium on Foundations of Computer Science* (1986).

[5] A. M. Gibbons and W. Rytter. An optimal parallel algorithm for dynamic evaluation and its applications. *Sixth Conference on Foundations of Software Technology and Theoretical Computer Science*. Lecture Notes in Computer Science 241. Springer-Verlag (1986), 453–69.

[6] J. Hopcroft and J. Ullman. *Introduction to Automata Theory, Languages and Computations*. Addison-Wesley (1979), Chapter 2.

[7] G. Kindervater and J. Lenstra. An introduction to parallelism in combinatorial

optimization. Report OS-R8501. Centre for Mathematics and Computer Science, Amsterdam (1985).

[8] G. Miller, V. Ramachandran and E. Kaltofen. Efficient parallel evaluation of straight-line code and arithmetic circuits. 'Workshop on Parallel Algorithms' (1986), *Theoretical Computer Science.*

[9] G. L. Miller and J. Reif. Parallel tree contraction and its application. *26th IEEE Symposium on Foundations of Computer Science* (1985), 478–89.

[10] W. Rytter. The complexity of two way pushdown automata and recursive programs. *Combinatorial Algorithms on Words* (eds. A. Apostolica and Z. Galil), NATO ASI Series F:12. Springer-Verlag (1985).

[11] W. Rytter. Remarks on pebble games on graphs. 'Combinatorial analysis and its applications' (1985) (ed. M. Syslo), to appear in *Zastosowania Matematyki* (1987).

[12] W. Rytter. A note on parallel transformations of regular expressions to nondeterministic finite automata. 'International workshop on parallel algorithms and architectures' (1987), final version to appear in *Theoretical Computer Science.*

[13] W. Rytter. Fast parallel computations for some dynamic programming problems. Research Report, Department of Computer Science, University of Warwick, June 1987.

[14] W. Rytter and R. Giancarlo. Optimal parallel parsing of bracket languages. 'International workshop on parallel algorithms and architectures' (1987), final version to appear in *Theoretical Computer Science.*

[15] R. Sedgewick. *Algorithms.* Addison-Wesley (1983), Chapter 20.

[16] R. E. Tarjan and U. Vishkin. Finding biconnected components and computing tree functions in logarithmic parallel time. *25th IEEE Symposium on Foundations of Computer Science* (1984), 12–22.

[17] L. Valiant, S. Skyum, S. Berkowitz and C. Rackoff. Fast parallel computation of polynomials using few processors. *SIAM Journal of Computing* 12, 4 (1983), 641–4.

# CHAPTER 4

# PARALLEL RECOGNITION AND PARSING OF CONTEXT-FREE LANGUAGES

The class of context-free languages (cfls) is probably the most interesting class of formal languages, certainly from an applications point of view. Despite a lot of research the sequential complexity of general cfl recognition is not well understood. An obvious lower bound for sequential time is linear, while the best known algorithms have more than quadratic complexity. Moreover the known lower bound for space complexity is $\log n$, while the best upper bound is $\log^2 n$. This holds even if we restrict ourselves to deterministic cfls, and moreover we do not know how to reduce this space through the use of non-determinism.

In the case of parallel computations our knowledge is also at present not very satisfactory. The best algorithms for parallel cfl recognition work in $O(\log^2 n)$ time using $n^6$ processors on a P-RAM (or $O(\log n)$ time on a W-RAM). In this chapter we describe such an algorithm. We note however that the product (parallel time * number of processors), although polynomial in the problem size, is too large to be satisfactory. There are two non-trivial subclasses of cfls, bracket languages and input-driven languages,[3] for which recognition can be achieved by optimal parallel algorithms (that is, in $O(\log n)$ time using $n/\log n$ processors on a P-RAM). The recognition problem for these languages can be reduced to the problem of evaluating certain algebraic expressions.

Problems about cfls are suitable for parallel processing because they are mostly concerned with the existence or construction of certain (syntactic) trees. Following normal conventions (see [4] for example) we formally specify a context-free grammar $G$ by the 4-tuple $G = (V_N, V_T, P, S)$, where

$V_N$ is the set of non-terminals

$V_T$ is the set of terminal symbols

$P$ is the set of productions

$S$ is the starting non-terminal

For the non-terminal $A$ and the string $u$ (in general containing non-terminals and terminals), we write $A \to u$ if and only if $A \to u$ is a production, and we write $A \to *u$ if and only if $u$ can be derived from $A$ after the application of one or more productions of the grammar. We shall assume throughout the chapter that any context-free grammar we consider is in Chomsky normal form. This will greatly facilitate our reasoning and, as is well known, any cfg is easily transformed into this form.[4] In Chomsky normal form each production of the grammar is of the type $A \to BC$ or of the type $A \to a$. Here $A$, $B$ and $C$ are arbitrary non-terminals whilst $a$ is a terminal symbol.

The *context-free recognition problem* for a given context-free grammar $G$ is to decide whether or not $S \to *w$, for a given string $w$ of terminal symbols. The problem size $n$ is the length of the string $w$. The size of $G$ is treated as a constant.

If $w = a_1 a_2 \dots a_n$ is a given input string, then by $w[i{:}j]$ we denote the substring $a_{i+1} \dots a_j$ for $0 \leqslant i < j \leqslant n$ while by $w[i{:}i]$ we denote the empty word. (This is in contrast to the convention used in the chapter on string matching where $w[i \mathinner{.\,.} j]$ means the substring $a_i \dots a_j$.)

# 4.1 Parallel recognition of general context-free languages

Almost all algorithms for context-free language recognition are (in some sense) based on syntactic trees. A syntactic tree represents a derivation of a string $x$ (in general consisting of both terminal and non-terminal symbols) from some non-terminal symbol. The internal nodes of such a tree are non-terminals and the leaves are labelled by consecutive symbols of $x$ (from left to right). If $A$ is the label of a particular node, and if its left and right sons are respectively labelled $B$ and $C$, then $A \to BC$ is a production of the grammar.

*Example 4.1*

Let us consider the grammar $G = (V_N, V_T, P, S)$, where $V_N = \{S, A, B\}$, $V_T = \{a, b\}$ and $P = \{S \to SS, S \to AB, S \to b, B \to SB, B \to b, A \to a\}$. Now take the string $w = aabbb = a_1 a_2 a_3 a_4 a_5$. A syntactic tree for the derivation of the substring $x = abb$ is shown in figure 4.1.

Any syntactic tree can be obtained by the successive composition of pairs of syntactic trees. An initial syntactic tree in this process is a derivation tree of height 1, generating one non-terminal symbol, as illustrated in figure 4.2.

The recognition problem is equivalent to the problem of determining for a given string $w$ if there is a syntactic tree with root $S$ and with leaves spelling $w$. Then a brute-force solution to the problem is to generate all possible syntactic trees starting from initial trees and applying simple rules of composition. The number of leaves is limited by $n$. The main drawback of this algorithm is the volume of possible data, since the number of trees with at most $n$ leaves is not polynomially bounded. Specifically we note that the number of distinct binary trees with $n$ leaves is given by the so-called Catalan number $C(n)$:

$$C(n) = \frac{1}{n}\binom{2n-2}{n-1} \geqslant 2^{n-2}$$

It is possible, however, to refine this method and to obtain satisfactory algorithms. The main strategy is to make use of *partial syntactic trees* instead of syntactic trees. A partial syntactic tree is described only by its root $R$ and by an interval $[i:j]$. This interval specifies the substring $w[i:j]$ as a sequence of leaf labels. The partial syntactic tree corresponding to figure 4.1 is presented in figure 4.3. Notice that the volume of data is now polynomially bounded since there are only $O(n^2)$ partial syntactic trees. This follows from the observation

*Figure 4.1.* The syntactic (or parse) tree of *abb*

*Figure 4.2.* An initial syntactic tree. Such a tree corresponds to a triple $(A, i, i+1)$, where $a_{i+1} = a$

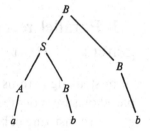

*Figure 4.3.* The partial syntactic tree corresponding to the syntactic tree of figure 4.1.

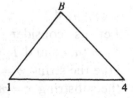

that the number of non-terminals for a given grammar is a constant and that there are $O(n^2)$ intervals $[i{:}j]$.

A triple, $(R, i, j)$, is used to denote the partial syntactic tree with root labelled $R$ and with interval $[i .. j]$. Such a triple is called a *node*. We bear in mind that these nodes will be the vertices of a graph to be described later. We say that the node $(A, i, j)$ is *realisable* iff there is a derivation $A \to {}^*w[i{:}j]$. We shall write $y, z \vdash x$ or $z, y \vdash x$ iff $(A \to BC$ and $x, y, z$ are of the form $x = (A, i, j)$, $y = (B, i, k)$, $z = (C, k, j))$.

The relation denoted by $\vdash$ is a rule of composition by which a bigger partial syntactic tree may be obtained from two smaller ones. The *initial* partial syntactic trees are $(A, i, i + 1)$, where $A \to a_{i+1}$ is a production. We have to determine whether or not the node $(S, 0, n)$ can be generated from the initial nodes after (possibly many) applications of the composition rule which is graphically represented in figure 4.4.

Consider the following straightforward algorithm in which $M$ is a set of nodes (partial syntactic trees):

> initialise $M$ to contain exactly the initial nodes
> **repeat** 'several' **times**
>   **begin**
>   **for** all nodes $x, y, z$ **in parallel do**
>     **if** $(x, y \in M$ and $x, y \vdash z)$ **then** add $z$ to $M$
>   check if $(S, 0, n) \in M$
>   **end**

We have to determine what 'several' means. If we take the grammar with $P = \{S \to AS, S \to a, A \to a\}$, then we can easily see that 'several' must mean $\Omega(n)$ in this case. Such a slow parallel algorithm is not very interesting.

However, we shall use the same approach successfully by taking slightly more complicated objects and rules of composition. These more complicated objects are partial syntactic trees with *gaps*. A partial syntactic tree with a gap is a tree deriving some substring $w[i{:}j]$ of $w$, in which an internal substring $w[k{:}l]$, $i \leqslant k < l \leqslant j$, is missing. This substring is replaced with a non-terminal

*Figure 4.4.* A graphical presentation of the composition of partial syntactic trees

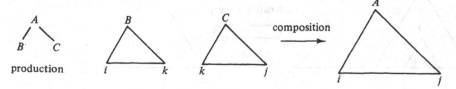

symbol $B$. Hence it is a tree corresponding to a derivation of a string $w[i:k]Bw[l:j]$ from some non-terminal $A$. Graphically such a tree may be represented as in figure 4.5.

It is convenient to represent a partial syntactic tree with root $A$ and leaves $w[i:k]Bw[l:j]$ by a pair of nodes $((A, i, j), (B, k, l))$. Such a pair of nodes can be interpreted as an edge in a graph whose vertices are partial syntactic trees.

There are three basic ways to compose bigger partial syntactic trees with gaps from smaller ones. These are presented in figure 4.6. We show later that these compositions allow us to construct a fast parallel algorithm using the same philosophy as the naive algorithm already described (augmenting the set of generated elements by applying compositions simultaneously whenever possible).

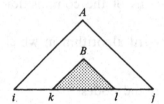

*Figure 4.5*

*Figure 4.6.* The three ways to construct larger partial trees with gaps

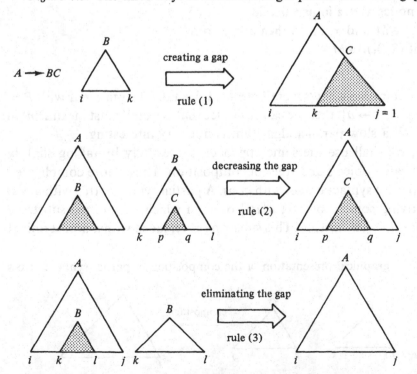

We say that a pair of nodes $\langle (A, i, j), (B, k, l) \rangle$ is realisable iff $(A \to {}^* w[i{:}k] B w[l{:}j], i \leqslant k < l \leqslant j,$ and $(A, i, j) \neq (B, k, l))$. In general the pair of nodes $\langle x, y \rangle$ can be interpreted as the syntactic tree $x$ with the gap $y$. We use diamond brackets here to emphasise that, in the graph we are about to define, an edge does not necessarily exist between $x$ and $y$, although (as example 4.2 illustrates) if $\langle x, y \rangle$ is realisable then a path will exist from $x$ to $y$ in that graph.

For the grammar $G$ and string $w$ we define a directed graph $U_{G,w} = (V, E)$, where $V$ is the set of all nodes (partial syntactic trees without gaps) and $(x, y)$ is in $E$ iff for some realisable node $z$ we have $y, z \vdash x$ (or equivalently $z, y \vdash x$). Thus the edges of $U_{G,w}$ correspond to partial syntactic trees with gaps which can be created *only* by using rule (1) of figure 4.6. Graph-theoretic and syntactic terminologies are used simultaneously for the same set of objects as figure 4.7 implies.

### Example 4.2

Let us consider the grammar $G$ and the string $w = aabbb$ from example 4.1. Node $(S, 0, 5)$ is the goal node, which is to be derived from initial nodes in order to prove that $w$ can be generated by the grammar. Figure 4.8 presents the

*Figure 4.7.* The edge $((B, 1, 5), (B, 3, 5))$ corresponds to the partial syntactic tree $(B, 1, 5)$ with the gap $(B, 3, 5)$

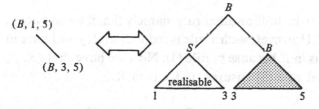

*Figure 4.8*

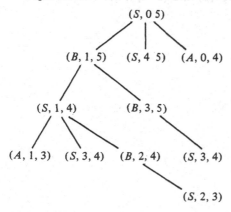

subgraph of $U_{G,w}$ spanned by the set of nodes reachable from $(S, 0, 5)$. All edges are directed downwards. The input string $w$ can be derived from $S$ iff the node $(S, 0, 5)$ is realisable. In the graph there is an edge $((S, 0, 5), (B, 1, 5))$ because $((A, 0, 1), (B, 1, 5) \vdash (S, 0, 5)$ and $(A, 0, 1)$ is realisable). There is an edge $((B, 1, 5), (B, 3, 5))$ because $((S, 1, 3), (B, 3, 5) \vdash (B, 1, 5)$ and $(S, 1, 3)$ is realisable). Adding edges in a similar manner we can see that there is a path from $(S, 0, 5)$ to $(S, 2, 3)$. This means that there is a derivation $S \to *w[0{:}2]Sw[3{:}5]$. The pair $\langle (S, 0, 5), (S, 2, 3) \rangle$ can be interpreted as a tree with a gap, as figure 4.9 illustrates. The gap corresponds to the partial syntactic tree $(S, 2, 3)$ which derives $a_3 = b = w[2{:}3]$ from $S$. Thus, incidentally, $S \to *w$.

Let $R$ be the set of all realisable nodes and realisable pairs of nodes. Lemma 4.1 follows from the definitions. Rules (1)–(3) correspond to the composition rules presented in figure 4.6.

*Lemma 4.1*
$R$ is the smallest set satisfying the rules
(0)    for each $A$ in $V_N$, $0 \leqslant i < n$, if $A \to a_{i+1}$ then $(A, i, i+1)$ is in $R$,
(1)    if $z$ is in $R$ and $y, z \vdash x$ then $\langle x, y \rangle$ is in $R$,
(2)    if $\langle x, y \rangle, \langle y, z \rangle$ are in $R$ then $\langle x, z \rangle$ is in $R$,
(3)    if $\langle x, y \rangle$ is in $R$ and $y$ is in $R$ then $x$ is in $R$.

It might be thought natural to include another rule, namely that if $y$ and $z$ are in $R$ and $y, z \vdash x$ then $x$ is in $R$. However, such a rule is redundant. If $y$ and $z$ are in $R$ and $y, z \vdash x$, then $\langle x, y \rangle$ is in $R$ because of rule (1). Now we have that $\langle x, y \rangle$ is in $R$ and $y$ is in $R$ so that rule (3) ensures that $x$ is in $R$.

*Figure 4.9.* A tree with a gap. There is a path from $(S, 0, 5)$ to $(S, 2, 3)$ in figure 4.8 because the trees $(A, 0, 1)$, $(A, 1, 2)$, $(B, 4, 5)$ and $(B, 3, 4)$ are realisable

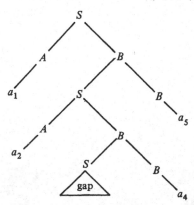

We say that an element $x$ of $R$ is *initial* iff it belongs to $R$ because of rule (0). Hence initial elements are of the form $(A, i, i + 1)$. Every other element of $R$ will be generated from the initial elements after a (finite) number of applications of the rules (1)–(3) of lemma 4.1.

*Example 4.3*
Figure 4.10 shows how the pair $\langle(S, 0, 5), (S, 2, 3)\rangle$ can be derived from initial elements using the rules expressed in lemma 4.1. Notice that this tree is shorter than the tree of figure 4.9.

We assume the following terminology. Inserting a node $x$ into $R$ is called *pebbling* this node. We introduce the logical tables $COND$, *pebbled* and $EDGE$. Pebbling a node $x$ consists of executing $pebbled(x) \leftarrow$ **true**. A node is pebbled if we know that it is realisable. Here the table $EDGE$ is redundant; later it will play a crucial role to eliminate write conflicts in the case of unambiguous grammars. Assume that initially all tables contain the values **false**.

We define the following operations.

*activate1*
 **for** all $x, y, z$ such that $y, z \vdash x$ and $pebbled(z)$ **in parallel do**
$$EDGE(x, y) \leftarrow COND(x, y) \leftarrow \textbf{true}$$
*square1*
 **for** all $x, z, y$ such that $COND(x, z)$ and $COND(z, y)$ **in parallel do**
$$COND(x, y) \leftarrow \textbf{true}$$
*pebble1*
 **for** all $x, y$ such that $COND(x, y)$ and $pebbled(y)$ **in parallel do**
$$pebbled(x) \leftarrow \textbf{true}$$

*Figure 4.10*

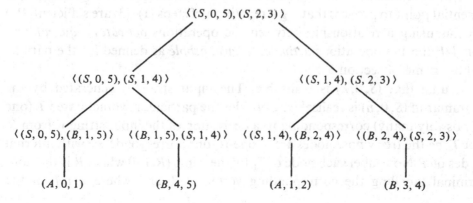

*Algorithm 4.1*
{parallel context-free recognition}

**begin**
0. **for** all $i$, $0 \leqslant i < n$, $A$ in $V_N$ such that $A \rightarrow a_{i+1}$ **in parallel do**
$$pebbled((A, i, i + 1)) \leftarrow \textbf{true}$$

**repeat** $\log_2 n$ **times**
   **begin** {invariants}
1.   *activate1*
      {invariants}
2.   *square1*
      {invariants}
    *square1*
      {invariants}
3.   *pebble1*
  **end**
**if** node $(S, 0, n)$ is pebbled **then** *ACCEPT*
**end** of algorithm 4.1

*Lemma 4.2*
Algorithm 4.1 accepts an input string (of length $n$) if and only if node $(S, 0, n)$ is realisable.

*Proof*
Instructions (0)–(3) of the algorithm are in correspondence with the rules of Lemma 4.1. Note that instruction (2) consists of two applications of rule (2). If the algorithm accepts then it follows from lemma 4.1 that $(S, 0, n)$ can be generated and is therefore realisable. It remains to be shown that if $(S, 0, n)$ is realisable then the algorithm accepts. In other words we must show that if $(S, 0, n)$ is realisable then it is pebbled on completion of the algorithm. The essential point to prove is that $\log n$ repetition of steps (1)–(3) are sufficient. We do this using a relationship between the operations *activate1*, *square1* and *pebble1* and the operations *activate*, *square*, *pebble* as defined for the parallel pebble game of section 3.2.

    Assume that $(S, 0, n)$ is realisable. The input string is generated by the grammar iff $(S, 0, n)$ is realisable. Consider the particular syntactic tree $T$ (one of possibly many) corresponding to a derivation of the input string $w$ from $S$. Let $T_1$ be the tree whose nodes are in one-to-one correspondence with internal nodes of $T$. Now label each node of $T_1$ by the triple $(R, i, j)$ where $R$ is the non-terminal labelling the corresponding vertex of $T$ and where $w[i, j]$ is the segment of $w$ spelled by the leaves of the subtree of $T$ rooted at the same vertex. Clearly $T_1$ is a subgraph of $U_{G,w}$ with the leaves of $T_1$ being initial nodes of the form $(R, i, j)$. Let $T_2$ be a disjoint copy of $T_1$ in which $x'$ denotes a copy of the node $x$ in $T_1$. Now consider the following algorithm in which the operations *activate*, *square* and *pebble* are applied to $T_2$ whilst *activate1*, *square1* and *pebble1* are applied to $T_1$. We assume that initially all the leaves of $T_2$ are pebbled.

**repeat** log $n$ **times**
    **begin** *activate*, *activate1*, *square*, *square1*, *square*, *square1*,
                                                    *pebble*, *pebble1* **end**

It is evident that the following invariant holds after each of the operations *activate1*, *square1*, *pebble1*.

    (If $x'$ is pebbled then $x$ is) and (if $cond(x') = y'$ then $COND(x, y)$)

Notice that it is possible for node $x$ to be pebbled whilst $x'$ is not; this is likely to happen for some $x$, for example if there is a second topologically different parse tree for $w$. We know from section 3.2 that on completion of the algorithm the root of $T_2$, that is node $(S, 0, n)'$, will be pebbled. Hence, because of the invariant, node $(S, 0, n)$ must also become pebbled. It follows that $(S, 0, n)$ will be pebbled on termination of algorithm 4.1. That completes the proof.   □

The algorithm uses $O(n^6)$ processors. For example, in the operation *square1* we have to assign a processor to each triple $(x, y, z)$. There are $O(n^2)$ possible nodes, hence there are $O(n^6)$ such triples. The algorithm as described works on a W-RAM. Write conflicts occur, for example, when for two distinct nodes $y$ and $y'$ we have $COND(x, y)$, $COND(y, z)$, $COND(x, y')$ and $COND(y', z)$ and both processors assigned to $(x, y, z)$ and $(x, y', z)$ try to assign the value **true** to $COND(x, z)$ during the operation *square1*. Thus we have two distinct processors which try to write simultaneously to the same location.

*Example 4.4*
Consider the (new) grammar with $P = \{S \rightarrow SS \,|\, AS \,|\, SA \,|\, b, A \rightarrow a\}$ and the input $w = abab$. Initially nodes $(A, 0, 1)$, $(S, 1, 2)$, $(A, 2, 3)$ and $(S, 3, 4)$ are pebbled. The effect of the first sequence of operations (*activate1*, *square1*, *square1*) is illustrated (in three stages) in figure 4.11. All edges are directed top down. We disregard edges with endpoints $(A, i, j)$ for which $j > i + 1$, because no such nodes are realisable (we know this in advance from a simple inspection of the grammar). After the second of the *square1* operations there is a link from

*Figure 4.11.* The first graph is induced by those edges created during the first operation *activate1*. The second (third) graph consists of edges added by the first (second) operation *square1*. In the first graph the initially pebbled nodes are underlined

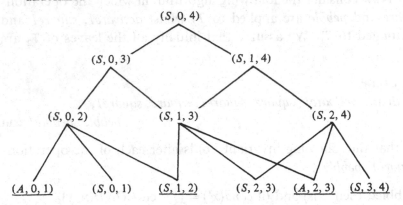

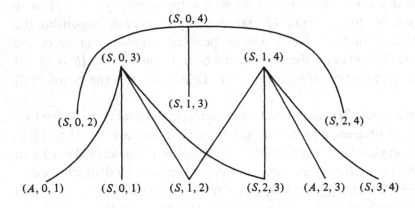

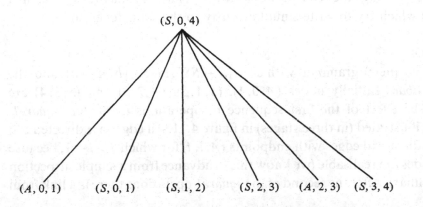

the goal node $(S, 0, 4)$ to the pebbled node $(A, 2, 3)$. In fact there are links to all pebbled nodes. Hence in the next operation, *pebble1*, node $(S, 0, 4)$ is pebbled. Thus the algorithm accepts the input string after a single iteration of the **repeat** statement. The first graph in figure 4.11 is a subgraph of $U_{G,w}$. The example grammar is ambiguous and in this graph there are three distinct paths from $(S, 0, 4)$ to $(A, 2, 3)$. Each of these paths corresponds to a distinct derivation tree for the string *abab*. These can be identified in figure 4.12 which shows all the distinct parse trees for *abab* and indicates the associated paths in $U_{G,w}$.

For general context-free grammars the instructions (1)–(3) of algorithm 4.1, as we implied earlier, cause write conflicts. These can easily be removed by simulating the instructions on a P-RAM. This requires the same number of processors; however, the time is multiplied by a factor of log *n*. We therefore have the following theorem.

*Figure 4.12.* All possible derivation trees for $w = abab$ in the ambiguous grammar with the set of productions $\{S \rightarrow SS \mid SA \mid AS \mid b, \ A \rightarrow a\}$. Each derivation tree corresponds to two paths (defined here below the figures) in that subgraph of $U_{G,w}$ shown at the top of figure 4.11

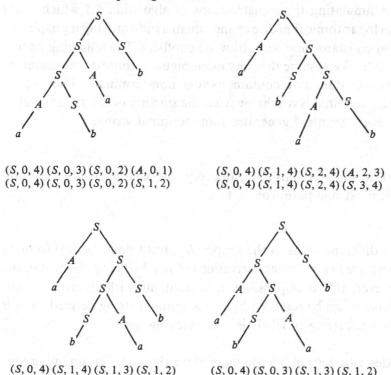

$(S, 0, 4) \, (S, 0, 3) \, (S, 0, 2) \, (A, 0, 1)$
$(S, 0, 4) \, (S, 0, 3) \, (S, 0, 2) \, (S, 1, 2)$

$(S, 0, 4) \, (S, 1, 4) \, (S, 2, 4) \, (A, 2, 3)$
$(S, 0, 4) \, (S, 1, 4) \, (S, 2, 4) \, (S, 3, 4)$

$(S, 0, 4) \, (S, 1, 4) \, (S, 1, 3) \, (S, 1, 2)$
$(S, 0, 4) \, (S, 1, 4) \, (S, 1, 3) \, (A, 2, 3)$

$(S, 0, 4) \, (S, 0, 3) \, (S, 1, 3) \, (S, 1, 2)$
$(S, 0, 4) \, (S, 0, 3) \, (S, 1, 3) \, (A, 2, 3)$

*Theorem 4.1*
Every context-free language can be recognized in $O(\log^2 n)$ time using $n^6$ processors on a P-RAM.     □

*Remark*
Algorithm 4.1 also gives $O(\log^2 n)$ space recognition of cfls.

We conclude this section by noting that the recognition problem can be solved by optimal parallel algorithms for two subclasses of context-free languages, namely bracket languages and input-driven languages. The recognition of bracket languages is considered later in this chapter and is based upon an optimal algorithm for expression evaluation. Similarly input driven languages are also considered later.

## 4.2 Parallel recognition of unambiguous context-free languages

If the context-free grammar provided in a recognition problem is unambiguous then, instead of simulating those instructions of algorithm 4.1 which cause write conflicts in logarithmic time, we change them a little making it possible to simulate them in constant time without write conflicts. The following lemma makes this possible. We assume that any unambiguous context-free grammar under consideration does not contain useless non-terminals. That is, we assume that every terminal is reachable from the starting non-terminal and in particular that every terminal generates some terminal string.

*Lemma 4.3*
If the grammar $G$ is unambiguous then, for every pair of nodes $x$, $y$ in the graph $U_{G,w}$, there is at most one path from $x$ to $y$.

*Proof*
If there are two different paths in the graph $U_{G,w}$ from node $(A, i, j)$ to node $(B, k, l)$ then there are two different derivations of $w[i:k]Bw[l:j]$ from $A$ in the grammar. However, this is impossible in a grammar without useless non-terminals, because $B$ can be replaced by some terminal string derived from $B$ (not necessarily a substring of $w$). This completes the proof.     □

We shall now describe certain invariants of algorithm 4.1. For unambiguous context-free grammars we can use these to eliminate write conflicts. There are no write conflicts in instruction 0. We also claim that there are no write conflicts in instruction 1. This follows from the following invariant of the algorithm:

(A1)  if $EDGE(x, y) =$ **true** then there is exactly one pebbled node $z \neq y$ such that $y, z \vdash x$.

This follows directly from the unambiguity of the grammar and the definition of the relation $\vdash$.

Now we define $H = (V, E)$ to be the directed graph in which $V$ is the same as the vertex set of $U_{G,w}$ and in which $E = \{(x, y) \mid EDGE(x, y) = \textbf{true}\}$. $H$ is clearly a subgraph of $U_{G,w}$. We write $x \Rightarrow y$ iff $EDGE(x, y) = \textbf{true}$, and let $\Rightarrow^*$ be the transitive closure of $\Rightarrow$. If $W$ is a subset of $V$, then we say that a node $y$ of $W$ is maximal in $W$ iff there is no $x$ in $W$ such that $EDGE(x, y) = \textbf{true}$.

### Lemma 4.4

For an unambiguous grammar the following are invariants of algorithm 4.1.

(A2)  (key invariant) for every two nodes $x, y$ there is at most one path from $x$ to $y$ in the graph $H$.

(A3)  if $COND(x, y) = \textbf{true}$ then $x \Rightarrow^* y$.

(A4)  if $x \Rightarrow^* z \Rightarrow^* y$ and $COND(x, y) = \textbf{true}$ then $COND(x, z) = \textbf{true}$ and $COND(z, y) = \textbf{true}$.

(A5)  if $COND(x, z) = \textbf{true}$ and $COND(z, y) = \textbf{true}$ and **not** $(COND(x, y) = \textbf{true})$ then there is exactly one pair of nodes $y_1, y_2$ satisfying the following condition, which we refer to as $c_1(x, y_1, y_2, y)$.

$$COND(x, y_1) \textbf{ and } COND(y_1, y) \textbf{ and } (\textbf{not } COND(x, y_2))$$
$$\textbf{and } (COND(y_2, y) \textbf{ or } y_2 = y) \textbf{ and } EDGE(y_1, y_2)$$

(A6)  if $x \Rightarrow y_1$, $x \Rightarrow y_2$, $y_1 \neq y_2$, and there are paths from $y_1, y_2$ to pebbled nodes, then $y_1, y_2$ are pebbled.

(A7)  for every $x$ in $V$ the set $\{y \mid x \Rightarrow^* y$ and $pebbled(y)\}$ has at most two maximal elements. If it has two maximal elements then they are brothers (that is, sons of the same father).

### Proof

(A2) $H$ is a subgraph of $U_{G,w}$, hence (A2) follows from lemma 4.3.

(A3) Table $COND$ is changed in instructions 1 and 2. Whenever we set $COND(x, y) \leftarrow \textbf{true}$ in instruction 1 then we set also $EDGE(x, y) \leftarrow \textbf{true}$, hence $x \Rightarrow^* y$. If the invariant holds before instruction 2 then it also holds after executing this instruction, because $(COND(x, y) \textbf{ and } COND(y, z)) = \textbf{true}$ implies $x \Rightarrow^* y \Rightarrow^* z$ and $x \Rightarrow^* z$.

(A4)  Proof is by induction on the number of iterations. When $COND(x, y)$ is set to **true** in instruction 2 then there must be a $u$ with $(COND(x, u)$ **and** $COND(u, y)) =$ **true**. Since there is only one path from $x$ to $y$, $z$ and $u$ both lie on this path, say $x \Rightarrow^* z \Rightarrow^* u \Rightarrow^* y$. By the induction hypothesis we therefore had $(COND(x, z)$ **and** $COND(z, u)) =$ **true** at the end of the previous iteration. Hence $(COND(x, z)$ **and** $COND(z, y)) =$ **true** at the end of the current iteration.

(A5)  We have $x \Rightarrow^* z \Rightarrow^* y$. From (A4) we know that all nodes $u$ before $z$ (on the path from $x$ to $y$) satisfy $COND(x, u)$, and all nodes $u$ after $z$ satisfy $COND(u, y)$. We also know from (A4) that all the nodes $u$ with $COND(x, u)$ form a contiguous segment of the path. Hence $y_1$, $y_2$ as defined exist and are the unique pair of nodes with this property.

(A6)  If $x \Rightarrow y_1$ then there is a pebbled node $y_1'$ with $y_1, y_1' \vdash x$. If $x \Rightarrow y_2$ then there is a pebbled node $y_2'$ with $y_2, y_2' \vdash x$. Since there is a path from $y_1$ to a pebbled node $y_1$ is realisable; similarly for $y_2$. Hence $y_2 = y_1'$ and $y_1 = y_2'$ because the grammar is unambiguous. Thus $y_1$ and $y_2$ are pebbled.

(A7)

(1)  First we prove that if $x \Rightarrow^* y$ and $x$, $y$ are pebbled then all nodes on the path from $x$ to $y$ are also pebbled. Suppose that this is not true. Then there are two pebbled nodes $x$, $y$ and a path $x \Rightarrow y_1 \Rightarrow y_2 \Rightarrow \cdots \Rightarrow y_k \Rightarrow y$ such that $y_1, y_2, \ldots, y_k$ are not pebbled. We shall derive a contradiction. Consider the moment when $x$ was first pebbled. It was pebbled through instruction 3 because for some pebbled node $z$ we had $COND(x, z) =$ **true**. There are two cases:

Case 1.  One of $y_i$ lies on the path from $x$ to $z$. Then $COND(y_i, z) =$ **true** also held because of (A4) and $y_i$ was pebbled when $x$ was pebbled.

Case 2.  No $y_i$ lies on the path from $x$ to $z$. Take the immediate successor $v$ of $x$ on the path from $x$ to $z$. Now $v$ and $y_1$ are sons of $x$ lying on the paths leading to pebbled nodes. Invariant (A6) implies that both of them are pebbled. Hence $y_1$ is pebbled. This proves the claim.

(2)  Let $W = \{y \mid x \Rightarrow^* y$ and $y$ is pebbled$\}$ and $Y = \{y$ in $W \mid y$ is maximal in $W\}$, and let $T$ be the minimal subtree of $H$ containing $x$ and all $y$ in $Y$. Assume that $Y$ has more than two elements and let $x_1$ be the lowest common ancestor in $T$ of the nodes in $Y$. It follows from what was proved in part (1) that no path connects two nodes in $Y$. Hence $x_1$ is not an element of $Y$. Node $x_1$ has at least two sons and so by (A6) all sons of $x_1$ are pebbled. It then follows from what was proved in part (1) and from the definition of maximality that every $y$ in $Y$ must be a son of $x_1$. But by the reasoning of the proof of (A6) $x_1$ can have only two pebbled sons. These sons are the only elements of $Y$ and they are brothers. This completes the proof. $\qquad\square$

## Theorem 4.2

Every unambiguous context-free language can be recognised on a P-RAM in $O(\log n)$ time using a polynomial number of processors.

## Proof

It is enough to eliminate write conflicts from instructions 2 and 3 in algorithm 4.1. We make use of invariant (A5) and condition $c_1(x, y_1, y_2, y)$ of lemma 4.3. We replace instruction 2 by instruction 2' defined as follows.

2'.  **for all** $x, y_1, y_2, y$ such that $c_1(x, y_1, y_2, y)$ **in parallel do**
$$COND(x, y) \leftarrow \textbf{true}$$

Invariant (A5) implies that this instruction is equivalent to instruction 2 and there are no write conflicts. For each $x, y$ there is at most one pair $y_1, y_2$ satisfying $c_1(x, y_1, y_2, y)$. Notice that if $COND(x, y)$ already holds then there is no such pair, however in this case we can omit the execution of $COND(x, y) \leftarrow \textbf{true}$.

We define the condition $c_2(x, y_1, y)$ as

$COND(x, y)$ **and** $(COND(x, y_1)$ **or** $y_1 = x)$ **and** $EDGE(y_1, y)$ **and**
$pebbled(y)$ **and** (**not** $pebbled(y_1)$) **and** (**not** $pebbled(x)$)

If $x$ is not pebbled then $c_2(x, y_1, y)$ expresses the fact that $y$ is maximal in the set specified by $\{y \mid COND(x, y)$ and $pebbled(y)\}$. Moreover for each $x, y$ there is at most one $y_1$ with $c_2(x, y_1, y)$. Here $y_1$ is the immediate predecessor of $y$ on the path from $x$ to $y$. Using $c_2(x, y_1, y)$ we can eliminate write conflicts in which more than two processors attempt to write into the same location in the same step, because of (A7).

We introduce an auxiliary table $ALLOWED$ to eliminate write conflicts completely. Let $\ll$ be any linear order on the vertices of $U_{G,w}$ computable on a RAM in $O(1)$ time. We replace instruction 3 by instruction 3' defined as follows.

3'.  **for all** $x, y$ **in parallel do** $ALLOWED(x, y) \leftarrow \textbf{true}$
    **for all** $x, y_1, y, z$ such that $y \ll z$ and $c_2(x, y_1, y)$ and $c_2(x, y_1, z)$
        **in parallel do** $ALLOWED(x, z) \leftarrow \textbf{false}$
        $\{y, z$ are maximal nodes reachable from $x$ and pebbled$\}$
    **for all** $x, y_1, y$ such that $c_2(x, y_1, y)$ and $ALLOWED(x, y)$
        **in parallel do** $pebbled(x) \leftarrow \textbf{true}$

Invariant (A7) implies that there are at most two nodes $y, z$ such that for some $y_1$ the conditions $c_2(x, y_1, y), c_2(x, y_1, z), y \ll z$ hold for a given $x$. These nodes should be sons of a uniquely determined node $y_1$. Table $ALLOWED$ 'eliminates' the second maximal element corresponding to a given node $x$. This proves that there are no write conflicts in instruction 3' and this instruction is equivalent to instruction 3 (disregarding the table *ALLOWED*). After replacing instructions 2 and 3 by instructions 2' and 3' respectively, we obtain the required algorithm. This completes the proof.　　　　　□

We note that although the number of processors is polynomial, the degree of the polynomial is very high. There are $O(n^2)$ nodes. Hence implementing instructions 2' and 3' directly we use $O(n^8)$ processors. However, we can reduce this number using the following observation. There are $O(n)$ nodes which can be a son of a specific node. Observe also that if $c_1(x, y_1, y_2, y)$ holds then $y_2$ is a son of $y_1$, and if $c_2(x, y_1, y)$ holds then $y$ is a son of $y_1$. Hence only tuples with such properties need be considered in instructions 2' and 3'. These two observations allow us to reduce the number of processors to $n^7$.

## 4.3 Parallel parsing of general context-free languages

The problem of parsing for context-free languages seems to be more costly than the problem of recognition. Ruzzo[9] proved that if $T(n)$ is the sequential recognition time for context-free languages on a RAM then the sequential parsing time is $O(T(n) \log n)$. We show that when parallel time is considered then parsing can be achieved in the same order of time as the best algorithms for recognition although we require a considerably larger (although still polynomial) number of processors.

Algorithms for general context-free recognition use the so-called *parsing matrix* which we define later. Using this matrix we show that a parse tree can be constructed in $O(\log n)$ time using a cubic number of processors. Even if recognition does not construct the parsing matrix then we can construct it by executing simultaneously $O(n^2)$ parallel recognising algorithms. Parallel time does not increase; however, the number of processors required increases by a factor of $n^2$. As in the previous sections, we shall assume that the grammars are in Chomsky normal form.

The *parsing problem* is to construct, for a given grammar and input string, a parse tree $PT$ if such a tree exists. In the following formal definition $PT$ is (informally) precisely the tree obtained in a generation of the given terminal string except that leaves (corresponding to terminal symbols) have been removed. Thus $PT$ is that part of the generation tree induced by the non-terminals.

For an input string of length $n$ $PT$ is a directed binary tree with $2n - 1$ nodes numbered $1, \ldots, 2n - 1$. Each vertex except the root has in-degree of 1 whilst the root has zero in-degree. We associate the following information with each node $x$: $Father[x]$, $Left[x]$ and $Right[x]$. Here $Left[x]$ ($Right[x]$) is the left (right) son of $x$. We also associate a label, denoted by $Label[x]$, with each node $x$. The rules of the grammar are locally satisfied within the tree, in other words

(a)  $Label[root] = S$ where $S$ is the start symbol of the grammar,

(b)  $Label[x] \to Label[Left[x]]Label[Right[x]]$ is a production of the grammar if $x$ is not a leaf,

(c)  $Label[x] \to a[i]$ is a production of the grammar if $x$ is the $i$th leaf from the left and the input string is $w = a[1]a[2] \ldots a[n]$.

In order to obtain $PT$ it is sufficient to compute only the tables $Father$ and $Label$. $Left$ and $Right$ can then be computed easily on a P-RAM in constant time using a small number of processors. On the other hand, if we have $Left$ and $Right$ then this does not determine $Father$, since an attempt to construct $PT$ from these relations might lead to a directed acyclic graph having some vertices of in-degree greater than 1.

The parsing table $Tab$ is an $n$ by $n$ array whose elements are subsets of $V_N$:

$$Tab[i, j] = \textbf{if } i < j \textbf{ then } \{A \,|\, A \to^* a[i+1] \ldots a[j]\} \textbf{ else } \varnothing$$

In other words, for $i < j$, the $(i, j)$th element of $Tab$ is the subset of non-terminals of the grammar from each of which the substring of non-terminals $a[i+1] \ldots a[j]$ can be derived.

*Example 4.5*

If $G$ is the grammar with $P = \{S \to CS \,|\, AS \,|\, CA \,|\, DD \,|\, AC,\ C \to AA \,|\, BB,\ D \to AA \,|\, DC,\ A \to a,\ B \to b\}$, $V_N = \{S, C, D, A\}$ and $V_T = \{a, b\}$ then, for the input *aabba*, the parsing table is shown in figure 4.14, and a parse tree in figure 4.13.

Let $G$ be a directed acyclic graph defined by the relation $R$, where $R(u, v)$ holds

*Figure 4.13*. A parse tree and its representation. The edges are directed top down

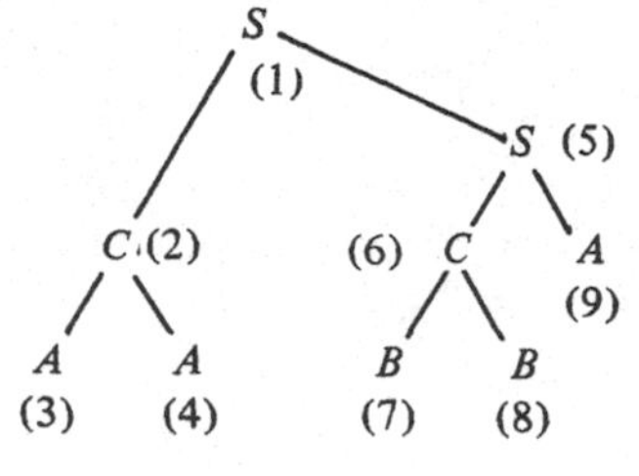

| Node | Label | Father | Left | Right |
|---|---|---|---|---|
| 1 | S | – | 2 | 5 |
| 2 | C | 1 | 3 | 4 |
| 3 | A | 2 | – | – |
| 4 | A | 2 | – | – |
| 5 | S | 1 | 6 | 9 |
| 6 | C | 5 | 7 | 8 |
| 7 | B | 6 | – | – |
| 8 | B | 6 | – | – |
| 9 | A | 5 | – | – |

whenever $(u, v)$ is an edge of $G$. We say that $G$ satisfies the *unique path condition* (UPC) iff for every two nodes $x, y$ there is at most one path from $x$ to $y$.

*Lemma 4.5*

If the directed acyclic graph $G$ with $n$ nodes satisfies UPC then the transitive closure of $G$ can be computed in $O(\log n)$ parallel time on a P-RAM using $n^3$ processors.

*Proof*

Let $R$ be the relation corresponding to a directed acyclic graph $G$ satisfying UPC, and $V$ be the set of nodes. Assume that the nodes are numbered $1, \ldots, m$. We say that a node is a sink iff it has zero out-degree. Let $s = \log n$. First we define and compute the tables $R_k[v]$, for $0 \leqslant k \leqslant s$, as follows.

> $R_0 \leftarrow R$
> **for all** sinks $v$ **in parallel do** $R_0[v, v] \leftarrow$ **true**
> **for** $k \leftarrow 1$ **to** $s$ **do**
>     **for** all $v_1, v_2, v_3$ **in parallel do**
>         **if** $(R_{k-1}[v_1, v_2]$ **and** $R_{k-1}[v_2, v_3])$ **then** $R_k[v_1, v_3] \leftarrow$ **true**

We claim that there are no write conflicts in the above computation and secondly that $R_s[v_1, v_2]$ is true if and only if there is a path from $v_1$ to $v_2$ and $v_2$ is a sink. The first claim follows from the following (easily proved) invariant

> for $0 \leqslant k \leqslant s$: [if $(R_k[v, v_1]$ and $R_k[v, v_2]) =$ **true**
>                        and $v, v_1, v_2$ are lying on the same path in $G$ then $v_1 = v_2$]

This invariant implies that whenever all of $R_{k-1}[v_1, v_2]$, $R_{k-1}[v_2, v_3]$, $R_{k-1}[v_1, v_2']$ and $R_{k-1}[v_2', v_3]$ are true then $v_2 = v_2'$, because UPC guarantees

*Figure 4.14.* The parsing table. Blank entries correspond to empty subsets of nonterminals

|   | 0 | 1 | 2 | 3 | 4 | 5 |
|---|---|---|---|---|---|---|
| 0 |   | $A$ | $C\,D$ |   | $D\,S$ | $S$ |
| 1 |   |   | $A$ |   | $S$ | $S$ |
| 2 |   |   |   | $B$ | $C$ | $S$ |
| 3 |   |   |   |   | $B$ |   |
| 4 |   |   |   |   |   | $A$ |
| 5 |   |   |   |   |   |   |

that all the nodes involved lie on the same path. The second claim follows because we are using a standard doubling technique. We double the distances between $v_1$ and $v_2$ for which $R_k[v_1, v_2] = $ **true** holds until ultimately $v_2$ becomes a sink. The following invariant is easily proved.

if $R_k[x, y]$ and $y$ is not a sink then $dist(x, y) = 2^k$

where $dist(x, y)$ is the length of the path from $x$ to $y$ in $G$.

We have partially computed $R^*$; if $y$ is a sink then $R^*(x, y) = R_s[x, y]$. Now we compute $R^*$ for all non-sink nodes. We introduce two relations $R'_k$ and $D_k$ ($k = 0, \ldots, s$), represented by two-dimensional tables similarly named.

$R'_k[x, y]$ holds iff $R_k[x, y]$ holds and $y$ is not a sink
$D_k[x, y]$ holds iff $dist(x, y) < 2^{k+1}$, for non-sink nodes $x, y$

Let $ID$ denote the identity relation and $\cdot$ denote the composition of relations. We consider only those nodes which are not sinks. The relations $D_k$ can be computed using the following recurrence formula (which follows from the last mentioned invariant).

$$D_0 = R + ID, \quad D_{k+1} = D_k + D_k \cdot R'_{k+1}$$

We can easily compute $R'_0$ and $D_0$. Next we apply the recurrence equation $\log n$ times.

> **for** $k \leftarrow 1$ **to** $s$ **do**
>   **begin**
>     **for all** $x, z$ **in parallel do if** $D_{k-1}[x, z]$ **then** $D_k[x, z] \leftarrow$ **true**
>     **for all** $x, y, z$ such that $D_{k-1}[x, y]$ **and** $R'_k[y, z]$ **in parallel do**
>                                            $D_k[x, z] \leftarrow$ **true**
>   **end**

There are no write conflicts here because if $x, y, z$ are lying on the same path and $R'_k[y, z]$ holds then $y$ is uniquely determined by $x$ and $z$ (as a node lying on the path from $x$ to $z$, whose distance to $z$ is $2^k$). Observe that in this algorithm $D_k$ could be replaced by $D$ (in fact the subscript $k$ is not needed, though it helps to apply the recurrence formula directly). Now we can compute $R^* = R_s + D_s$ in one parallel step. This completes the proof. $\quad\square$

Let $Q$ be a boolean vector of length $n$. Assume that at least one entry of $Q$ contains the value **true**. We define the operation

$$first(Q) = \min\{k \mid 0 \leqslant k \leqslant n, Q[k] = \textbf{true}\}$$

*Lemma 4.6*

The operation $first(Q)$ can be computed on a P-RAM in $O(\log n)$ time using $O(n)$ processors, provided $Q$ contains at least one entry containing the value **true**.

*Proof*

The following algorithm fulfils the lemma.

1.  **for all** $k$, $1 \leqslant k < n$, **in parallel do if** $Q[k]$ **then** $P(k) \leftarrow k$ **else** $P(k) \leftarrow k + 1$
2.  **for** $i \leftarrow 1$ **to** $\log_2 n$ **do**
    **for all** $k$, $1 \leqslant k < n$, **in parallel do if** $Q[P(k)] \neq$ **true and** $P(k) \neq n$ **then**
    $$P(k) \leftarrow P(P(k))$$
3.  $first(Q) \leftarrow P(1)$

For all $k$, $P(k)$ is a pointer from that location containing $Q[k]$ to a location containing $Q[j]$ for some $j \geqslant k$. Initially (statement 1) $P(k)$ points to the $k$th location of $Q$ if this contains the value **true**, otherwise it points to the $(k + 1)$th location. Thereafter (statement 2) $P(k)$ is 'doubled' to higher and higher indices provided the currently pointed at location of $Q$ does not contain the value **true** or is not the $n$th location. It is easy to see that, after $p$ iterations of the body of statement 3, $P(k)$ points to the location containing $Q[k + 2^p]$ provided that no $Q[j] =$ **true** exists for $k \leqslant j < k + 2^p$. Hence $\log_2 n$ iterations are sufficient for $P(1)$ to find $first(Q)$. This completes the proof. $\square$

*Theorem 4.3*

If context-free recognition can be achieved in $T(n)$ parallel time with $R(n)$ processors on a P-RAM and if $T(n) = \Omega(\log n)$, then a representation of a parse tree (if one exists) can be found in $O(T(n))$ parallel time with $O(R(n)n^2 + n^3)$ processors. If the recognition procedure constructs the parsing table then $O(R(n) + n^3)$ processors are sufficient.

*Proof*

First the parsing table *Tab* is constructed for the given input string $w = a[1]a[2] \ldots a[n]$, and a given grammar $G$ in Chomsky normal form. This can be achieved in $T(n)$ parallel time with $O(n^2 R(n))$ processors. We simply check simultaneously whether $A \to^* a[i + 1] \ldots a[j]$ for each $A$, $i < j$. If $S \to^* w$ then we start to construct a parse tree; otherwise we stop because in such a case no parse tree exists.

For a non-terminal $A$ and sets of non-terminals $X_1, X_2$ we define the operation $find(A, X_1, X_2)$:

$$find(A, X_1, X_2) = (B, C)$$

where $(B, C)$ is lexicographically the first pair of non-terminals such that there is a production $A \rightarrow BC$, $B$ in $X_1$, and $C$ in $X_2$. If no such pair $(B, C)$ exists then $find(A, X_1, X_2)$ takes the special value 'undefined'. The operation $find$ can be computed in $O(1)$ time with one processor because the size of the grammar is constant. We now construct the following acyclic directed graph $G$ representing the relation $R$ (the relation is 'a possible father'). The set of nodes of $G$ is $V$:

$$V = \{(A, i, j) \,|\, i < j, A \text{ in } Tab[i, j]\}$$

With each pair $(i, j)$, $0 \leqslant i < j \leqslant n$, we associate a boolean vector $mark_{ij}$ of length $n$. All these vectors contain initially only the values false. Initialisation is made in one parallel step for each entry simultaneously. Next we execute

**for** all nodes $(A, i, j)$, $i < j - 1$, **in parallel do**
  **begin**
  **for** all $k$, $i < k < j$, **in parallel do**
    **if** $find(A, Tab[i, k], Tab[k, j]) \neq$ 'undefined' **then** $mark_{ij}[k] \leftarrow$ **true**
  $k \leftarrow first(mark_{ij})$
  $(B, C) \leftarrow find(A, Tab[i, k], Tab[k, j])$
    {there is a production $A \rightarrow BC$ with $B$ in $Tab[i, k]$ and $C$ in $Tab[k, j]$}
  $R[(B, i, k), (A, i, j)] \leftarrow R[(C, k, j), (A, i, j)] \leftarrow$ **true**
    {$(A, i, j)$ becomes a possible father of $(B, i, k)$ and $(C, k, j)$}
  **end**

It follows from the definition of the parsing matrix that for each $(A, i, j)$ in $V$ there exist suitable $(B, i, k)$ and $(C, k, j)$. The grammar does not have to be unambiguous because we choose the first suitable pair of nodes $(B, i, k), (C, k, j)$ when applying the operations $first$ and $find$. The above algorithm works in $O(\log n)$ time.

The graph corresponding to the grammar of example 4.3 and the string *aabba* is shown in figure 4.15. Notice that the tree from figure 4.13 corresponds to a subgraph of this graph.

Next we compute the transitive closure of $R$. The graph $G$ satisfies UPC and we can use the algorithm of lemma 4.5. Let $v_0 = (S, 0, n)$. The parse tree $PT$

consists of all nodes $v$ such that $R^*(v, v_0)$ holds. The root of $PT$ is $v_0$. The function *Father* is computed as follows.

**for** all $u, v$ in $PT$ **in parallel do if** $R(u, v)$ **then** $Father[u] \leftarrow v$

The tables *Left* and *Right* can be computed in $O(\log n)$ parallel time using the table *Father*. The nodes are not yet numbered (from 1 to $2n - 1$) as required. Each node is a triple of the form $(A, i, j)$, and all tables have entries indexed by such triples. The set of these triples which belong to $PT$ can be numbered from 1 to $2n - 1$ by arranging all possible triples in any initial order (for example, lexicographically), then the final numbering of a triple belonging to $PT$ could be obtained by counting the number of preceding triples which are elements of $PT$ (using a prefix computation). If *num* is the numbering obtained, then $Label[num(A, i, j)] \leftarrow A$. The constructed tree now satisfies all the requirements. This completes the proof.  $\square$

We have proved that every context-free language can be recognized in $O(\log^2 n)$ time using $n^6$ processors and that every unambiguous context-free language can be recognized in $O(\log n)$ time on a P-RAM using a polynomial number of processors. In both cases the parsing matrix can be computed as a side effect without extra cost. We therefore have the following corollary.

*Corollary 4.1*
Every context-free language can be parsed on a P-RAM in $O(\log^2 n)$ time using $n^6$ processors. Every unambiguous context-free language can be parsed on a P-RAM in $O(\log n)$ time using a polynomial number of processors.

Figure 4.15. The edges of $G$ are directed top down

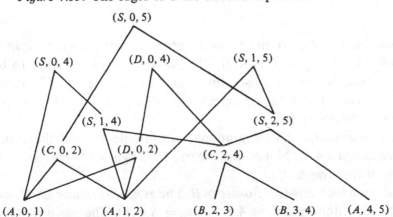

## 4.4 Optimal parallel recognition and parsing of bracket languages

We now consider a special subclass of context-free languages for which the recognition and parsing problems can be solved by optimal parallel algorithms (using $n/\log n$ processors in $O(\log n)$ time). The subclass of languages we consider are bracket languages, the parsing of which can be treated as an optimal conversion of expressions into parse trees (if we assume that the expressions are fully parenthesised).

Bracket languages are one of the few subclasses of context-free languages which are known to be sequentially recognisable in logarithmic space. We might therefore expect that the problem can be solved by a fast parallel algorithm.

A context-free grammar $G$ is a bracket grammar iff each of its productions is of the form $A \rightarrow (u)$, where the string $u$ (of terminals and non-terminals) does not contain the brackets '(', ')'. A language is a bracket language iff it is generated by a bracket grammar. A natural example of a bracket language is the set of parenthesised arithmetic expressions with constants $a$ and $b$. The productions of the corresponding grammar are

$$E \rightarrow (E) \,|\, (E * E) \,|\, (E + E) \,|\, (E - E) \,|\, (E/E) \,|\, (a) \,|\, (b)$$

Any terminal string generated by a bracket grammar implicitly contains, through the embedding of the brackets in the text, the topology of the parse tree. However this does not give directly all the details of the parse tree. In particular the labels associated with the internal nodes are missing. The essential aim of the algorithm we describe is to compute these labels in optimal parallel fashion. The number of possibly correct labellings can be exponentially large. Although for each text the shape of its parse tree is uniquely determined, the grammar can have a very large degree of ambiguity. For example, the grammar with the following productions certainly demonstrates this:

$$S \rightarrow (SA) \,|\, (AS) \,|\, (SS) \,|\, (AA), \quad A \rightarrow (a)$$

We shall essentially be concerned with finding *any* correct labelling.

We shall assume that $G$ is in a Chomsky-like normal form, each production being of the type $A \rightarrow (BC)$ or $A \rightarrow (a)$, where $B$ and $C$ are non-terminals whilst $a$ is a terminal. The algorithm is easily extended to arbitrary bracket grammars in which case, instead of binary trees, we have to consider trees with constant-bounded vertex degrees.

*Example 4.6*
Consider the grammar

$$S \rightarrow (BA)\,|\,(BC)\,|\,(AS)$$
$$A \rightarrow (BA)\,|\,(AA)\,|\,(BB)\,|\,(a)$$
$$B \rightarrow (CC)\,|\,(CS)\,|\,(b)$$
$$C \rightarrow (AB)\,|\,(CA)\,|\,(BC)\,|\,(a)$$

and the input text $w = ((b)(((a)(a))((b)(a))))$.

The bracket structure of $w$ can be represented as in figure 4.16. Every node corresponds to two matching brackets. Sons of a given pair are pairs enclosed between them. Figure 4.16 illustrates how this uniquely determines the shape of the parse tree. Non-terminals corresponding to the internal nodes of such a parse tree are as yet unknown.

From section 3.2 we know that such a tree can be constructed by an optimal parallel algorithm. At this stage (that is, in computing the 'shape' of the tree) we can ignore all symbols except brackets.

We define the operation * on sets $S_1$ and $S_2$ of non-terminals as follows.

$$S_1 * S_2 = \{A\,|\,A \rightarrow (BC) \text{ is a production and } B \text{ is in } S_1 \text{ and } C \text{ in } S_2\}$$

Thus, for the grammar of example 4.4, we have that $\{A, B\} * \{B, C\} = \{A, S, C\}$.

A node in the parse tree is called a *bottom node* if it corresponds to a derivation $X \rightarrow (x)$, where $X$ is a non-terminal and $x$ a terminal symbol. Bottom nodes are indicated in figure 4.17.

Each node $v$ covers a substring consisting of all those symbols corresponding to leaves of the tree rooted at $v$. For a given tree and input text $w$ we denote this substring by $sub(v)$. For each internal node $v$ we now define $val(v) =$

*Figure 4.16*

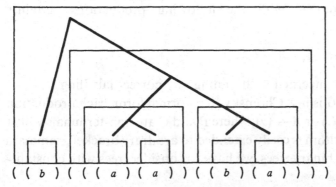

( ( *b* ) ( ( ( *a* ) ( *a* ) ) ( ( *b* ) ( *a* ) ) ) )

$\{X \mid X \to^* sub(v)\}$. It is easy to compute $val(v)$ for each bottom node in $O(1)$ time because the size of the grammar is constant. Hence $val(v)$ can be computed for all bottom nodes in $O(1)$ time using $n$ processors or in $O(\log n)$ time with $n/\log n$ processors.

If $v$ is an internal node which is not a bottom node then it has two sons which we denote by $v_1$ and $v_2$. It follows from the definition that $val(v) = val(v_1)^* val(v_2)$. Thus the problem of computing $val(v)$ for all $v$ is the problem of computing the values of all the nodes of a tree of an algebraic expression. The underlying algebra is not very regular. The operation $*$ can, for example, be non-associative. However, the carrier of the algebra is finite. In chapter 3 we showed that such a computation can be carried out by an optimal parallel algorithm.

In the present case we can consecutively number the bottom nodes in $O(\log n)$ time using $n/\log n$ processors. Each bottom node $v$ corresponds to a position $i$ containing a terminal symbol $x$. Such positions can be easily numbered by assigning 1 to each position of the input string with a terminal symbol which is not a bracket and 0 to other positions. Now for a given position $i$ we can compute the sum of all the assigned integers to the left of $i$ (including $i$). This gives the correct number for the bottom node $v$ corresponding to $i$. Such a computation is a classical prefix computation as described in chapter 1. Hence we can assume that $val(v)$ is computed for each node $v$.

Now we have to choose one non-terminal from each set $val(v)$. We cannot make this choice locally, since many conflicts (with respect to the grammar) would occur. We associate with each node $v$ a partial function $D_v$, called the dependency function. The arguments and values of this function are non-terminals. The interpretation of $D_v(A) = B$ is that if $label(father(v)) = A$ then

*Figure 4.17*

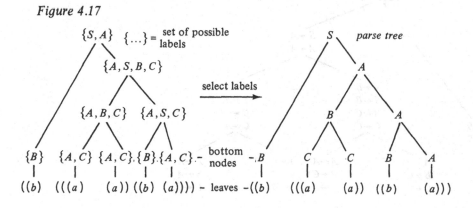

$label(v) = B$. We now execute the following algorithm, where $v_1$ and $v_2$ are the left and right son of $v$, respectively.

**for** all internal non-bottom nodes $v$ **in parallel do**
    **for** all $X \in val(v)$ choose $Y \in val(v_1)$ and $Z \in val(v_2)$
                                such that $X \rightarrow (YZ)$ is a production
      **do begin** $D_{v_1}(X) \leftarrow Y$, $D_{v_2}(X) \leftarrow Z$ **end**
      {invariant: suitable $Y, Z$ can always be found}

*Example 4.7*
Let $val(v) = \{A, S, B, C\}$, $val(v_1) = \{A, B, C\}$ and $val(v_2) = \{A, S, C\}$. Then for $A$ we can choose $B \in val(v_1)$, $A \in val(v_2)$, since $A \rightarrow (BA)$ is a production. We set $D_{v_1}(A) = B$ and $D_{v_2}(A) = A$. For $S \in val(v)$ we can choose also $B, A$ and set $D_{v_1}(S) = B$, $D_{v_2}(S) = A$. Analogously we can set $D_{v_1}(B) = C$, $D_{v_2}(B) = C$ and $D_{v_1}(C) = C$, $D_{v_2}(C) = A$.

The function $D_{v_1}$ can also be written in the form.

$A \rightarrow B$
$S \rightarrow B$
$B \rightarrow C$
$C \rightarrow C$

The functions associated with each node, in this form, are shown in figure 4.18 for our example tree. The functions $D_v$ for all nodes $v$ can be easily computed in $O(1)$ time with $n$ processors or in $O(\log n)$ time with $n/\log n$ processors.

Notice that we resolve the (possible) ambiguity of the grammar when computing the functions $D_v$. We have many possibilities to choose

*Figure 4.18.* $A \rightarrow B$ means here that if the father has the label $A$ then this node should have the label $B$. We know that the root should have label $S$

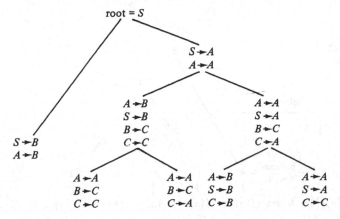

corresponding non-terminals and we fix one of them. It might seem that there are write conflicts; however, this is not so. Each local search is in a set of possibilities (pairs $Y, Z$) whose cardinality is bounded by a constant. The choice can be made sequentially for a given node in $O(1)$ time, and determinism can be achieved by selecting (for example) the pair corresponding to a production with the smallest number. Whenever we compute $D_v$ then $val(v) = val(v_1) * val(v_2)$. This guarantees that for each $X \in val(v)$ there are suitable $Y \in val(v_1)$, $Z \in val(v_2)$.

If we require that the root has the label $S$ then the functions $D_v$ determine uniquely the label for each node in a top-down way. The value in the root determines the values in the sons of the root through their functions $D$, this determines values for their sons and so on.

We define the composition of functions $f \cdot g(x) = g(f(x))$. For each internal non-root node $v$ let $F_v$ be $f_1 \cdot f_2 \cdot \ldots \cdot f_k$, where $f_1, \ldots, f_k$ are the functions $D$ associated with the nodes on the path (top-down) from the root to $v$ (excluding the root and including $v$). For each node $v$ in parallel we set $label(v) = F_v(S)$. This gives the full parse tree. The parse tree determined by the functions in figure 4.18 is shown in figure 4.17. The selection of labels can be done in $O(1)$ time with $n$ processors, or in $O(\log n)$ time with $n/\log n$ processors if the values of $F_v$ are already computed for each $v$. Hence the parse tree can be constructed by an optimal parallel algorithm if the functions $F_v$ can be computed by an optimal parallel algorithm.

We say that a path from $v_1$ to $v_2$ (in a given tree $T$) is reducible if each node on this path, except maybe $v_1$ and $v_2$, has a son which is a leaf. (Formally, a single edge is also a reducible path, though there is no significant use of such a type of reducibility.)

The reducible path $p$ can be compressed into single edge as illustrated in figure 4.19. We call this operation *compress(p)*. The compression does not affect the value of $F_v$ for any nodes $v$ except those eliminated. If the value of $F_{v_1}$ is computed then the values of $F_v$ for all eliminated nodes can easily be computed in $O(\log n)$ time using one processor. We have to decompress the compressed path and compute values $F_v$ going along this path top down.

Our aim is to find $n/\log n$ edge-disjoint reducible paths whose removal will reduce the tree by a factor of $\log n$. Our approach will utilise the methodology of Bar-On and Vishkin as described for the algorithm of section 3.1. We assume here familiarity with the details explained there.

At this point we have the parse tree $T$ without labels (but with the functions $D_v$ computed). Such a tree and the bracket structure of the input text are two different representations of the same object. The bracket structure will help to

find a good decomposition into reducible paths. We illustrate the method using
the following example input string.

$$w = (((((a)((a)(((a)(((a)(((a)(a))(a)))((a)(a))))((a)(((a)(a))(a))))))$$
$$((((a)((a)((a)(a))))(a))(a)))(a))(a))$$

In general we partition the string into $n/\log n$ segments of length
(approximately) $\log n$. For ease of presentation let us disregard for a moment
the true value of $\log n$ and assume that the partition is as follows.

$$(((((a)((a)(((a)(((a)(((a)\,|\,(a))(a)))((a)(a))))((a)(((a)\,|$$
$$(a))(a))))))(((((a)((a)((a)\,|\,(a))))(a))(a)))(a))(a))$$

We assign a processor to each segment. Within each segment there are some
matching pairs of brackets and some brackets whose matches are outside the
segment. The processor (assigned to a given segment) finds which brackets
have their matches inside the segment. Let us define the maximal matching pair
in a given segment to be a pair of matching brackets, both within this segment,
which is not enclosed by any pair with the same property. The subsegment
whose endpoints are such brackets (including them) is called the maximal
subsegment. Consider the second segment $(a))(a)))((a)(a))))((a)(((a$. This
segment (with maximal subsegments enclosed in '[', '])' is
$[(a)][(a)]))[((a)(a))]))([(a)](([(a)]$. The maximal matching pair corresponds to
a subtree all of whose leaves are within the given segment. If we know the value
of $F_v$ for the root of each such tree in a given segment then one processor can
easily compute the values of $F_v$ for all other nodes in this segment.

*Figure 4.19*

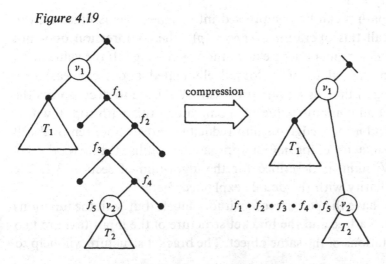

Our first step is the replacement of all such trees by new single leaves. In terms of symbols we replace each maximal subsegment by a special symbol ·. Hence the second segment will be transformed into ·)·))·))(·((·. For the whole string we obtain the following sequence.

$$w' = ((((·(·((·((·((·\,|\,·)·))·))(·((·\,|\,·)·)))))((·(·(·\,|\,·)))·)·))·)·)$$

This sequence corresponds to the tree with some subtrees replaced by leaves. Denote this tree by *T*. The symbols · correspond to leaves of the tree and each pair of matching brackets corresponds to an internal node of *T*. The tree *T* for our example string is illustrated in figure 4.21 and the bracket structure in figure 4.20. The numbering of rectangles (corresponding to matching brackets) in figure 4.20 corresponds to the numbering of nodes of the tree *T* shown in figure 4.21.

Let *w″* be the string *w′* with the symbols · erased and with the same partition into segment. A crucial property of *w″* is that each segment of *w″* is of the form )) ... )(( ... (, possibly with only one type of bracket. In each segment we mark each leftmost and each rightmost left and right bracket. Thus there are at most four brackets marked in any one segment. Next for each marked bracket (using the method of Bar-On and Vishkin) we mark its corresponding matching bracket. In figure 4.20 all marked brackets are arrowed.

We define the following transformation for the tree *T*.

*Transformation* (tree compression)

(1)   For each pair of marked matching brackets we mark the corresponding node of *T*.

*Figure 4.20*

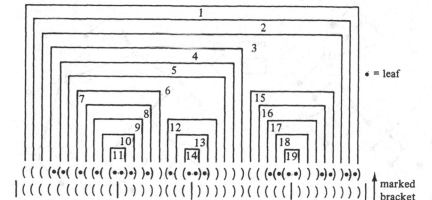

(2)  Additionally for each node of the tree (in parallel) we mark it if both of its sons were marked in step (1).

(3)  For each marked non-root node $v$, if *father(v)* is not marked, denote by *path(v)* the path from $v$ (bottom up) to the next marked node. If no such path exists, then *path(v)* is undefined. Now compress each defined path $p = path(v)$ into a single edge using the operation *compress(p)*.

For our example, in step (1) we mark the nodes 1, 4, 15, 7, 12, 19, 14 and 11. Then in step (2) we additionally mark the nodes 3 and 6. Then figure 4.21 illustrates the compressing of paths as required in step (3).

### Theorem 4.4
For each marked node $v$ $path(v)$ is a reducible path and its length is $O(\log n)$. If we compress the paths $path(v)$ for all marked nodes $v$ then the resulting tree $RT$ will have $O(n/\log n)$ nodes.

### Proof
Let us look at the bracket structure. We consider first the paths from marked nodes down. Let $v'$ be a marked node and let $(_{v'}$ and $)_{v'}$ be its corresponding pair of brackets. These brackets are marked. Assume that one of the descendants of $v'$ is marked and the son of $v'$ is not marked. Let us go, in the bracket sequence $w''$, to the left of $)_{v'}$ until we find a marked bracket [it will be some bracket $)_{v_2}$ corresponding to a node $v_2$], and to the right of $(_{v'}$ until we find

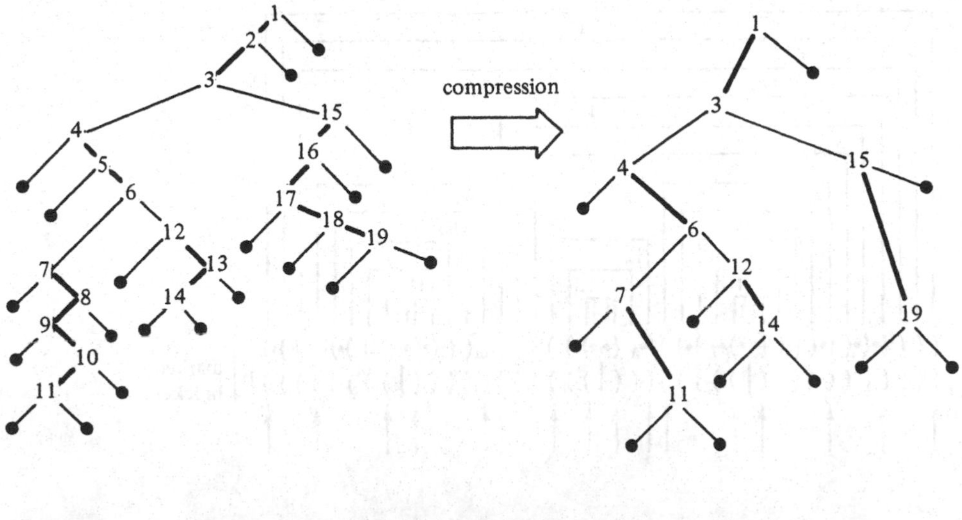

*Figure 4.21.* The tree corresponding to the bracket structure in our example string and its compressed version

a marked bracket [which will be some bracket $($ corresponding to a node $v_1$]. We then have the following bracket sequence.

$$(_{v'}(_1(_2(_3((\cdots (_{v_1}\cdots )_{v_2}\cdots )))_3)_2)_1)_{v'}$$

*Case 1.* $v_1 = v_2 = v$, say (this occurs in our example for $v' = 7$)
Nodes $v'$ and $v$ are marked and the brackets corresponding to $v'$ enclose the brackets corresponding to $v$. If we disregard the symbol $\cdot$ we have the following situation.

$$(_{v'}(_1(_2(_3((\cdots (_v\cdots )_v\cdots )))_3)_2)_1)_{v'}$$

All brackets between $(_{v'}$ and $(_v$ are left brackets and all brackets between $)_v$ and $)_{v'}$ are right brackets. Moreover, as can be seen from the corresponding detailed reasoning of section 3.1, bracket $(_1$ matches bracket $)_1$, $(_2$ matches $)_2$, and so on.

Now consider two consecutively enclosed pairs of brackets, for example $(_1 \ldots )_1$ and $(_2 \ldots )_2$. Node $x$ corresponding to the first pair is the father of node $y$ corresponding to the second pair. We denote the other son of node $x$ by $z$. We claim that $z$ is a leaf. If we look at these pairs of brackets in the string $w'$ then there are only two possible situations: $(_1 \cdot (_2 \ldots )_2)_1$ or $(_1(_2 \ldots )_2 \cdot )$. The son $z$ should correspond to $\cdot$. If it were not a leaf then it could be reduced to a leaf during the preprocessing of a segment, because all its leaves are in the same segment (they are between brackets lying in the same segment). Hence the path from $v$ to $v'$ is reducible.

*Case 2.* $v_1 \neq v_2$ (this occurs in our example for $v' = 4$)
We have the following situation.

$$(_{v'}(_1(_2(_3((\cdots (_k(_{v_1}\cdots )_{v_1}(_{v_2}\cdots )_{v_2})_k\cdots )))_3)_2)_1)_{v'}$$

Now node $v''$ corresponding to $(_k)_k$ has both sons marked (because of marking corresponding brackets), hence it is itself a marked node (after additional marking). It follows that the path from $v'$ to $v''$ is reducible using the same argument as that in case 1.

Take any non-root marked node $v$ and its path *path*$(v)$ which ends at $v'$ (a proper ancestor of $v$). We have proved that if we go down from $v'$ then at some moment we encounter a marked node $x$ and the path from $v'$ to $x$ is reducible. However $x$ must be equal to $v$, because there are no marked nodes between $v$ and $v'$ and $v$ is not a leaf. Hence *path*$(v)$ is reducible.

It is easy to see that there are only $O(n/\log n)$ marked brackets (there are a constant number in each segment), hence there are also only $O(n/\log n)$

marked nodes. There can be in fact more marked nodes than pairs of matching marked brackets (because of the additional marking of nodes in step (2) of the tree compression transformation). However it is of the same order. Hence the size of the compressed tree is $O(n/\log n)$. This completes the proof. □

### Theorem 4.5
Every bracket language can be parsed in $O(\log n)$ time using $n/\log n$ processors on a P-RAM.

### Proof
It is enough to show that the functions $F_v$ for all internal non-root nodes $v$ can be computed in $O(\log n)$ time using $n/\log n$ processors. One possibility is to extend the method used in chapter 3 for optimal dynamic evaluation of expressions. However we develop a slightly different method, which is more suitable in this case. We first show how to compute the functions $F_v$ in $O(\log n)$ time using $n$ processors. The method uses the doubling technique. Assume that $father(\text{root}) = \text{root}$ and that $F_{\text{root}}$ is the identity function.

Initially, for each non-root node $v$, set $F_v = D_v$ and then execute the following.

> **repeat** $\log n$ **times**
>     **for** all internal non-root nodes $v$ **in parallel do**
>         **begin**
>         $F_v \leftarrow F_{father(v)} \cdot F_v$
>         $father(v) \leftarrow father(father(v))$
>         **end**

One step of this algorithm is illustrated in figure 4.22. The above algorithm works in $O(\log n)$ time using $n$ processors. In order to reduce the number of processors by a factor of $\log n$ some preprocessing is required. The tree $T$ is

*Figure 4.22*

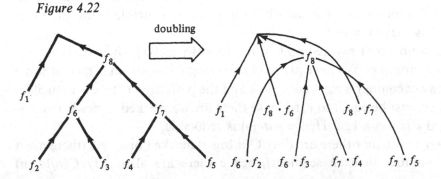

transformed to the reduced tree $RT$ with $n/\log n$ nodes and the functions $F_v$ are computed only for nodes of this tree using the above algorithm. Then the tree $RT$ is expanded and the functions are computed for all nodes.

Before this theorem we described an algorithm to compute all the functions $F$ in $O(\log m)$ time with $m$ processors for a tree with $m$ nodes. We compress our tree and compute the functions $F$ for the compressed tree $RT$. The size of $RT$ is $n/\log n$. If we take $m = n/\log n$ and the algorithm just mentioned, then we can compute the functions for $RT$ in $O(\log n)$ time using $n/\log n$ processors. Now we can assign a processor to $path(v)$, for each marked non-root node, and we can easily decompress each such path and compute the functions $F$ for reconstructed nodes in $O(\log n)$ time using one processor for each path. This requires time $O(\log n)$ and $n/\log n$ processors. This completes the proof. $\square$

## 4.5 Optimal parallel recognition of input-driven languages

A context-free language $L$ is said to be input-driven if and only if there is a pushdown automaton $A$ accepting $L$ such that in each move the change of the stack height of $A$ is determined by the scanned input symbol alone. Many standard texts ([4] for example) can be consulted for the definition of pushdown automata. A typical example of such language is the language of correct (matched) sequences of brackets '[', ']', '(' and ')'. An opening bracket corresponds to a push move and a closing bracket corresponds to a pop move. When the automaton $A$ encounters a closing bracket then it checks if this bracket and the bracket on the top of the stack are of the same type.

We say that the automaton $A$ is normalised if and only if it changes the height of its stack by 1 when scanning one input symbol. First we show that we can assume without loss of generality that the automaton $A$ (within the definition of input-driven language) is normalised. If $a$ is an input symbol which causes $k > 0$ symbols to be pushed then we can replace $a$ by the string $h(a) = a_1 a_2 \ldots a_k$, where each $a_i$ causes one symbol to be pushed and $h(a)$ makes the same change to the stack as the symbol $a$ alone. If the symbol $a$ does not change the height of the stack then we can replace it by $h(a) = a_1 a_2$ such that $a_1$ causes a push move and $a_2$ causes a pop move. In this way the automaton $A$, for the input $x$, is simulated by some normalised automaton $A'$ on the input $h(x)$.

Instead of checking if $A$ accepts $x$ we check if $A'$ accepts $h(x)$. The string $h(x)$ has $O(n)$ length and can be constructed easily from $x$ by an optimal parallel algorithm. Hence we can assume now that any pushdown automaton $A$ accepting an input-driven languages is normalised. It can be also assumed without loss of generality that when $A$ accepts the height of stack is 1 (by adding a sequence of extra symbols, if necessary).

*Theorem 4.6*
The recognition problem for input driven languages can be solved on a P-RAM using an optimal parallel algorithm.

*Proof*
We can assume that the pushdown automaton accepting an input-driven language $L$ is normalised. Now push symbols correspond to opening brackets and pop symbols correspond to closing brackets. These brackets implicitly describe the structure of a certain expression. The recognition problem can be again reduced to the problem of computing some algebraic expression. Let $P(M)$ be the set of all subsets of the set $M = (S \copyright W) \copyright (S \copyright W)$, where $\copyright$ denotes the cartesian product of sets, $S$ is the set of states and $W$ is the pushdown alphabet of the automaton $A$. The subsets of $M$ are values corresponding to certain substrings of the input string. The value corresponding to a substring $v$ of the input string is the set

$\{((s_1, q_1), (s_2, q_2)) |$automaton $A$ starting in the state $s_1$ with $q_1$ as the only element of its stack after reading $v$ is in state $s_2$ with $q_2$ as the only element of the stack$\}$

The operations on such sets (relations) can be made to reflect the behaviour of the automaton. Such an approach has been used by Rytter[13] to design a space-efficient algorithm. We now specify in more detail the relationship between input words and expressions. The input word will be transformed into an expression in a similar way to the case of bracket languages.

We introduce two operations * and &. The first operation is the composition of relations (elements of $P(M)$). The second operation is rather technical. Let $Q$ be the set of all pairs $[a, b]$ of symbols of the input alphabet such that $a$ is a push symbol and $b$ is a pop symbol. For each such pair $[a, b]$ and the relation $R \in P(M)$ we define

$[a, b] \& R = \{((s_1, q_1), (s_2, q_2)) |A$ starting in state $s_1$ with $q_1$ as the only element on the stack after reading $a$ pushes a symbol $q_1'$ onto the stack and changes state to $s_1'$, and $A$ starting in state $s_2'$ with top element $q_2'$ after reading the symbol $b$ changes state to $s_2$, for some $((s_1', q_1'), (s_2', q_2')) \in R$, and moreover $q_1 = q_2\}$

Informally $[a, b]$ & $R$ is the set of all pairs which are 'below' pairs from $R$ in the 'context' $[a, b]$. For an input word $x$ we construct an expression $ex(x)$ involving the operations * and &. We demonstrate the construction with an example.

Let $x = a_1 a_2 \ldots a_{10}$ be the input word for which the history of the computation of the automaton $A$ is described in figure 4.23. We can see from the figure that the symbols $a_1, a_2, a_4, a_5$ and $a_8$ are push symbols whilst $a_3, a_6, a_7, a_9$ and $a_{10}$ are pop symbols.

First we insert the bracket '(' immediately before every push symbol and the bracket ')' immediately after every pop symbol. In this way the following string $x_1$ is obtained.

$$x_1 = (a_1(a_2a_3)(a_4(a_5a_6)a_7)(a_8a_9)a_{10})$$

Next for every substring of the form $(ab)$ we compute the relation

$$R(a, b) = \{((s_1, q_1), (s_2, q_2)) \mid A \text{ starting in the state } s_1 \text{ with the stack}$$
$$\text{containing only } q_1 \text{ after reading } ab \text{ is in state } s_2$$
$$\text{with the stack containing only } q_2\}$$

Every substring of the form $(ab)$ is replaced by $(R(a, b))$. Suppose that $R(a_2 a_3) = R_1, R(a_5, a_6) = R_2$ and $R(a_8, a_9) = R_3$. Then string $x_1$ is transformed into

$$x_2 = (a_1(R_1)(a_4(R_2)a_7)(R_3)a_{10})$$

Now for every position containing a push symbol in string $x_2$ we look for its corresponding pop symbol. For example the pop symbol $a_7$ corresponds to push symbol $a_4$. We replace every push symbol $a_i$ by a pair $[a_i, a_j]$, where $a_j$ is a

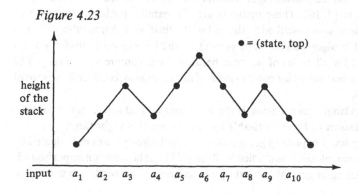

*Figure 4.23*

● = (state, top)

height of the stack

input    $a_1$   $a_2$   $a_3$   $a_4$   $a_5$   $a_6$   $a_7$   $a_8$   $a_9$   $a_{10}$

pop symbol corresponding to $a_i$, then we erase all pop symbols. The following string is obtained.

$$x_3 = ([a_1, a_{10}](R_1)([a_4, a_7](R_2))(R_3))$$

Finally the operation & is inserted after each pair $[a_i, a_j]$ and the operation * is inserted between each pair of brackets ')('. The operation * has higher priority than &. The resulting expression string is $ex(x)$. In our case we obtain

$$ex(x) = ([a_1, a_{10}] \& (R_1) * ([a_4, a_7] \& (R_2)) * (R_3))$$

The value of the expression $ex(x)$ is the set of all pairs $((s_1, q_1), (s_2, q_2))$ corresponding to the whole of the input word $x$. In order to check whether $A$ accepts we verify if a pair $((s_0, q_0), (s_2, q_2))$ is in $ex(x)$ for initial values $s_0$ and $q_0$ of state and top symbol and for some accepting state $q_2$. It is easy to see that the transformation $x \to ex(x)$ can be achieved by an optimal parallel algorithm. This is because the pop and push symbols give the bracket structure of $ex(x)$ and the correspondence between brackets '(' and brackets ')' can be computed by an optimal parallel algorithm – see [1] which was described in section 3.1. The corresponding algebra with operations & and * has a finite carrier and the algorithm for dynamic expression evaluation (algorithm 3.1) can be applied. This completes the proof.          □

### Bibliographic notes

The first *NC* algorithm for context-free language recognition was implicitly given by Ruzzo.[10] Ruzzo's method was simplified and generalised by Rytter,[14] where a method for transforming path systems to their 'bushy' versions was developed. The techniques from [14] were used later to construct fast parallel algorithms on more realistic models of computations[12] and to construct an $O(\log n)$-time algorithm for the recognition of unambiguous context-free languages. In the case of unambiguous languages the upper bound matches the lower bound of parallel time on a P-RAM. Optimal parallel algorithms for two theoretical subclasses of context-free languages were given in [2, 16]. These methods use the parallel pebble game and tree compression. The tree compression described at the end of the final section is an alternative to the compression described in algorithm 3.1. The present method is especially useful when a function is to be computed for *all* nodes of the tree, because the decompression is easy. The technique from section 3.3 is best suited for computation of the value associated with the root of the tree only.

Bracket and input-driven languages are actually the most complicated subclasses of context-free languages which are known to be recognisable by optimal parallel algorithms.

The sequential-time complexity of parsing general context-free languages was investigated by Ruzzo.[9] The parallel-time complexity was studied by Rytter.[11] The best known upper bounds for the recognition and parsing of general context-free languages are currently the same. The class of bracket languages is the most complicated subclass of context-free languages which are known to be parsable by optimal parallel algorithms.[16]

## Bibliography

[1] I. Bar-On and U. Vishkin. Optimal parallel generation of a computation tree form. *ACM Transactions on Programming Languages and Systems* **7**, 2 (1985), 348–57.

[2] S. Fortune and J. Wyllie. Parallelism in random access machines. *Proceedings of the 10th ACM Symposium on the Theory of Computation* (1978), 114–18.

[3] A. M. Gibbons and W. Rytter. An optimal parallel algorithm for dynamic expression evaluation and its applications. *Sixth Conference on the Foundations of Software Technology and Theoretical Computer Science* (1986). Lecture Notes in Computer Science 241. Springer-Verlag.

[4] J. E. Hopcroft and J. D. Ullman. *Introduction to Automata Theory, Languages and Computation.* Addison-Wesley (1979).

[5] G. Kindervater and J. Lenstra. An introduction to parallelism in combinatorial optimization. Report OS-R8501, Centre for Mathematics and Computer Science, Amsterdam (1984).

[6] R. Mattheyses and C. M. Fiduccia. Parsing Dyck languages on parallel machines. *20th Allerton Conference on Communication, Control and Computing* (1982).

[7] K. Mehlhorn. Bracket languages are recognizable in logarithmic space. *Information Processing Letters* **5**, 6 (1976), 169–70.

[8] J. Reif. Parallel time $O(\log(n))$ acceptance of deterministic context-free languages. *STOC 1982*, 290–6.

[9] W. Ruzzo. On the complexity of general context free language parsing and recognition. *Automata, Languages and Programming.* Lecture Notes in Computer Science **71**. Springer-Verlag (1979), 489–99.

[10] W. Ruzzo. Tree-size bounded alternation. *Journal of Computers and System Sciences* **21** (1980), 218–35.

[11] W. Rytter. On the complexity of parallel parsing of general context-free languages. *Theoretical Computer Science* **47** (1987), 315–22.

[12] W. Rytter. On the recognition of context free languages. *Computation Theory.* Lecture Notes in Computer Science 208. Springer-Verlag (1985), 318–25.

[13] W. Rytter. An application of Mehlhorn's algorithm for bracket languages to $\log(n)$ space recognition of input driven languages. *Information Processing Letters* **23**, 2 (1986), 81–4.

[14] W. Rytter. The complexity of two-way pushdown automata and recursive programs. *Combinatorial Algorithms on Words* (eds. A. Apostolico and Z. Galil). Springer-Verlag (1985), 341–56.

[15] W. Rytter. Parallel time $\log(n)$ recognition of unambiguous context-free languages. *Information and Computation* **73** (1987), 75–86.

[16] W. Rytter and R. Giancarlo. Optimal parallel parsing of bracket languages. To appear in *Theoretical Computer Science* (1987).

[17] R. Tarjan and U. Vishkin. Finding biconnected components and computing tree functions in logarithmic parallel time. *SIAM Journal of Computing* **14**, 2 (1985), 862–73.

# CHAPTER 5

# FAST PARALLEL SORTING

This chapter presents a few results from the very extensive literature on parallel sorting. One recently published bibliography[24] contains no less than three hundred and seventy-three references. In view of the model of parallel computation used commonly throughout our text, the most important algorithm we present here is Cole's optimal parallel merge sort on a P-RAM. However, for sorting, there is another model of parallel computation which has received such wide attention that we cannot properly ignore it. This model is that based on sorting networks. For completeness therefore we present some algorithms within this model also. This includes two sorting networks of Batcher and in addition a sketch of the celebrated sorter universally known as the three Hungarians' algorithm. This was the first to achieve (optimal) $\log n$ depth. The three Hungarians' algorithm is (from the point of proving correctness) perhaps the most difficult to be described in this book. Section 5.3 might therefore be properly regarded as optional reading.

Section 5.2 describes Cole's algorithm. In section 5.1 we describe the odd-even and the bitonic merge sorts of Batcher. For the purposes of both sections 5.1 and 5.3, we need to describe the basic unit of sorting networks, namely that of the *compare-exchange* operation. As is usual, we suppose that each element of the set of items to be sorted has a key which governs the sorting process. Let the keys of the items to be sorted be stored in a vector, $Key[1 .. n]$. For simplicity we shall (without loss of generality) generally assume that $n$ is a power of 2. The operation of *compare-exchange* is then as follows.

    *compare-exchange*$(i, j)$
       **if** $Key[i] > Key[j]$ **then** exchange values of $Key[i], Key[j]$

Figure 5.1 illustrates the network representation of one *compare-exchange* operation. The keys are entered ($x$ and $y$ in this case) from the left. The bold vertical line is a *compare-exchange* (or comparator) module. Its effect is to exchange the keys if and only if $x > y$. This simplest of possible networks therefore sorts two keys. Figure 5.5(b) shows a more complicated network with eight inputs and twelve *compare-exchange* modules. For a given $n$, algorithms performing a fixed sequence of *compare-exchange* operations are called sorting networks. The algorithms of both sections 5.1 and 5.3 can be implemented as sorting networks.

Two *compare-exchange* operations can be performed simultaneously if and only if they operate on disjoint entries of the vector *Key*. Hence in one step at most $n/2$ *compare-exchange* operations can be performed. The number of stages corresponds to parallel time and the maximum number of operations performed in one stage corresponds to the number of processors. Throughout this chapter we only consider the availability of a linear number of processors. Using pairwise key comparisons, it is well known that to sort a list of $n$ keys we need $\Omega(n \log n)$ comparisons (see [17] for example). Hence, using $O(n)$ processors, the best possible parallel time is $O(\log n)$.

The algorithms presented in section 5.1 (the odd-even and the bitonic merge sorts of Batcher) operate in $O(\log^2 n)$ time using $n$ processors. They are therefore not optimal algorithms for which (number of processors) * (parallel time) $= O(n \log n)$. It was shown recently in [7] that bitonic sorting can be modified to work in $O(\log^2 n)$ time with only $n/\log n$ processors. This gives an $O(\log^2 n)$ optimal parallel sorting algorithm. However, of greater interest are optimal parallel algorithms for which (parallel time) $= O(\log n)$. Two such algorithms are described, one in sections 5.2 and one in section 5.3. The first is Cole's efficient parallel merge sort for the P-RAM model of computation. The second is the sophisticated sorting network of Ajtai, Komlos and Szemeredi.

## 5.1 Batcher's sorting networks

In this section we describe two strategies, both due to Batcher, which lead to $O(\log^2 n)$ parallel time algorithms. Both are based on parallel merge sort and have the same underlying computational structure of a balanced binary tree.

*Figure 5.1.* The network representation of the *compare-exchange* operation

$x$ ——┬—— $\min(x, y)$

$y$ ——┴—— $\max(x, y)$

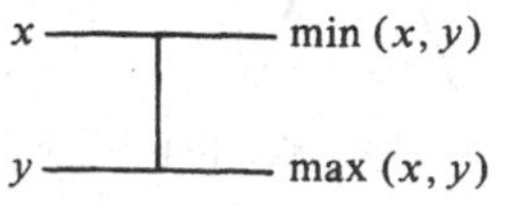

Leaves correspond to keys (one-element sequences) and the operation at non-leaf nodes is a merge of two sorted sequences. The result of each such node is a sorted sequence of those keys which are stored at leaf descendants of the node. Thus the final merge at the root of the tree produces the desired sorted sequence of all the inputs to the algorithm. Figure 5.2 illustrates this for the case that the number of keys, $n$, is 8. We shall presume in general that $n$ is a power of 2; otherwise we can always add a (minimum) number of dummy keys to achieve this.

The depth of the whole tree is $\log n$. By $M(n)$ we denote the time required to merge two sorted sequences with $n$ keys. Thus, if we perform in parallel all merges at the same depth in the tree, the algorithm will have $O(M(n) \log n)$ parallel time complexity. The two classical methods of Batcher which we now describe ensure that $M(n) = O(\log n)$.

*Odd-even merge*

Given a sequence $S$ of $n$ elements, let $odd(S)$ be the subsequence of $S$ consisting of elements with an odd index. Similarly let $even(S)$ be the subsequence of elements with even index. Thus if $S = (s_1, s_2, \ldots, s_n)$, then $odd(S) = (s_1, s_3, s_5, \ldots)$ and $even(S) = (s_2, s_4, s_6, \ldots)$. If we further let $S' = (s_1', s_2', \ldots, s_n')$ then we can define the operation $interleave(S, S') = (s_1, s_1', s_2, s_2', \ldots, s_n, s_n')$. Thus, for example, $interleave((1, 2, 3, 4), (5, 6, 7, 8)) = (1, 5, 2, 6, 3, 7, 4, 8)$.

Another operation we require is $odd-even(S)$. This consists of the parallel execution of $compare-exchange(i, i + 1)$ for each even value of $i$, $1 \leqslant i < n$. For example $odd-even(1, 6, 2, 4, 3, 10) = (1, 2, 6, 3, 4, 10)$. We also define the operation $join1(S, S')$. This consists of executing the two-command sequence $(interleave(S, S'), odd-even(S, S'))$. The operation $join1(S, S')$ is schematically illustrated in figure 5.3.

Figure 5.2

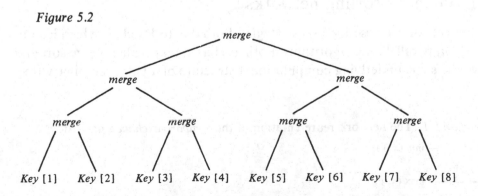

Having defined the basic operations required, we are now in a position to present Batcher's odd-even merge. The following functional description does this.

**function** *odd-even merge(S, S')* {The input is two sorted sequences}
**begin**
**if** the sequences are of length 1 **then** merge them using one
compare-exchange operation **else**
   **begin**
   **compute** $S_{odd}$ and $S_{even}$ **in parallel do**
      where $S_{odd} \leftarrow$ *odd-even merge(odd(S), odd(S'))*
      and $S_{even} \leftarrow$ *odd-even merge(even(S), even(S'))*
      *odd-even merge* $\leftarrow join1(S_{odd}, S_{even})$
   **end**
**end** of *odd-even merge*

The following example illustrates the procedure. Suppose that we start with $S = (2, 6, 10, 15)$ and $S' = (3, 4, 5, 8)$. Then $cdd(S) = (2, 10)$, $odd(S') = (3, 5)$, $even(S) = (6, 15)$ and $even(S') = (4, 8)$. We then see that $S_{odd} = (2, 3, 5, 10)$ and $S_{even} = (4, 6, 8, 15)$. The operation *join1* first requires an *interleave* computation with the result $interleave(S_{odd}, S_{even}) = (2, 4, 3, 6, 5, 8, 10, 15)$. Then completing the operation *join1* with an *odd-even* computation we obtain the final sorted list of keys given by $odd-even(2, 4, 3, 6, 5, 8, 10, 15) = (2, 3, 4, 5, 6, 8, 10, 15)$.

The recursive *odd-even merge* procedure has logarithmic depth. Using $n$ processors, the operations *interleave, odd-even* and *join1* can be performed in one parallel step. Therefore an odd-even merge of two sorted sequences takes $O(\log n)$ time using $n$ processors.

We delay verification of the *odd-even merge* sort until subsection 5.1.3. There the so-called zero-one principle is described. This greatly facilitates verifications in the area of sorting networks.

*Figure 5.3.* Graphical representation of the operation *join1*

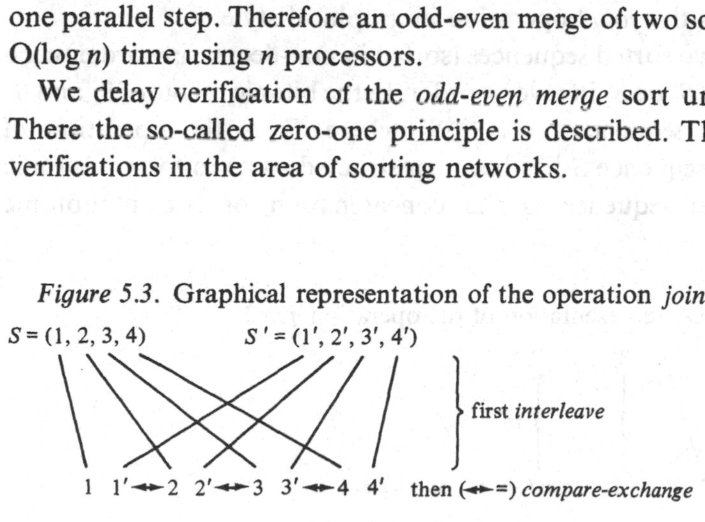

$S = (1, 2, 3, 4)$        $S' = (1', 2', 3', 4')$

first *interleave*

1  1' ↔ 2  2' ↔ 3  3' ↔ 4  4'   then (↔ =) *compare-exchange*

*Bitonic merge*

We come now to the second of Batcher's merge procedures which we describe. Like the odd-even merge of the last section the so-called bitonic merge described here has O(log $n$) depth. Our description starts by introducing the operation *join2(S)*, where $S$ is a sequence of length $n$. A component of this is the *shuffle* operation defined as follows.

**procedure** *shuffle(S)*
**begin**
partition $S$ into two sequences:
    $S_1$ consisting of the first $n/2$ elements of $S$, and
    $S_2$ consisting of the second $n/2$ elements of $S$
$S \leftarrow interleave(S_1, S_2)$
**end**

Shuffle is one of the basic operations for computers consisting of a fixed interconnection network. In these computers processors only communicate through the network. The perfect shuffle computer (see [26]) is a theoretical prototype of this class of machine. The operation *join2* can now be defined as follows.

**procedure** *join2(S)*
**begin**
*shuffle(S)*,
for all odd $i$, $1 \leqslant i \leqslant n$, **in parallel do** *compare-exchange(i, i + 1)*
**end**

Figure 5.4 illustrates the *join2* operation in graphical style.

Let $S_1$ and $S_2$ be two sorted sequences (sorted in non-decreasing order) each of length $n/2$. Also let $S_2'$ be $S_2$ in reverse order. In the bitonic merge of $S_1$ and $S_2$ we first obtain the sequence $S = S_1 \copyright S_2'$ where $\copyright$ is the operation of concatenation. The sequence $S$ has been constructed so as to form a bitonic sequence. A bitonic sequence is the concatenation of two monotonic

*Figure 5.4.* Graphical representation of the operation *join2*

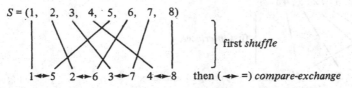

sequences, in this case $S_1$ and $S_2'$, the first of non-decreasing order and the second of non-increasing order. Given $S$ constructed in this way, the *bitonic merge* procedure is as follows.

> **procedure** *bitonic merge* {the input is the sequence $S$ formed from $S_1$ and $S_2$}
> **begin**
> **repeat** log $n$ **times** *join2* {after the first execution the input to *join2* is the
> sequence output from the previous execution}
> **end** of *bitonic merge*

We illustrate *bitonic merge* with the following example. Let $S_1 = (2, 6, 10, 15)$ and $S_2 = (3, 4, 5, 8)$ so that $S = (2, 6, 10, 15, 8, 5, 4, 3)$. Executing the *shuffle* operation within the first execution of *join2* we obtain *shuffle*$(S) =$ $(2, 8, 6, 5, 10, 4, 15, 3)$. Performing the *compare-exchange* operation on adjacent entries we obtain *join2*$(2, 6, 10, 15, 8, 5, 4, 3) = (2, 8, 5, 6, 4, 10, 3, 15)$. In turn, the second *join2* operation yields *join2*$(2, 8, 5, 6, 4, 10, 3, 15) =$ $(2, 4, 8, 10, 3, 5, 6, 15)$. Thus the third and final operation ($n = 8$ and so log $n = 3$) gives *join2*$(2, 4, 8, 10, 3, 5, 6, 15) = (2, 3, 4, 5, 6, 8, 10, 15)$. Figure 5.5 provides a network illustration for this example. In this figure, (a) and (b) show topologically equivalent versions of the same network. The *shuffle* operations are self-evident in (a), whereas (b) more conventionally emphasises the *compare-exchange* modules.

The operations *shuffle*, *odd-even* and *join2* can be performed in one parallel step using $n$ processors. Therefore a bitonic merge of two sorted sequences takes $O(\log n)$ time using $n$ processors.

We delay any consideration of a proof that the bitonic sort is valid until the end of the section.

*Figure 5.5.* A bitonic merge of two sequences, each of size 4

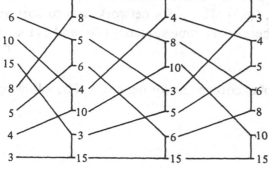
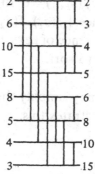

(a)                                                        (b)

## The zero-one principle

From a general point of view, proof of correctness of merging algorithms, of the type described earlier, can be considerably aided by the use of the so-called zero-one principle. The type of algorithms we refer to are algorithms which only use the operation of *compare-exchange* along with the permuting of elements. As we have already stated, such algorithms are called sorting networks. The fixed sequence of *compare-exchange* operations depends only upon the size of the input and not upon any particular order of the input elements. For the purposes of the following lemma, a zero-one sequence is a sequence of keys each of which is either 0 or 1.

## Lemma 5.1 (zero-one principle)

If a sorting network is valid for all zero-one input sequences then it is valid for any input sequence.

## Proof

Let $f(x)$ be any monotonic function. Thus $f(a_i) \leqslant f(a_j)$ if and only if $a_i \leqslant a_j$. Clearly, if a given network transforms a sequence $[a_1, a_2, \ldots, a_n]$ into the sequence $[b_1, b_2, \ldots, b_n]$, then it will transform the sequence $[f(a_1), f(a_2), \ldots, f(a_n)]$ into the sequence $[f(b_1), f(b_2), \ldots, f(b_n)]$. Thus, if in the transformation of $[a_1, a_2, \ldots, a_n]$ into $[b_1, b_2, \ldots, b_n]$ there exists some $i$ for which $b_i > b_{i+1}$, then in the transformation of $[f(a_1), f(a_2), \ldots, f(a_n)]$ into $[f(b_1), f(b_2), \ldots, f(b_n)]$ it will be the case that if $f(b_i) \neq f(b_{i+1})$ then $f(b_i) > f(b_{i+1})$. Now let $f(x)$ be the particular monotonic function for which $f(b_j) = 0$ for all $b_j < b_i$ and for which $f(b_j) = 1$ for all $b_j \geqslant b_i$. Now $[f(b_1), f(b_2), \ldots, f(b_n)]$ will be an unsorted sequence of 0s and 1s because $f(b_i) = 1$ and $f(b_{i+1}) = 0$. In other words, the network fails to sort the zero-one input sequence $[f(a_1), f(a_2), \ldots, f(a_n)]$. Thus, if a network fails to sort an arbitrary sequence of keys, then there exists some sequence of 0s and 1s that it will also fail to sort.                                                                                     □

Lemma 5.2 may simplify the proof of correctness for networks. The following corollary illustrates this.

## Corollary 5.1

Batcher's *odd-even merge* is valid.

*Proof*

The odd-even merge takes two sorted sequences $S$ and $S'$ and produces the sorted sequence *odd-even merge*$(S, S')$. In view of the zero-one principle (lemma 5.1) we need only consider $S$ and $S'$ having the forms $S = 0^p 1^{m-p}$ and $S' = 0^q 1^{n-q}$ for $0 \leqslant p \leqslant m$ and $0 \leqslant q \leqslant n$. In other words $S$ begins with $p$ 0s which are followed by $m - p$ 1s. $S'$ is $q$ 0s followed by $n - q$ 1s. We shall consider the case that $m$ is not necessarily equal to $n$ here, although previously (in our description of the odd-even merge) the length of $S$ was presumed to be the same as $S'$. Given $S$ and $S'$ as described, we now have to show that *odd-even merge*$(S, S')$ is sorted. In what follows, we use the definitions introduced within our description of *odd-even merge*.

Within the *odd-even merge* procedure $S_{\text{odd}}$ will consist of $\lceil p/2 \rceil + \lceil q/2 \rceil$ 0s followed by a string of 1s. Similarly, $S_{\text{even}}$ will consist of $\lfloor p/2 \rfloor + \lfloor q/2 \rfloor$ 0s followed by 1s. We define $d$ as follows –

$$d = (\lceil p/2 \rceil + \lceil q/2 \rceil) - (\lfloor p/2 \rfloor + \lfloor q/2 \rfloor)$$

and consider three cases.

(a) $d = 0$. In this case, after the *interleave step of the join1* command, we obtain

$$\text{interleave}(S_{\text{odd}}, S_{\text{even}}) = 0'00'0 \ldots 0'01^{m+n-p-q}$$

where the primed 0s are from $S_{\text{odd}}$ and the unprimed from $S_{\text{even}}$. Thus, we see *interleave*$(S_{\text{odd}}, S_{\text{even}})$ produces a sorted sequence in this case which the *compare-exchange* operations of the second step of the *join1* procedure will leave sorted.

(b) $d = 1$. In this case we obtain

$$\text{interleave}(S_{\text{odd}}, S_{\text{even}}) = 0'00'0 \ldots 00'1^{m+n-p-q}$$

and so we again obtain a sorted sequence.

(c) $d = 2$. In this case we obtain

$$\text{interleave}(S_{\text{odd}}, S_{\text{even}}) = 0'0 \ldots 0'10'1^{m+n-p-q-1}$$

This is a sorted sequence except for the 1 in position $2p$. If we exchange it with the 0 in position $2p + 1$ then we obtain a sorting. This exchange will be carried out by one of the *compare-exchange* operations of the second step of the *join1* operation. Thus we shall again obtain a sorted sequence. No other values of $d$ are possible and so the corollary is proved. $\square$

For merge sorts and because of the the zero-one principle, we only have to prove that we have correct merging for sequences $0^k 1^{n-k}$ and $0^{k'} 1^{n-k'}$, for all $k$

and $k'$ $(1 \leqslant k, k' \leqslant n)$. For fixed $n$, the number of possible inputs is reduced to $O(n^2)$. This gives a polynomial-time algorithm for verification of the network. In general, however, verification of sorting requires that all possible sequences of 0s and 1s should be considered. This number is of course exponential. In fact the problem of checking whether a general sorting network for a given $n$ is not correct is $NP$-complete.

Notice that the styles of our descriptions of the odd-even merge and of the bitonic merge were markedly different. The former was presented as a recursive procedure whilst the latter was not. The recursive description of the odd-even merge allowed a straightforward application of the zero-one principle in a verification of this merge. On the other hand, the particular presentation of the bitonic merge yields, in a relatively simple manner, the associated comparator network. Having verified the odd-even merge, we shall not include a proof that the bitonic merge is valid. If the bitonic merge is described in a recursive manner, then the proof follows in a manner very similar to that employed in corollary 5.1.

## 5.2 Cole's optimal parallel merge sort

Bearing in mind the emphasis on the P-RAM model of parallel computation throughout the text, this is the main section of this chapter. We shall presume throughout the section that the elements that are to be sorted are distinct.

Batcher's sorting, as described in the previous section, is parallel merge sorting where the parallel time for merging two sorted sequences of size $m$ is logarithmic. Cole[13] has invented an ingenious version of parallel merge sorting in which this merging is done in $O(1)$ parallel time. If we have no additional information about two sorted sequences $J$ and $K$ (each of size $m$) then it can be proved that in order to merge them we require non-constant parallel time with $m$ processors. However, Cole has shown that merging can be accomplished in constant time if we have at hand a third sequence $L$ which is a so-called good sampler for $J$ and $K$. Suppose that $K$ is the sorted sequence produced by merging two sorted sequences $L$ and $J$, where $|L| < |J|$. Informally, $L$ is then a good sampler for $J$ if the elements of $L$ are distributed uniformly (within certain tolerances) amongst the elements of $J$. In due course we shall provide an exact definition.

First we need two technical definitions. Let $a \leqslant b$, we say that $c$ is between $a$ and $b$ if and only if $a < c \leqslant b$. The rank of an element $e$ in the set $S$ is the number of elements of $L$ preceding $e$ (that is, which are smaller than $e$). We denote this number by $rank(e, L)$. Also, we denote by $R[A, B]$ the function for which

$R[A, B](e) = rank(e, B)$ for each $e$ in $A$. Such functions are called cross-ranks. The function $R[A, B]$ is represented as an array with $|A|$ entries. The $i$th entry contains the rank of the $i$th element of $A$ in $B$.

We say that the sorted sequence $L$ is a *good sampler* of the sorted sequence $J$ if and only if between any $k + 1$ adjacent elements of $\{-\infty\} \cup L \cup \{+\infty\}$ there are at most $2k + 1$ elements of $J$. In particular notice that there cannot be more than three elements of $J$ between any two elements of $\{-\infty\} \cup L \cup \{+\infty\}$. As an example consider the sorted sequence $S$. Let $S_1$ be a subsequence of $S$ consisting of each fourth element of $S$. Similarly, let $S_2$ be a subsequence of $S$ consisting of each second element. Then $S_1$ is a good sampler of $S_2$.

Assuming that $J$ and $K$ are sorted vectors of size $m$ and that $L$ is a good sampler for $J$ and $K$, then we can merge $J$ and $K$ with the help of $L$ as the following function describes. In this context, figure 5.6 illustrates the partitioning of $J$ and $K$.

> **function** *mergewithhelp*$(J, K, L)$
>
> $\qquad\qquad$ {$L$ is a good sampler of the sorted vectors $J$ and $K$}
> **begin**
> partition the set $J$ into $J(1), J(2), \ldots$, where $J(i)$ is the set of elements of $J$
> $\qquad$ lying between the $(i - 1)$th and the $i$th element of $L$; similarly partition $K$
> $\qquad$ into $K(1), K(2), \ldots$
> **for all** $i$, $1 \leqslant i \leqslant |L| + 1$, **in parallel do** $res_i \leftarrow merge(J(i), K(i))$
> *mergewithhelp* $\leftarrow res_1 res_2 res_3 \ldots res_{|L|}$ {concatenation of the $res_i$}
> **end**

*Figure 5.6.* Merging $J$ and $K$ with the help of $L$. We take $L_0 = -\infty$ and $L_9 = +\infty$. The crucial property of the input is that each of the sets $K(i)$ and $J(i)$ has at most three elements

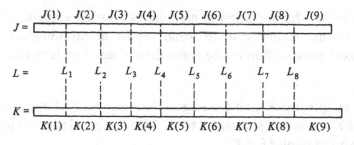

$$L = (L_1, L_2, L_3, L_4, L_5, L_6, L_7, L_8)$$

$J(i)$ = the set of elements of $J$ lying between the $(i-1)$th and $i$th elements of $L$

$K(i)$ = the set of elements of $K$ lying between the $(i-1)$th and $i$th elements of $L$

$merge(J, K) = merge(J(1), K(1))merge(J(2), K(2)) \ldots merge(J(9), K(9))$

Illustrating the function *mergewithhelp* let $K = [1, 4, 6, 9, 11, 12, 13, 16, 19, 20]$, $J = [2, 3, 7, 8, 10, 14, 15, 17, 18, 21]$ and $L = [5, 10, 12, 17]$. Now $L$ is a good sampler of $J$ and of $K$. The set $K$ is partitioned into $K(1) = [1, 4]$, $K(2) = [6, 9]$, $K(3) = [11, 12]$, $K(4) = [13, 16]$ and $K(5) = [19, 20]$. Similarly $J(1) = [2, 3]$, $J(2) = [7, 8, 10]$, $J(3) = \emptyset$, $J(4) = [14, 15, 17]$ and $J(5) = [18, 21]$. Hence

$$res_1 = merge([1, 4], [2, 3]) = [1, 2, 3, 4]$$
$$res_2 = merge([6, 9], [7, 8, 10]) = [6, 7, 8, 9, 10]$$
$$res_3 = merge([11, 12], \emptyset) = [11, 12]$$
$$res_4 = merge([13, 16], [14, 15, 17]) = [13, 14, 15, 16, 17]$$
$$res_5 = merge([19, 20], [18, 21]) = [18, 19, 20, 21]$$

and thus $mergewithhelp(J, K, L) = [1, 2, 3, 4, 6, 7, 8, 9, 10, 11, 12, 13, 14, 15, 16, 17, 18, 19, 20, 21]$. We have taken the 0th element of $L$ to be $-\infty$ and the $(|L| + 1)$th element to be $+\infty$.

The reader will find it an easy exercise to show that, if the cross-ranks $R[L, J]$, $R[L, K]$, $R[J, L]$ and $R[K, L]$ are already computed, then the partitions of $J$ and $K$, and the concatenation of the sorted sequences $res_i$ within the function *mergewithhelp* can be achieved in $O(1)$ time using $O(|J| + |K|)$ processors. In this context note that $L$ is a good sampler. This allows 'local' merges of $K(i)$ and $J(i)$ to be made in constant time since they are of constant-bounded size ($\leqslant 3$). We therefore have the following lemma.

### Lemma 5.2
If the cross-ranks $R[L, J]$, $R[L, K]$, $R[J, L]$ and $R[K, L]$ are already computed and $L$ is a good sampler for $J$ and $K$ then $mergewithhelp(J, K, L)$ can be computed in $O(1)$ time with $|J| + |K|$ processors on a P-RAM.               $\square$

We shall denote by '&' the operation of merging two sorted sequences. The next three lemmas are simple combinatorial results about samplers and merging. The whole construction of the algorithm is based on lemma 5.5.

### Lemma 5.3
Let $X$ be a good sampler for $X'$ and $Y$ be a good sampler for $Y'$. Suppose also that $X, X', Y$ and $Y'$ are sorted sequences, then $X \& Y$ is a good sampler for $X'$ and $X \& Y$ is a good sampler for $Y'$.

### Proof
It is easily seen that if $X$ is a good sampler for $X'$ then $X \& W$ is a good sampler of $X'$ for any set $W$.               $\square$

In contrast to the last lemma consider the following. Let $X$ be a good sampler for $X'$ and $Y$ be a good sampler for $Y'$. Also let $X$, $X'$, $Y$ and $Y'$ be sorted sequences. Then $X \& Y$ is not necessarily a good sampler for $X' \& Y'$. For example take $X = [2,7]$, $X' = [2,5,6,7]$, $Y = [1,8]$ and $Y' = [1,3,4,8]$. Then $X \& Y = [1,2,7,8]$ and $X' \& Y' = [1, 2, 3, 4, 5, 6, 7, 8]$. There are 5 elements in $X' \& Y'$ between 2 and 7.

If $X$ is a sorted sequence stored in a vector, then by $reduce(X)$ we denote the subsequence of $X$ consisting of every fourth element of $X$.

### Lemma 5.4
Let $X$ be a good sampler for $X'$ and $Y$ be a good sampler for $Y'$. Also let $X$, $X'$, $Y$ and $Y'$ be sorted sequences. Then there are at most $2r + 2$ elements of $X' \& Y'$ between $r$ consecutive elements of $X \& Y$.

### Proof
We can assume that $X$ and $Y$ contain special elements $-\infty$ and $+\infty$. Take a sequence $e_1, e_2, \ldots, e_r$ of $r$ consecutive elements of $X \& Y$. This sequence consists of some $h$ elements from $X$ and $j$ elements from $Y$. Without loss of generality we can assume that the first element $e_1$ of the sequence is from $X$. There are two cases to consider.

### Case 1: $e_r$ is from $X$
In this case, between $e_1$ and $e_r$ there are at most $2(h - 1) + 1$ elements from $X'$. There are also at most $2(j + 1) + 1$ elements from $Y'$ between $e_1$ and $e_r$, because these elements lie between $j + 2$ elements of $Y$ (we can add two boundary elements to the sequence of $j$ elements from $Y$ in $e_1, e_2, \ldots, e_r$). Hence, altogether there are $2(h - 1) + 1 + 2(j + 1) + 1 = 2r + 2$ elements of $X' \& Y'$ between $e_1, e_2, \ldots, e_r$.

### Case 2: $e_r$ is from $Y$
We can add the element $e_0$ from $Y$ preceding $e_1$ and the element $e_{r+1}$ from $X$ following $e_r$. Then elements from $X'$ and $Y'$ lying between $e_1, e_2, \ldots, e_r$ come from elements of $X'$ lying between $h + 1$ elements of $X$ and elements of $Y'$ lying between $j + 1$ elements of $Y$. Therefore we have altogether $(2h + 1) + (2j + 1) = 2r + 2$ elements.

That completes the proof. $\qquad\square$

### Lemma 5.5
Let $X$ be a good sampler for $X'$ and $Y$ be a good sampler for $Y'$. Also presume

that $X$, $X'$, $Y$ and $Y'$ are sorted sequences. Then $reduce(X \& Y)$ is a good sampler for $reduce(X' \& Y')$.

*Proof*
Let $Z = reduce(X \& Y)$ and $Z' = reduce(X' \& Y')$. Consider $k + 1$ consecutive elements $e_1, e_2, \ldots, e_{k+1}$ of $Z$. There are $4k + 1$ elements of $X \& Y$ which lie between $e_1, e_2, \ldots, e_{k+1}$ including $e_1$ and $e_{k+1}$. According to the previous lemma there are at most $8k + 4$ elements of $X' \& Y'$ between these $4k + 1$ elements $(r = 4k + 1)$. We take each fourth element when reducing the sequence, hence there are at most $(8k + 4)/4 = 2k + 1$ elements of $X' \& Y'$ between $e_1, e_2, \ldots, e_{k+1}$. This completes the proof.     □

The algorithm is described in terms of a complete binary tree with $n$ leaves. We assume, for simplicity, that $n$ (the number of elements) is a power of 2. In the course of the algorithm the nodes of the tree will contain sorted sets of elements. Initially the $i$th leaf contains the one-element sequence consisting of the $i$th element of the sequence to be sorted. Non-leaf nodes contain empty sets. By $val_v$ we denote the sequence associated with node $v$. Let $T_v$ be the subtree rooted at $v$ and $list_v$ be the list of elements stored initially at the leaves of $T_v$. The task of node $v$ is to sort the sequence $list_v$. The sequence $val_v$ will always be a sorted subsequence of $list_v$. We say that node $v$ is complete if and only if $val_v = list_v$. Otherwise $v$ is said to be incomplete. We describe how the algorithm works by explaining how it works for a typical internal node $v$.

Node $v$ receives from its left son a stream of sorted sequences $X_1, X_2, \ldots, X_r$. Similarly it receives from its right son the stream of sorted sequences $Y_1, Y_2, \ldots, Y_r$, receiving $X_i$ with $Y_i$. Consequently node $v$ produces, as well as an internal stream of values ($val_v$), the output stream of sorted sequences $Z_1, Z_2, \ldots, Z_{r+1}$. In each of these sequences the size of the next object is twice as big as the size of the preceding one.

If $X$ and $Y$ are sorted sequences input to $v$, then the internal and output values of $v$ are computed as described in figure 5.7. If $v$ is incomplete then every fourth element of $val_v$ is sent up. During the first step after $v$ becomes complete, every second element is sent up whilst in the step after that every element is sent up (for complete nodes $v$, the operation *reduce* is modified dynamically).

According to lemma 5.5, the following (main) invariant of the algorithm is preserved.

*Main invariant:* if each $X_i$ is a good sampler of $X_{i+1}$, and each $Y_i$ is a good sampler of $Y_{i+1}$ then each $Z_i$ is a good sampler of $Z_{i+1}$. The sizes of $X_i$, $Y_i$ and

$Z_i$ are, respectively, half the sizes of $X_{i+1}$, $Y_{i+1}$ and $Z_{i+1}$. The sizes of $X_1$, $Y_1$ and $Z_1$ are each 1.

Notice that lemma 5.5 works if, for the operation *reduce*, we take every fourth element. However, in the penultimate step we take every second element, and in the last step we take every element. Thus, if *val* is the last value of $val_v$, then $Z_{r-1}$ is obtained by taking every fourth element of *val* whilst $Z_r$ is obtained by taking every second element. Moreover, $Z_{r+1} = val$. Then (obviously) $Z_{r-1}$ is a good sampler for $Z_r$, and $Z_r$ is a good sampler for $Z_{r+1}$.

Figure 5.8 shows the local computation at node $v$ with $|list_v| = 8$. In step $i$ the inputs are the sorted sequences $X_i$ and $Y_i$.

The whole tree of processing nodes is synchronised as follows. If $X$ and $Y$ are inputs to $v$ at time $t$ then $reduce(merge(X, Y))$ is the input from $v$ to its father at time $t + 1$. In other words if *val* is the value associated with $v$ then $reduce(val)$ is first sent to the father and then $val \leftarrow merge(X, Y)$ is computed. Hence the output stream is shifted in time with respect to the input stream as follows.

$$X_1, X_2, X_3, X_4, \ldots, X_r$$
$$Z_1, Z_2, \ldots, Z_{r-2}, Z_{r-1}, Z_r, Z_{r+1}$$

Therefore, if node $x$ finishes its output stream at time $t$, then its father $v$ finishes its output stream at time $t + 3$. The height of the tree is $\log n$. Hence the total number of stages is $3 \log n$. In one stage the processors associated with each active (incomplete) node perform simultaneously according to figure 5.7. After $3 \log n$ stages, the root will contain the whole set of $n$ elements as a sorted sequence. This presumes that each *mergewithhelp* operation takes O(1) time. Let us estimate the number of processors. We need O($|val_v|$) processors for each node $v$. However we need processors only for incomplete nodes $v$. It is easily

*Figure 5.7.* The local action of processing streams of sorted sequences. First $val_v$ is computed, and then the output to the father

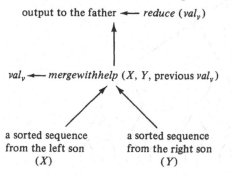

output to the father ◀— *reduce* ($val_v$)

$val_v$ ◀— *mergewithhelp* ($X$, $Y$, previous $val_v$)

a sorted sequence   a sorted sequence
from the left son    from the right son
      ($X$)                  ($Y$)

seen that the sum of $|val_v|$ over all incomplete nodes $v$ is $O(n)$. The typical structure of the capacities of $|val_v|$ is illustrated in figure 5.9.

We have almost finished our presentation of Cole's algorithm. It works in logarithmic time with $O(n)$ processors. However we should look more carefully

*Figure 5.8.* The history of the computation associated with a node $v$, starting from the moment when its input sequences are non-empty. Node $v$ sends every fourth element of the computed sequence up to its father until such time as $v$ becomes complete. This happens in step 3. Then, in step 4, $v$ sends every second element up, whilst in step 5 every element is sent up. This guarantees that, in the stream sent to the father of $v$, each sequence (if it is not the last) is succeeded by a sequence of twice the size. In steps 4 and 5, because $v$ is complete, $v$ ignores its inputs

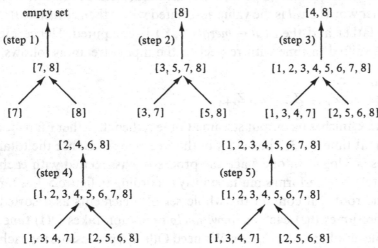

*Figure 5.9.* The typical structure of sizes of values (sequences) associated with the nodes

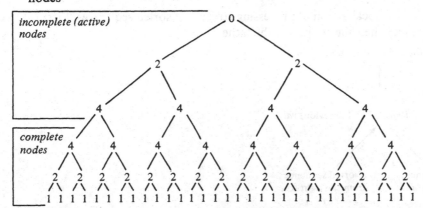

at our application of the operation *mergewithhelp*. The crucial point is that the merging of the sequences $J$ and $K$ with the help of $L$ can be done in O(1) time. The essential condition that $L$ is a good sampler of $J$ and $K$ is satisfied because of the main invariant. We compute $mergewithhelp(X_{i+1}, Y_{i+1}, X_i \& Y_i)$. In other words $L = X_i \& Y_i$, $J = X_{i+1}$ and $K = Y_{i+1}$. $L$ is a good sampler of $J$ and $K$ because of lemma 5.3. In order to complete the proof of the complexity claim we need to prove the technical condition of lemma 5.2. That is, we need to know the crossranks $R[L, J]$, $R[L, K]$, $R[J, L]$, $R[K, L]$. The following invariant helps with this.

*Auxiliary invariant:* if $[S_1, S_2, \ldots, S_p]$ is a stream of input or output sequences for a given internal node $v$ then the corresponding stream of crossranks $R[S_{i+1}, S_i]$ is known.

We assume that for each sorted sequence $S$ we know the crossrank $R[S, S]$. In other words we know the index of each element in the sorted sequence. This is computed as a part of the representation of the sorted sequence $S$. We need some technical lemmas at this point.

## Lemma 5.6

If $S = [b_1, b_2, \ldots, b_k]$ is a sorted sequence then the rank of a given element $a$ in $S$ can be computed in O(1) time using O(k) processors on a P-RAM.

## Proof

Take $b_0 = -\infty$ and $b_{k+1} = +\infty$. Then the required rank is computed as follows.

> **for** all $i$, $0 \leqslant i \leqslant k$, **in parallel do if** $b_i < a \leqslant b_{i+1}$ **then** $rank \leftarrow i$

There are no write conflicts here because only one processor (corresponding to the index $i$) will fix the value of *rank*. This completes the proof. □

## Lemma 5.7

If we have the three sorted sequences $S_1$, $S_2$ and $S$, where $S = S_1 \& S_2$ and $S_1 \cap S_2 = \varnothing$, then we can compute $R[S_1, S_2]$ and $R[S_2, S_1]$ in O(1) time with $O(|S|)$ processors.

## Proof

We assume that whenever we have a sorted sequence $S$ then we know also the crossrank $R[S, S]$, stored in an array. That is, we know the index of each element and we know what the $i$th element is. Then, since $rank(a, S_2) = rank(a, S_1 \& S_2) - rank(a, S_1)$, the lemma follows trivially. □

**Lemma 5.8**

Suppose that we have the sorted sequences $X, Y, U = X \& Y, X'$ and $Y'$. Let $X$ be a good sampler of $X'$ and $Y$ be a good sampler of $Y'$. Given the crossranks $R[X', X]$ and $R[Y', Y]$, then we can compute the crossranks $R[X', U]$, $R[Y', U]$, $R[U, X']$ and $R[U, Y']$ in O(1) time using O($|X| + |Y|$) processors on a P-RAM.

**Proof**

We show first how $R[X', U]$ may be computed. Figure 5.10 illustrates the computation. Let $X = [a_1, a_2, \ldots, a_k]$. We partition the sequence $X'$ into segments $X'(1), \ldots, X'(k + 1)$, where $X'(1)$ is the set of elements of $X'$ lying between $-\infty$ and $a_1$, $X'(2)$ is the set of elements of $X'$ lying between $a_1$ and $a_2$ and so on. Such a partition is easily done in O(1) time with O($|X|$) processors because we know $R[X', X]$. Let $U(i)$ be the sequence of all elements of $Y$ which lie between $a_{i-1}$ and $a_i$ in $U$ (we take $a_0 = -\infty$ and $a_{k+1} = +\infty$). We compute the rank of $x$ in $U$ (denoted by $rank(x, U)$) for each element $x$ of $X'$ as follows.

> **for** all $i$, $1 \leqslant i \leqslant k + 1$, **in parallel do**
>    **for** all $x \in X'(i)$ **do**
>      **begin**
>      compute $rank(x, U(i))$ {use the method of lemma 5.6}
>      $rank(x, U) \leftarrow i + rank(x, U(i))$
>      **end**

For each $i$ we use $|U(i)|$ processors. Altogether we therefore require O($|U|$) processors. The time is O(1) because $X$ is a good sampler of $X'$ (the size of each $X'(i)$ is therefore bounded by 3). We have therefore computed $R[X', U]$. We can compute $R[Y', U]$ in similar fashion.

Now we see how $R[X, X']$ and $R[Y, Y']$ can be computed. Consider an element $a_i$ from $X$ and take the minimal element $a'$ in $X'(i + 1)$. The rank of $a_i$ in $X'$ is the same as the rank of $a'$ in $X'$. This rank is already computed as a part

*Figure 5.10.* The computation of $R[X', U]$

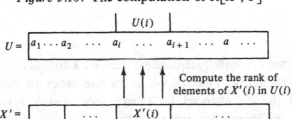

of the representation of the sorted sequence $X'$. Hence we can compute $rank(a_i, X')$ in O(1) time using one processor. Similarly we can compute the rank of each element of $Y$ in $Y'$. $U = X \& Y$, hence the computation of $R[U, X']$ requires the computation of the rank of each element of $X$ in $X'$ and of each element of $Y$ in $X'$. The first ranks are already computed. We show how to compute the rank of each element $a$ of $Y$ in $X'$. However we can easily compute the rank of each element $a$ in $Y$ in $X$ (according to lemma 5.7). Then we can compute $rank(a, X')$ using $rank(a, X)$ and $R[X, X']$. In this way we compute $R[U, X']$ in O(1) time with O($|U|$) processors. We can compute $R[U, Y']$ by a similar means. This completes the proof. □

Now we can finish the description of Cole's algorithm. Suppose that we are computing $mergewithhelp(X_{i+1}, Y_{i+1}, X_i \& Y_i)$. Let $L = X_i \& Y_i$, $J = X_{i+1}$ and $K = Y_{i+1}$. We should know the crossranks $R[L, J]$, $R[L, K]$, $R[J, L]$ and $R[K, L]$. However the auxiliary-invariant implies that we know the crossranks $R[J, X_i]$ and $R[K, Y_i]$. Using the algorithm from lemma 5.8 with $X = X_i$, $Y = Y_i$, $X' = J$, $Y' = K$, and $U = L$ we can compute all the required crossranks in O(1) time with O($|L|$) processors.

Finally we explain how the auxiliary invariant is preserved. We show how to compute $R[next, previous]$, where $previous = reduce(X_i \& Y_i)$ and $next = reduce(X_{i+1} \& Y_{i+1})$. Figure 5.11 illustrates the situation.

We already know the rank of each element of $X_{i+1}$ and $Y_{i+1}$ in $X_i \& Y_i = L$. It is easy now to compute the rank of each element of $X_{i+1}$ and $Y_{i+1}$ in $reduce(X_i \& Y_i)$. Hence we can compute $R[X_{i+1} \& Y_{i+1}, previous]$ within the stated complexity. This automatically gives $R[next, previous]$, because $next$ is a subset of $X_{i+1} \& Y_{i+1}$. This completes the description of the algorithm. We therefore have the following theorem.

Figure 5.11

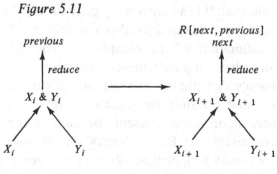

*Theorem 5.9*

Using $n$ processors, $n$ keys can be sorted in $O(\log n)$ time on a P-RAM.

Cole's algorithm is without write conflicts. However there are read conflicts (which are allowed in our P-RAM model). Such conflicts appear in the computational statement in lemma 5.6. There many processors simultaneously read the same value of an element $a$ (in order to compute its rank in a sequence in constant time). Cole[13] has also described a more complicated version of his algorithm in which no read conflicts occur. This version of the algorithm is therefore implementable on an EREW P-RAM. Cole's algorithm (in its present version) is not a sorting network. The sequence of comparisons is not fixed for a given size $n$. This sequence can depend on the actual values of the data.

## 5.3 A theoretical optimal sorting network: Paterson's version of the algorithm of Ajtai, Komlos and Szemeredi

We present here a sketch of the sorting network of Ajtai, Komlos and Szemeredi as simplified and improved by Paterson.[21] This section is the most advanced and the most theoretical in the book. It is included because of the celebrated nature of the three Hungarians' algorithm. However, in view of the fact that the model of computation employed here is outside the main stream of the book, some readers may prefer to regard this section as optional. The general sketch presented here provides sufficient insight for an understanding of the basic ideas behind the algorithm.

The algorithm of Ajtai, Komlos and Szemeredi,[3] which we also refer to as the AKS algorithm, was the first sorting network to achieve $\log n$ depth. The algorithm was based on the fact that using special bipartite graphs (called expanders) we can split a sequence into two halves in $O(1)$ time. Verification of the AKS algorithm is rather complicated. It is a surprisingly general rule that the most difficult part of analysing many advanced parallel algorithms is the correctness proof and not the estimation of the complexity. The AKS algorithm is commonly thought of as being a purely theoretical achievement. In this respect it is similar to Strassen's algorithm for the fast multiplication of matrices. It is rather too intricate and certainly the huge constants in the complexity make it an impractical algorithm at present. Because of these constants, for problem sizes of practical interest, Batcher's networks are faster.

We present Paterson's version of the AKS algorithm. Within this ingenious version of the algorithm the complexity constants are considerably reduced.

However, they remain impractically large, The AKS algorithm was a milestone in the theory of parallel sorting networks. Once the asymptotic $O(\log n)$ parallel time was achieved (with $n$ processors) there was and remains the possibility of future improvements which may close the gap between its theoretical importance and its practical use.

The algorithm uses an interesting family of bipartite graphs, called $(k, \varepsilon)$-expanders. Let $G$ be a bipartite graph. The two sets of nodes of the bipartition are $A$ and $B$, and we require that $|A| = |B|$. By $\Gamma_X$ we denote the set of all vertices adjacent to vertices in the subset $X$. Then $G$ is a $(k, \varepsilon)$-expander if it is $k$-regular (that is, every vertex has exactly $k$ neighbours) and if for each $X$ such that $A \supseteq X$ or $B \supseteq X$ we have that $|\Gamma_X| \geq ((1 - \varepsilon)/\varepsilon) \min\{\varepsilon |A|, |X|\}$. In this sketch we omit the difficult proof of the fact (see [5, 15, 19]) that there exists a $(k, \varepsilon)$-expander for every $\varepsilon > 0$. For fixed $\varepsilon$, $k$ is generally a very large constant. We are essentially interested in cases where $(1 - \varepsilon)/\varepsilon > 1$. Then every sufficiently small subset of vertices $X$ is 'expanded' $(1 - \varepsilon)/\varepsilon$ times. By this we mean that $|\Gamma_X|/|X|$ is $(1 - \varepsilon)/\varepsilon$. Figure 5.12 illustrates this.

Another common definition of an expander is as follows. A graph $G$ with maximum vertex degree $k$ is a $(k, \beta_1, \beta_2)$-expander if for every subset $X$ of vertices $|\Gamma_X| \geq \beta_2 |X|$ and if $|X| \leq \beta_1 n$. In other words every sufficiently small set of nodes has 'many' neighbours. For bipartite graphs the definition we employ is equivalent to this if we take $\beta_2 = (1 - \varepsilon)/\varepsilon$ and $\beta_1 = \varepsilon$.

We assume that a given expander is partitioned into $k$ disjoint perfect matchings $M_1, \ldots, M_k$. This is always possible because, as we saw in subsection 2.4.1, every bipartite graph with maximum vertex degree $k$ has a $k$ edge-colouring. Then the edges of each colour form a disjoint matching. The

Figure 5.12. The small subset $X$ of $A$ is 'expanded' into a larger subset $\Gamma_X$ of $B$

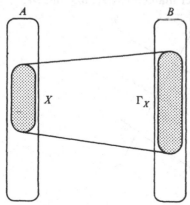

expander of figure 5.13 is so partitioned in figure 5.14. Notice that for $G$ of figure 5.13 $|\Gamma_X|/|X| = (1 - \varepsilon)/\varepsilon = 3$ and so $\varepsilon = \frac{1}{4}$. Let $X = \{x_1, \ldots, x_n\}$ where $x_i \in A$ for $i \leqslant n/2$ and $x_i \in B$ for $i > n/2$. Also $|A| + |B| = n$. For a particular set of disjoint perfect matchings we construct the so-called splitting network for the set $X$ as follows. In step $i$, $1 \leqslant i \leqslant k$, the operations *compare-exchange* are performed between initial positions of elements joined by an edge from $M_i$. The splitting network corresponding to the perfect matchings of figure 5.14 is presented in figure 5.15.

The splitting of $X$ into two subsets, $X_1$ and $X_2$, as indicated in figure 5.15, is 'correct' if and only if each element of $X_1$ is no larger than any element of $X_2$. In this sense, any element wrongly placed by the splitting network is said to be a stranger in $X_1$ or $X_2$. Observe that the splitting performed in figure 5.15 using our expander graph in not correct. A stranger appears in each of $X_1$ and $X_2$. However, such splittings are always, as we see in lemma 5.10 and within a

*Figure 5.13.* The $(3,\frac{1}{4})$-expander $G$ with $|A| = |B| = 4$

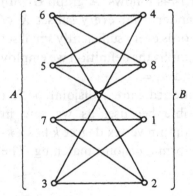

*Figure 5.14.* The partition of $G$ into three perfect matchings $M_1$, $M_2$ and $M_3$

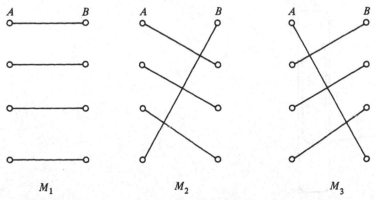

known tolerance, approximately correct. A splitting which is not correct is therefore called an approximate splitting.

The comparator network (that is, a network of *compare-exchange* modules) which performs a splitting of the set of $n$ elements according to the $(k, \varepsilon)$-expander $G$ is called an $\varepsilon$-halver. Lemma 5.11 expresses the main property of $\varepsilon$-halvers.

*Lemma 5.10*

Let $G$ be a $(k, \varepsilon)$-expander. After performing a splitting of $X$ using $G$, the number of strangers in $X_1$ (or in $X_2$) is at most $\varepsilon n/2$. Thus, the total number of strangers is at most $\varepsilon n$.

*Proof*

Let $\{1, 2, \ldots, n\}$ be the set of keys exchanged between the nodes of the expander $G$ during the splitting procedure. Also let $S$ be the subset of those elements of $X_1$ which are strangers. For $G$ of figure 5.13, given the initial distribution of keys shown in that figure, $S$ consists only of the key 5 (see figure 5.15). All elements of $S$ are in the range $(n/2 + 1 .. n)$. After termination of the splitting procedure let $\Gamma_S$ be the keys placed at those nodes in $B$ which are adjacent to nodes containing the elements of $S$. Every element of $\Gamma_S$ is greater than some element of $S$. Hence all elements of $\Gamma_S$ are also in the range $(n/2 + 1 .. n)$. We therefore have the inequality that $|S| + |\Gamma_S| \leqslant n/2$.

*Figure 5.15.* The approximate splitting of $X = [6, 5, 7, 3, 4, 8, 1, 2]$ into $X_1 = [3, 5, 1, 2]$ and $X_2 = [6, 8, 7, 4]$. The element 5 is a stranger in $X_1$ and 4 is a stranger in $X_2$

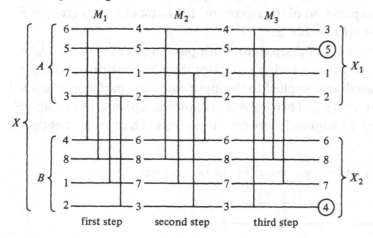

Two cases need now to be considered. First suppose that $|S| \leqslant \varepsilon |A| = \varepsilon n/2$. Then it follows from the definition of a $(k, \varepsilon)$-expander that $|\Gamma_S| \geqslant ((1 - \varepsilon)/\varepsilon)|S|$. Taking the inequality along with $|S| + |\Gamma_S| \leqslant n/2$ it follows that $|S| \leqslant \varepsilon n/2$. Thus in this case the number of strangers is as stated by the theorem. Secondly suppose that $|S| \geqslant \varepsilon |A| = \varepsilon n/2$. In this case $|\Gamma_S| \geqslant (1 - \varepsilon)n/2$. Again, from taking this inequality along with $|S| + |\Gamma_S| \leqslant n/2$ it follows that $|S| \leqslant \varepsilon n/2$, and the number of strangers is once more as stated by the theorem. This completes the proof.                                                                                  $\square$

The following lemma is proved in the same way as lemma 5.10.

*Lemma 5.11*

Let $G$ be a $(k, \varepsilon)$-expander. After performing a splitting of $X$ using $G$, the number of elements from the $K \leqslant n/2$ smallest (largest) in the ordering which are strangers in $X_2$ ($X_1$) is at most $\varepsilon K$.                                        $\square$

We shall use a more complicated comparator network introduced by Paterson and called a $(\lambda, \varepsilon, \varepsilon_0)$-separator. This separator returns a partition of the $n$ input values into four parts called $FL$, $CL$, $CR$, and $FR$ of respective sizes $\lambda n/2$, $(1 - \lambda)n/2$, $(1 - \lambda)n/2$ and $\lambda n/2$. Figure 5.16 depicts this division of the output vector into the parts 'far-left' ($FL$), 'centre-left' ($CL$), 'centre-right' ($CR$) and 'far-right' ($FR$). The separator produces an approximation to a sorting of the inputs which would place them in ascending order (left to right) in the vector of figure 5.16. Again, we use the term 'stranger' to describe an element which (after an application of the separator) appears outside its 'natural' division ($FL$, $CL$, $CR$ or $FR$) of the output vector.

A $(\lambda, \varepsilon, \varepsilon_0)$-separator has the following properties. It is an $\varepsilon_0$-halver and in addition, after an application of the separator, the number of strangers in $FR$ or in $FL$ is at most $\varepsilon |FR| = \varepsilon \lambda n/2$.

We shall be using a $(\lambda, \varepsilon, \varepsilon_0)$-separator with parameters $\varepsilon_0 = \frac{1}{72}$, $\varepsilon = \frac{1}{18}$ and $\lambda = \frac{1}{8}$. Figure 5.17 shows how such a separator may be constructed using $\varepsilon_0$-halvers. First an $\varepsilon_0$-halver is applied to the input causing a partition into a left half ($L_1$) and a right half ($R_2$). Then halvers are applied separately to $L_1$ and $R_1$ and so on as figure 5.17 implies. There are three levels of halvers in that figure.

*Figure 5.16.* The partitioning induced by the $(\lambda, \varepsilon, \varepsilon_0)$-separator

| $\lambda n/2$ | $(1 - \lambda)n/2$ | $(1-\lambda)\,n/2$ | $\lambda n/2$ |
|---|---|---|---|
| $FL$ | $CL$ | $CR$ | $FR$ |

In general, for $x$ levels and using the same form of construction, we obtain a $(2^{1-x}, x\varepsilon_0, \varepsilon_0)$-separator.

Precisely in order to introduce gently some of the notions required later, we first describe a solution to a somewhat contrived (partial) sorting problem. Given a vector of $n$ elements, this *partial sorting problem* is to output a sorted subsequence of $O(\sqrt{n})$ elements. In fact this length is not important. What is important is that the algorithm has certain features in common with the algorithm for complete sorting which will be the main subject of this section. Consider a $(\Delta, \mu, \mu_0)$-separator with parameters satisfying the following partial sorting problem inequality.

(*I0*)): $\mu\Delta + \mu_0 \leqslant ((1 - \Delta)/2)\Delta/2$

for very small $\Delta$. We shall later determine what small means here.

We now construct a binary tree and we associated with each of its nodes a bag containing some of the elements to be sorted.

**Algorithm** {partial sorting}
**begin**
{At time 0, all the elements to be sorted are in the bag at the root of the tree
    and only the root (that is, level 0) is active. At time $t$ only level $t$ is active}
**while** (the size of each bag at the active level) $> c$

                            {$c$ is a constant to be determined later} **do**

*Figure 5.17.* The construction of a $(\frac{1}{8}, \frac{1}{18}, \frac{1}{72})$-separator using $\frac{1}{72}$-halvers

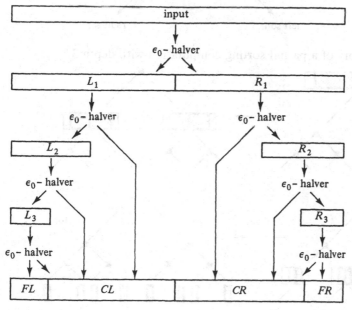

**for** all bags at the active level **in parallel do**
 **begin**
 apply the separator to the bag
 {The bag is now partitioned into parts *FL*, *CL*, *CR* and *FR*}
 pass *CL* to the left son and *CR* to the right son of the node and discard
   parts *FR* and *FL*
 {Figure 5.18 illustrates this}
 **end**
{The bags at the active level are now 'sufficiently' small (smaller than the
 constant $c$). Let $S_i$ be the contents of the $i$th bag at this final level}
**for** all sets $S_i$ **in parallel do** sort $S_i$
{This sorting takes constant time (because the sets are of constant bounded
 size). We can use one of Batcher's networks from section 5.1 for this}
**output** $S_1 S_2 S_3 \ldots$ {the concatenation of $S_1, S_2, S_3, \ldots$}
**end** of the algorithm

The partial sorting algorithm is schematically illustrated in figure 5.19 for a
computation with depth 3.

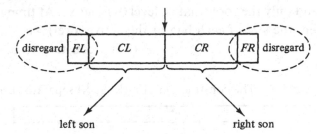

*Figure 5.18*                    left son                    right son

*Figure 5.19.* A history of a partial sorting computation with depth 3

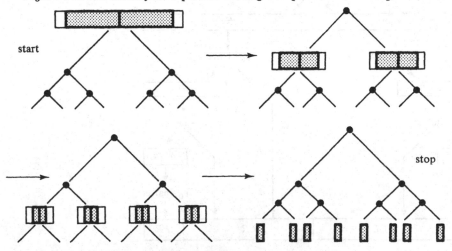

*Theorem 5.10*

There exists a value for the constant $c$, of the partial sorting algorithm, such that the algorithm obtains a sorted subsequence of size $O(\sqrt{n})$ in $O(\log n)$ time.

*Proof*

To each bag of the tree there corresponds a natural interval of the elements in sorted order. For example, the root bag corresponds to the complete set of elements, its left and right sons correspond to the left and right halves of the ordered sets and so on. Figure 5.20 illustrates this. A given element $x$ is a stranger in a given bag of the tree if $x$ is not within the natural interval corresponding to this bag.

The main invariant of the algorithm is

> *invariant:* the proportion of strangers in a given bag at the active level is at most $\Delta/2$

We first prove that this invariant holds. Initially the invariant holds because it refers to the root bag where there can be no strangers. Assume that the invariant holds at the active level $t$. Let us consider a bag $B$ with actual contents $S$ at this level. We calculate the number of strangers which may appear in a son $B'$ of $B$. These strangers arise from two sources.

(i)  $B$ contains strangers whose number is bounded by the invariant. If any of these are sent to $B'$, they will continue to be strangers. It follows from the invariant that, if the contents of $B$ were sorted, then these strangers would all appear in $FL$ and/or $FR$. Hence, after the application of the separator, the number of these strangers that are sent to $B'$ is certainly bounded by $\mu(|FL| + |FR|) = \mu\Delta|S|$. The other strangers in $B$ will be contained in $FR$ or $FL$ and disregarded.

(ii)  $B'$ will also receive strangers from $B$ because the separator will place some elements of $B$ in the wrong half of the approximately sorted vector that it

*Figure 5.20.* The natural intervals for two bags are indicated in the tree on the left. The set of elements in sorted order is $\{1, 3, 4, 6, 7, 8, 9, 10\}$. Elements 7 and 3 are strangers in the tree on the right

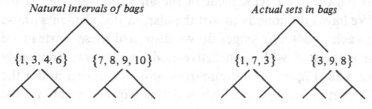

| *Natural intervals of bags* | *Actual sets in bags* |

produces. There are at most $\mu_0|S|$ of these. Hence the total number of strangers in a son $B'$ of $B$ will be bounded by $\mu\Delta|S| + \mu_0|S|$. The number of elements sent to $B'$ will be $|S|(1 - \Delta)/2$. We have to prove that the proportion of strangers in $B'$ is at most $\Delta/2$. It is enough to prove $\mu\Delta|S| + \mu_0|S| \leqslant (|S|(1 - \Delta)/2)\Delta/2$. However, this is equivalent to partial sorting problem inequality (I0), and so if (I0) holds then so does the invariant. We can take $\mu$ to be very small compared with $\Delta$ to satisfy (I0). Let $A = (1 - \Delta)/2$ and $A' = 1/A$. A bag at level $t$ has size $nA^t$. Let $c_0$ be the bag size at time $t_0$ when $c_0\Delta/2 < 1$. Then there are no strangers at time $t_0$, because the number in each bag is less than 1. It follows that the algorithm produces a sorted subsequence of the input. Let us consider the length of this sequence. Now $t_0 > \log_{A'}(n\Delta/2)$ and the number of bags at time $t$ is $2^t$. It is then easy to see (taking the length $L$ of the sequence to be at least the number of bags) that $L = \Omega(n^k)$, where $k = \log_{A'} 2$. We can then fix $\Delta$ (which fixes $A'$) so that $k \geqslant \frac{1}{2}$ and then $L = O(\sqrt{n})$. In fact we could decrease the value of $\Delta$ making $k > \frac{1}{2}$. Observe that $A' > 2$; however, $A' \to 2$ when $\Delta \to 0$. This completes the proof.                                                                    □

Notice that the proof above is incomplete. We analysed and designed the algorithm as if the sizes of the bags were real numbers of infinite precision. However, they are actually integers and the effect of rounding should be considered. We return to this problem later when analysing the (complete) sorting network. The theorem is of no independent value; its main purpose was to demonstrate how separators work, how to calculate proportions and to prepare the reader for the more complicated construction of the complete sorting algorithm.

We proceed now to the construction of the network for *complete sorting*. The main theorem in this section is the following.

*Theorem 5.11*
There exists a sorting network with $O(\log n)$ depth.

The rest of this chapter is devoted to a sketch of the proof of theorem 5.11. The network we describe is Paterson's version of the network of Ajtai, Komlos and Szemeredi.[3] This network is a refinement of the algorithm for the partial sorting problem. We have additionally to sort the disregarded elements (those in $FL$ and $FR$ for each node). No longer do we disregard these. Instead we modify the action associated with each active node which was previously described in figure 5.18. Figure 5.21 summarises (for one active node) the modification to the partial sorting algorithm which is required to obtain the complete sorting algorithm. The following statement also defines the modification.

> **for** all active nodes $v$ **in parallel do**
> **begin**
> partition the elements of the bag associated with $v$ using a $(\Delta, \mu, \mu_0)$-separator
> {We shall presume the following parameters: $\Delta = \frac{1}{8}$, $\mu = \frac{1}{18}$ and $\mu_0 = \frac{1}{72}$}
> send $CL$ and $CR$ respectively to the left and right son of $v$
> return $FL$ and $FR$ to the father of $v$
> **end**

Figure 5.22 schematically shows three initial stages of a computation on the network. A further modification concerns a special situation at the root of the binary tree. For technical reasons (which we shall return to) an artificial new root-node (called the *cold storage*) is added to the tree. The (normal) root will send and will receive elements from the cold storage. Another special situation occurs at the bottom nodes and we shall be explaining that situation later. We take the $(\Delta, \mu, \mu_0)$-separator from figure 5.17 and hence the parameters are $\Delta = \frac{1}{8}$, $\mu = \frac{1}{18}$ and $\mu_0 = \frac{1}{72}$.

We have specified Paterson's network except for the boundary situations at the root and at bottom nodes. As in the partial sorting algorithm there is a bag associated with each node. Within the specifications to be made, the capacities of bags can be non-integers whilst the actual sizes of bags are integral. At the beginning, in order to simplify the calculations and to provide some intuition, let us disregard the difference between the actual sizes and the capacities of bags.

*Figure 5.21.* The action associated with an active (non-bottom) node in the final algorithm. A proportion $(=\Delta)$ of elements is sent up and all other elements are sent down

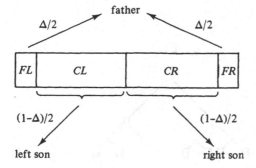

It will be convenient to have some simple formula for the capacities of the bags. Let $r_t$ denote the capacity of the root at time $t$. For each active bag which is above the bottom level, we require the following invariants.

(I1) The capacity of a bag at level $d$ is $r_t A^d$, where $A = 3$
(I2) $r_{t+1} = \beta r_t$, where $\beta = \frac{43}{48}$

These invariants work well when the tree is upwards infinite (we 'assume' levels of the tree above the root of $-1, -2, \ldots$. The initial root then becomes an internal node). We can make such an assumption if we can guarantee that the cold storage stores the same number of elements whose natural location is the subtree rooted at the root as the nodes of the infinite tree above the root.

However, if the root is active then every second ancestor in the infinite branch up to the 'root' is active. The cold storage should then be $UP_{odd}(r) = B_2/4 + B_4/16 + \cdots$ (see figure 5.23), where $r$ is the capacity of the root. Hence

$$UP_{odd}(r) = r/(4A^2) + r/(16A^4) + \cdots$$

because the invariant implies that the capacity of the $i$th bag above the root is $r/A^i$. If the root is not active then the cold storage should be

$$UP_{even}(r) = r/(2A) + r/(8A^3) + \cdots$$

*Figure 5.22.* Three stages of Paterson's sorting network. Initially all elements are at the root or in cold storage and only the root is active. Then odd and even levels are active alternatively

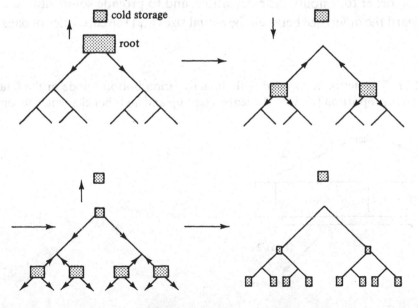

Therefore we maintain the capacity of the cold storage to be equal to $UP_{odd}(r)$ at odd stages and to $UP_{even}(r)$ at even stages. For the first (odd) stage only the root is active. Hence we maintain above the root the special cold storage node whose capacity allows us to make all calculations on the assumption that the tree is infinite upwards. The root treats the cold storage as though it were its father.

The same argument applies to every node of the tree. If the capacity of a non-bottom node $v$ is $B$ and there are actually $C$ elements in bags of $T_v$ (excluding $v$) then the number of elements whose natural location is in $T_v$ is

$UP_{even}(B) + B + C$ at stages when $v$ is active

and

$UP_{odd}(B) + C$ at other stages

The bags at the bottom level can have less elements than required; however, they send back the number of elements as if they were full. This implies that they send enough elements up and in the calculations (involving father nodes) we can assume that they have the number of elements according to the invariant, or that they do not have enough elements. However, in the latter case the level above will become the bottom level (because nothing will be sent down from the old bottom active level). This also proves that we have always one (possibly partially filled) bottom level.

Notice that this strategy would seem to run counter to intuition which would suggest that the bottom level should not move up. It can in fact happen that

*Figure 5.23.* If $C$ is the set of elements actually stored in the successors of $v$ and $B_i$ is the number of elements in the $i$th (bottom-up) ancestor of $v$ then the number of elements whose natural location is in the leaves of the subtree $T_v$ (rooted at $v$) is $|C| + B + B_1/2 + B_2/4 + B_3/8 + \cdots$

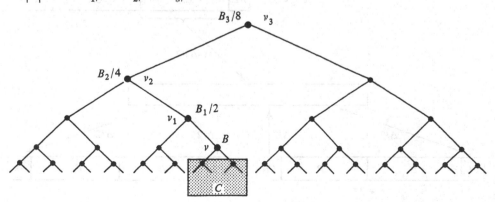

during some stages the bottom level oscillates between the same neighbouring levels.

The invariants I1 and I2 follow directly from our rule for distributing the elements in a given node. Figures 5.21 and 5.24 illustrate this distribution.

A main property of the algorithm is that after a logarithmic number of steps there will be no elements in the wrong half of the tree and the size of the root together with the cold storage will be bounded by a constant. At this moment we can split the tree into two trees and the same process will be repeated for these trees independently. Immediately after splitting, the two resulting subtrees will be at some advanced computational stage. To analyse this we introduce a concept of the measure of the strangeness of an element. We also estimate the number of elements with a given strangeness (a similar idea was used in the case of partial sorting).

The strangeness of some element in a given bag is defined as the number of steps up the tree from that bag towards the root which are needed to arrive at a bag within whose natural interval the element lies. Hence all elements in the root bag have strangeness 0. The strangeness of an element decreases (if it was positive) when the element is passed to the bag of the father. The strangeness of an element increases by 1 if the element is passed to the wrong son of a given node.

In figure 5.25 the natural location of element $i$ is the $i$th leaf. For example, element 14 has to be moved to the root (two steps up) to arrive at the node whose subtree contains the fourteenth leaf.

*Figure 5.24.* At time $t + 1$ the bag at level $d$ becomes active and its capacity becomes $2\Delta r_t \cdot 3^{d+1} + \frac{1}{2}(1 - \Delta)r_t \cdot 3^d$. Hence $r_{t+2} = Br_t$ and $B = 43/48$

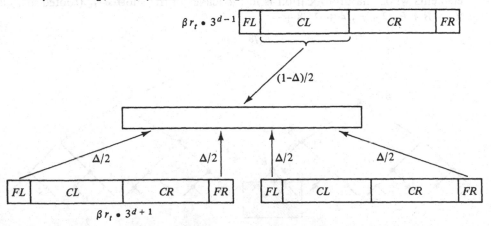

For any node $v$ and integer $j > 0$, we define $S_j(v)$ at a given stage to be the number of elements currently in the bag at $v$ with strangeness at least $j$. This is expressed as a proportion of the capacity of the bag. Let $s_j = f\delta^{j-1}$, where $f = \frac{1}{36}$, $\delta = \frac{1}{40}$ and $j > 0$. Then the *main invariant* is

(I3) $\quad S_j(v) < s_j$

*Claim*
Invariant (I3) is preserved by the algorithm.

*Proof*
At the outset, the invariant is trivially true. Then all the elements are at the root or in cold storage and therefore have strangeness 0. Therefore assume that (I3) holds at some stage. Consider node $v$ whose bag has capacity $b$ and which immediately after this stage has capacity $B = \beta b$. Its parent has (before the given stage) capacity $b/A$ and both sons together have capacity $2bA$.

*Case 1: $j > 1$*
We have that $f < \Delta/2$. Hence the elements of non-zero strangeness would all be contained in $FL$ and $FR$ if the separation were perfect. However, due to the approximate ordering of the separator applied to the parent bag, at most a proportion $\mu$ of such elements will be placed in $CL$ or $CR$ and sent down.

Thus at most $\mu s_{j-1} b/A$ elements of strangeness $j - 1$ can pass to $v$. There are at most $2bAs_{j+1}$ elements sent from the sons to $v$ which will have strangeness $j$ in $v$. Let $S_j(v)$ be the proportion of the number of elements of strangeness at least $j$ in the bag of $v$ after performing the given stage. We have $S_j(v)\beta b <$

*Figure 5.25.* The bag at node $v$ has capacity $B = 3$. Elements 11 and 14 are of strangeness 2 and element 2 has strangeness 1. Hence there are $S_1 B$ elements of strangeness at least 1 and $S_2 B$ elements of strangeness at least 2 at $v$, where $S_1 = 1$ and $S_2 = \frac{2}{3}$

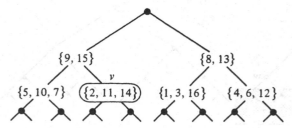

$2bAs_{j+1} + \mu s_{j-1}b/A$. It is a matter of simple calculation to derive the inequality

(In1)  $2bAs_{j+1} + \mu s_{j-1}b/A < s_j \beta b$

Hence for $j > 1$ we have that $S_j(v) < s_j$.

*Case 2: $j = 1$*

The situation now is more complicated. As before we can receive at most $2bAs_{j+1}$ elements from sons which can contribute to $S_j(v)$. Let $p$ be the father of $v$ and $w$ be the brother of $v$. For a node $z$, let $range_z$ denote the set of elements whose natural location is in the leaves of $T_z$. We estimate how many elements from $range_w$ can be in the bag of $p$. Only such elements can contribute to $S_1(v)$ passing from $p$ to its son $v$. Denote the number of these elements by $R$. We refer to figures 5.23 and 5.26; the latter is obtained by replacing $v$ by $w$ in the former.

Node $w$ is not active. Its capacity is $b$ (the same as that of its brother $v$); however, it actually contains no elements. We have that $|range_w| = |C| + UP_{even}(b) = |C| + (b/A)/2 + UP_{odd}(b/A)$, where $C$ is the number of elements currently in $T_w$ (see figures 5.23 and 5.26).

The crucial point is to estimate the number of elements from $range_w$ which can be in the bag of $p$ instead of being in $C$. It is equivalent to estimate the total number of elements out of $range_w$ which are in the bags of $T_w$. Any such element at a node $v_1$ in $T_w$ has strangeness at least $dist(v_1, w) + 1$. Hence the proportion of such elements at this node is bounded (from above) by $s_{j+1}$, where $j = dist(v_1, w)$. There are $2^j bA^j$ elements at the nodes $v_1 \in T_w$ with $dist(v_1, w) = j$. They can have in total at most $2^j bA^j s_{j+1}$ elements out of $range_w$.

**Figure 5.26.** Node $p$ is active and its bag can have *too many* elements appropriate to $w$. $C$ is the set of elements currently in $T_w$. We need to estimate the number of elements in $C - range_w$. They can be in the bag of $p$

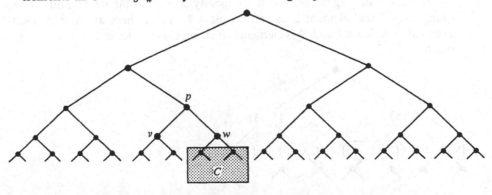

If we sum for all nodes in $T_w$ then we have at most $\sum 2^j b A^j s_{j+1} < 2f\delta bA/(1 - 4\delta^2 A^2)$ elements from $range_w$ which could be in the bag of $p$ instead of in $C$. Hence the number of elements in $p$ with strangeness 0 whose natural location should be in $T_w$ is bounded by $(b/A)/2 + 2f\delta bA/(1 - 4\delta^2 A^2) + UP_{odd}(b/A)$. Additionally at $p$ can be at most $s_1 b/A$ elements which are not in $range_v$ as strangers in $p$. Hence at $p$ there are at most

$$(b/A)/2 + 2f\delta bA/(1 - 4\delta^2 A^2) + UP_{odd}(b/A) + s_1 b/A$$

elements which are not in $range_v$. The rest are in $range_v$. We estimate how many elements outside $range_v$ can pass from $p$ to $v$ after applying the separator.

Now $2f\delta bA/(1 - 4\delta^2 A^2) + UP_{odd}(b/A) + s_1 b/A$ can pass to $v$ as an excess of half of the bag of $p$. Additionally $\mu_0 b/(2A)$ elements can pass because of the approximate nature of the 'sorting' of the separator. Together with strangers sent from the son (at most $2bAs_2$) this gives the following bound on the number of strangers which arrive at $v$.

(In2) $\quad 2f\delta bA/(1 - 4\delta^2 A^2) + UP_{odd}(b/A) + s_1 b/A + \mu_0 b/(2A) + 2bAs_2 < f\beta b$

It is an easy matter to prove this inequality with our parameters. Hence $S_1(v) < s_j$.

This completes the proof of the lemma. □

The root is at level 0. At odd stages the root bag is active, and only bags at even levels $2j$ can be active. The number of elements in a bag at level $2j$ is $rA^{2j}$, where $r$ is an actual size of the root bag. An element in a bag at level $2j$ is in the wrong half of the tree if and only if its strangeness is $2j$. Because $A\delta \leqslant 1$, the number of such elements in a bag at level $2j$ is bounded by

(In3) $\quad rA^{2j}S_{2j} < rA^{2j}s_{2j} \leqslant rA^2 f\delta$

Hence the number of these elements is less than 1 if $r \leqslant 1/(A^2 f\delta)$. The value $r = 160$ satisfies this. Thus, if the size of the root bag is at most 160, we know that there are no elements in a wrong half of the tree. The size of the cold storage is at this moment also bounded by 160. At such a stage we exactly separate the elements in cold storage and in the root bag into a left and a right half. The root and cold storage for each subtree (whose root is a son of the previous root) is formed from these halves. The reader can check that the sizes are correct here by checking with the formula for the size of the cold storage. The correctness of sizes of the separated parts follows from the fact that the cold storage simulates an infinite upward branch.

The root bag will be reduced to a size not exceeding 160 after a logarithmic number of stages. In each stage it decreases by a factor $\beta < 1$. Then the roots of two separated subtrees will have bag sizes bounded by a constant, and after $O(1)$ steps they will go below 160. Again we separate subtrees of the root in each tree. In this way a new root-splitting is performed at time intervals bounded by a constant and after logarithmic time we will be left with many subtrees whose sizes are bounded by a constant. Then we can apply to each subtree any sorting network which within this context will operate in $O(1)$ time to accomplish the final sorting. One of Batcher's networks described at the beginning of this chapter will be adequate for this.

We can estimate the total number of computational stages as follows. Theoretically the bags at level $\log n$ are initially of capacity $O(nA^{\log n})$. (Our logarithms are to the base 2.) At the outset of the computation they are empty. In the final step these bags contain one element each. Their capacity at stage $k$ is $(nA^{\log n}\beta^k) = O(1)$. This implies that the bound on the number $k$ of stages is $k < 17 \log n + O(1)$. The coefficient of $\log n$ is not big here. However, this constant does not include a very huge additional constant factor arising from the depth of the separators. It is this constant which makes the algorithm of little practical value. We regard any discussion of this constant as beyond the scope of this book. Paterson[21] introduced the new halvers briefly introduced here and has shown that the (total) constant is then under 6100. We also refer the reader to [5, 15, 19] for constructions of expanders.

We have specified the 'ideal' sizes of bags. However, these sizes can be non-integer, whereas the actual sizes are integer. Hence we have a problem of integer rounding. It is enough to show that the actual sizes can be very close to the ideal ones (the difference need not be bigger than 4). Then the crucial inequalities (In1), (In2), and (In3) can be maintained because the smallest non-bottom bag is the root bag, and it can always be kept big enough to absorb the effects of rounding. The bottom bags can be actually smaller (they can be partially filled and have less elements than their ideal capacity requires) but their capacity always exceeds the capacity of the root. The parameters $S_j$ are expressed as proportions of capacities of bags.

We indicate Paterson's resolution of the rounding problem. Assume that $n$ is an even number. It is also convenient and efficient that the actual number of elements in each bag be even. Paterson's recipe is as follows. Each ideally empty bag is actually empty. Whenever the ideal total content of some subtree rooted at a non-empty node is $x$ then the actual content is to be $2\lceil x/2 \rceil$. Suppose that for some non-empty node $v$, whose grandsons are $v_1, v_2, v_3, v_4$, the ideal content of $T_v$ is $x$ and the ideal content of each $T_{v_1}, \ldots, T_{v_4}$ is $y$. If the ideal and actual contents of the bag at $v$ are denoted by $b$ and $Z(b)$, respectively, then $b = x - 4y$, and $Z(b) = 2\lceil x/2 \rceil - 8\lceil y/2 \rceil$. Hence $b - 8 < Z(b) < b + 2$. It can be proved that such a close correspondence between the actual size $b$ and the ideal size $Z(b)$ for each non-empty bag solves the integer-rounding problem.

This completes the sketch of the proof of theorem 5.11.

### Bibliographic notes

The book of Knuth[17] is an excellent source of information concerning sorting networks. Our description of Batcher's sorting networks is from [25] and [27]. The first sorting network of depth $\log n$ was presented by Ajtai, Komlos and Szemeredi.[2,3] Our exposition follows a simplified version.[21] The construction of expanders is the most complicated part of the AKS algorithm, especially concerning the proofs of correctness of the constructed graphs. The literature on this subject is rich and is mathematically advanced.[5,15,19,20]

From the point of view of this book (which is largely concerned with P-RAM algorithms) Cole's algorithm is the best solution to the parallel sorting problem. It is optimal and reasonably simple. The constants are small, compared with the AKS algorithm.

Merging, selection and finding the median are all problems related to sorting. There are many results concerning parallel computations for these problems.[1,4,10,13,14] Valiant[28] has presented complexity results for parallel problems related to sorting in the abstract setting of a comparison model.

### Bibliography

[1] M. Ajtai, J. Komlos and E. Szemeredi. An O($n \log(n)$) sorting network. *STOC 1983*, 1–9.

[2] M. Ajtai, J. Komlos, W. Steiger and E. Szemeredi. Deterministic selection in O($\log \log n$) parallel time. *STOC 1986*, 188–95.

[3] M. Ajtai, J. Komlos and E. Szemeredi. Sorting in $c \log(n)$ parallel steps. *Combinatorica* **3** (1983), 1–19.

[4] S. Akl. An optimal algorithm for parallel selection. *Information Processing Letters* **19** (1984), 47–50.

[5] N. Alon. Expanders, sorting in rounds and superconcentrators of limited depth. *STOC 1985*, 98–102.

[6] K. Batcher. Sorting networks and their applications. *AFIPS Spring Joint Computing Conference* **32** (1968), 307–14.

[7] G. Bilardi and A. Nicolau. Bitonic sorting with O($n \log n$) comparisons. *Proceedings of the 20th Annual Conference on Information Science and Systems* (1986).

[8] G. Bilardi and F. Preparata. The VLSI optimality of the AKS sorting network. *Information Processing Letters* **20** (1985), 55–9.

[9] B. Bollobás. Sorting algorithms. *Random Graphs*. Academic Press (1985), 377–98.

[10] A. Borodin and J. Hopcroft. Routing, merging and sorting on parallel models of computation. *Journal of Computer and System Science* **30** (1985), 130–45.

[11] R. Bose and R. Nelson. A sorting problem. *Journal of the ACM* **9** (1962), 282–96.

[12] R. Cole. Slowing down sorting networks to obtain faster sorting algorithms. *FOCS 1984*, 255–60.

[13] R. Cole. Parallel merge sort. *FOCS 1986.*

[14] R. Cole and C. Yap. A parallel median algorithm. *Information Processing Letters* **20** (1985), 137–9.

[15] O. Gabber and Z. Galil. Explicit constructions of linear sized superconcentrators. *Journal of Computer System Sciences* **22** (1981), 407–20.

[16] D. Hirschberg. Fast parallel sorting algorithms. *Communications of the ACM* **21** (1978), 657–61.

[17] D. Knuth. *Sorting and Searching*. Addison-Wesley (1973).

[18] T. Leighton. Tight bounds on the complexity of parallel sorting. *IEEE Transactions on Computing* **C-34** (1985), 344–54.

[19] A. Lubotzky, L. Phillips and P. Sarnak. Ramanujan conjecture and explicit construction of expanders and superconcentrators. *STOC 1986.*

[20] G. Margulis. Explicit constructions of concentrators. *Problems of Information Transmission* **9** (1973), 325–32.

[21] M. S. Paterson. Improved sorting networks with O(log n) depth. Research Report 89, Department of Computer Science, University of Warwick (1987).

[22] J. Reif. An optimal parallel algorithm for integer sorting. *FOCS 1985*, 496–504.

[23] J. Reif and L. Valiant. A logarithmic time sort for linear size networks. *STOC 1983*, 10–6.

[24] D. Richards. Parallel sorting – a bibliography. *ACM SIGACT News*, Summer 1986, 28–48.

[25] R. Sedgewick. *Algorithms*. Addison-Wesley (1983), Chapter 35.

[26] H. Stone. Parallel processing with perfect shuffle. *IEEE Transactions on Computing* **C-20** (1971), 152–61.

[27] J. Ullman. *Computational Aspects of VLSI*. Computer Science Press (1984).

[28] L. Valiant. Parallelism in comparison problems. *SIAM Journal of Computing* **4** (1975), 348–55.

# CHAPTER 6

# PARALLEL STRING MATCHING

The string matching problem is defined as follows. Given two strings *pattern* and *text*, of lengths $m$ and $n$ respectively (with $n \geq m$), we have to find all occurrences of *pattern* in *text*. The size of the problem is defined to be $n$. We shall commonly use the abbreviation *pat* for *pattern*. The strings *pat* and *text* are provided as arrays whose elements are characters. We say that *pat* occurs at position $i$ in *text* if and only if $pat = text[i .. i + m - 1]$, where $text[i .. j]$ denotes the substring of text starting at $i$ and ending at position $j$. Let $match(i) =$ **true** if *pat* occurs at $i$ whilst otherwise $match(i) =$ **false**.

The string-matching problem is one of the most studied problems in complexity theory. There are several algorithms which solve the problem sequentially in linear time (see [5]), or even in average sublinear time (when the text is a random string) – see [2]. The most interesting sequential algorithm for this problem is a linear-time algorithm using very small memory (five integer variables of logarithmic size, or five heads of two-way deterministic finite automata) – see [4]. This algorithm is possible because of certain interesting combinatorial properties of periods in strings. The known linear-time sequential algorithms are not easy to parallelise. However, the same mathematical properties of periods are used in efficient parallel algorithms.

It is easy to construct an algorithm which solves the string-matching problem in $O(\log n)$ time using $nm/\log m$ processors on a P-RAM. We can assign $m/\log m$ processors to each position $i$, $1 \leq i \leq n - m + 1$, of the text. These processors check whether *pat* starts at position $i$. The processors can be organised in a binary tree to compute the boolean **AND** of $m$ values $match(i) = (text[i + k - 1] = pat[k]$ for $k = 1, \ldots, m)$. This is schematically illustrated in figure 6.1.

Using the powerful W-RAM model of computation we can solve the string-matching problem in O(1) time using *nm* processors. As before we assign *m* processors to each position *i* to check $pat = text[i..i + m - 1]$. Using simultaneous writes the boolean **AND** of *m* values can be computed in constant-time (see chapter 1). This perhaps suggests that the W-RAM model can be more pathological than powerful.

The algorithms mentioned so far are not optimal. The product of parallel time, *t*, and the number of processors, *p*, is not linear. We have that $p = n^2$ and that $t = O(\log n)$ (or, for a W-RAM, *t* is a constant).

The first optimal parallel algorithm was described by Galil,[3] for fixed-size alphabets. His algorithm works in O(log *n*) time using $n/\log n$ processors on a W-RAM, or in $\log^2 n$ time using $n/log^2 n$ processors on a P-RAM. In order to obtain an optimal algorithm a trick of encoding small subsegments of the string into integers is used. The input strings are divided into segments of length O(log *n*) which are later encoded by small integers. In this way the size of the input is reduced by a factor of log *n*. The algorithm makes heavy use of the combinatorics of periods in strings and is not strictly optimal since there exist linear-time sequential algorithms whose complexity does not depend on the size of the alphabet.

Vishkin has refined Galil's algorithm in such a way that the resulting algorithm is also optimal when the size of the alphabet is not fixed. He introduced the new idea of a duel between positions in the string. Both algorithms (of Galil and Vishkin) compute arrays which for each position *i* contain information about whether the prefix of *pat* of size $2^k$ occurs at *i*, for $k = 1, 2, \ldots, \log m$. The main difference between the algorithms is that in Galil's this information is only a boolean value, whilst in Vishkin's it also contains (in the case of a mismatch) an integer pointing to a mismatch. We follow Vishkin's presentation.[7] The reader is referred to [3] for a comparison of these algorithms.

Given two strings *u* and *w*, *u* is called a period of *w* if *w* is a prefix of $u^k$ (for some *k*). Here $u^k$ is the concatenation of *k* copies of *u*. The period size of *w* is the length of the shortest period of *w*.

*Figure 6.1.* Computing the value of *match*(*i*), *m* = 7, using a tree with **and** nodes

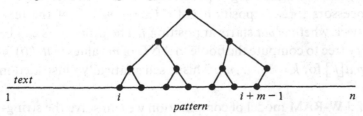

For a given $j$, suppose that $pat[j..m]$ is not a prefix of $pat$ (that is, $pat[j..m] \neq pat[1..m-j+1]$). Then there is an integer $w$, $1 \leqslant w \leqslant m-j+1$, such that $pat[w] \neq pat[s]$, where $s = j-1+w$. Figure 6.2 schematically shows this.

We say that $w$ is a witness to this mismatch. Let $WIT[j]$ be any such $w$. When there is no such $w$, we write $WIT[j] = 0$. For example, if $pat = abaababa$, then $WIT[1] = 0$, $WIT[2] = 1$, $WIT[3] = 2$ and $WIT[4] = 4$.

We say that the pattern is aperiodic if and only if $WIT[j] \neq 0$ for each $2 \leqslant j \leqslant m/2$. In other words the pattern is aperiodic if the size of its smallest period is at least $m/2$. The example $pat = abaababa$ is aperiodic. The probability that the pattern is aperiodic is very close to 1. However, we must later consider the periodic case also because we are concerned with the complexity of the worst case.

## 6.1 Analysis of the text

Here we analyse the text. First we consider the case of the pattern being aperiodic and then in subsection 6.1.2 we look at the periodic case. The complexity results of both cases are brought together in a single theorem presented in subsection 6.1.3.

### 6.1.1 THE APERIODIC CASE

We start then with the aperiodic case and we assume (for the time being) that the table $WIT$ has already been computed for $1 \leqslant j \leqslant m/2$. We shall show how to find *pattern* in *text* very quickly using this information. As we shall see later, the computation of $WIT$ is the most difficult part of the algorithm. Let $n' = n - m + 1$; we need only consider positions $1, \ldots, n'$ in the text as candidates for an occurrence of the pattern.

Let $WIT1$ denote a table (defined in a manner similar to $WIT$) for the string *text*. $WIT1[i]$ is a witness to a mismatch if the pattern placed at position $i$ does not match the text; otherwise $WIT1[i] = 0$. It can be zero even if there is a mismatch. The entries with zeros are called candidates (they are candidates for

*Figure 6.2*

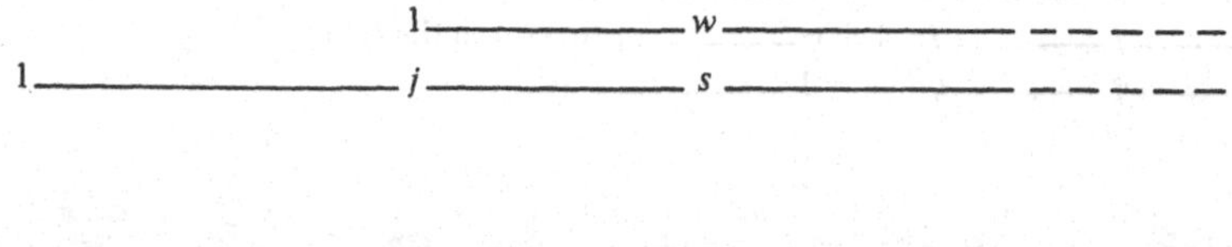

a match). Initially all entries of *WIT1* will contain zeros. The table *WIT1* is not really needed here, however we shall make use of its construction later when computing the table *WIT* for the pattern. In this section we can just assume that *WIT1* is a vector with entries indicating which position is a candidate.

A crucial concept within the algorithm is that of a duel between two positions. Let $p$ and $q$ be two positions in the text such that $1 \leqslant p < q \leqslant n'$ and $q - p < m/2$. We claim that an occurrence of *pat* cannot start both on $p$ and on $q$ and in one step we can eliminate at least one of them as a possible candidate for a match. Let $j = q - p + 1$ and $WIT[j] = w$.

Suppose that the pattern starts at $p$, $text[p .. p+m-1] = pat$ (see figure 6.3). Then, according to the definition of *WIT*, $pat[j-1+w] \neq pat[w]$, hence $text[q+w-1] \neq pat[w]$ and *pat* does not occur at $q$. We can set $WIT1[q] = w$. On the other hand if $pat[w] = text[q+w-1]$ and $text[p+q-p+w-1] \neq pat[q-p+w]$, then *pat* does not occur at $p$ and we can set $WIT1[p] = q - p + w$.

Consider the following example. Let *text = abaababaababaababaababa* and *pat = abaababa*. We then have that $WIT[1] = 0$, $WIT[2] = 1$, $WIT[3] = 2$ and $WIT[4] = 4$. Consider the positions $p = 6$ and $q = 9$. Let $j = q - p + 1$ and $j = 4$. We have that $WIT[4] = w = 4$. In our case $text[q+w-1] = text[9+4-1] = b \neq pat[w] = pat[4] = a$. Hence we can set $WIT1[9] = 4$. We also set $duel(6, 9) = 6$; the value of the duel is the surviving position (it can happen that both positions are 'shot' and the value of *WIT* could be set for them if the alphabet has at least three letters. For simplicity of exposition we only 'shoot' one position at a time). We use a special symbol denoted by *null* which indicates that one of $p$ and $q$ is absent. The function *duel* returns the survival position or *null*; its side effect is computing the value of *WIT1* for at least one position if both $p, q$ are not equal to *null*.

**function** *duel*$(p, q)$ $\{WIT[q - p + 1] \neq 0\}$
**begin**
**if** $p = null$ **then** $duel \leftarrow q$ **else**
  **if** $q = null$ **then** $duel \leftarrow p$ **else**
    **begin**
      $j \leftarrow q - p + 1$, $w \leftarrow WIT[j]$

*Figure 6.3*

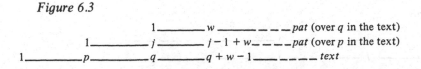

```
        if text[q + w − 1] ≠ pat[w]
            then begin WIT1[q] ← w, duel ← p end
            else begin WIT1[p] ← q − p + w, duel ← q end
    end
end
```

Assume for simplicity that both $m$ and $n'$ are powers of 2. We shall be successively dividing the set of indices $1, \ldots, n'$ into disjoint blocks of size $2^k$ for $k = 0, 1, \ldots, \log m − 1$. The $k$th partition is $[1 .. 2^k][2^k + 1 .. 2 . 2^k]$ ... $[i . 2^k + 1 .. (i + 1) . 2^k] \ldots$.

In the aperiodic case we know that two occurrences, $p$ and $q$, of the pattern have to satisfy $q − p > m/2$. In every $k$-block there will be at most one position $i$ where an occurrence of *pat* starts. This position satisfies $WIT1[i] = 0$. Such a position is a candidate for a match. Initially $k = 0$ and $WIT1[i] = 0$ for each $i$. In every $k$-block there is one candidate. If we set $k ← k + 1$ then in every $k$-block there are now two candidates. We perform duels between two candidates of each $k$-block in parallel. Then in every $k$-block we are left with only one candidate again. We iterate this procedure $\log m − 1$ times. The computation has a tree structure. Figure 6.4 shows such a computation for our example strings. Initially each position is a candidate; after a duel between two candidates one of them ceases to be a candidate.

We say that the table $WIT1$ is $k$-sparse if and only if in every $k$-block there is at most one entry $j$ with $WIT1[j] \neq 0$. The above process achieves $\log m − 1$ sparsity and can be more formally expressed as a procedure:

```
procedure moresparse(text, k) {WIT1 is (k − 1)-sparse}
begin
for all k-blocks in parallel do
    begin
```

Figure 6.4

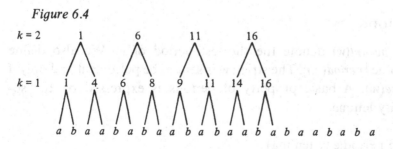

```
k = 1,    WIT1 = [0,1] [2, 0] [2, 0] [2,0] [0,1] [0,1] [2,0] [2,0]
k = 2,    WIT1 = [0, 1, 2, 4] [2, 0, 2, 4] [4, 1, 0, 1] [2, 4, 2, 0]
```

let $p$ and $q$ be two candidates in this block {entries with zero value of
  *WIT1*}
*candidate* ← *duel*(*p, q*) {let $r$ be the eliminated candidate in this block; now
  *WIT1*[$r$] = 0}
**end**
**end** {*WIT1* is $k$-sparse}

**procedure** *makesparse*(*text, sparsity*)
**begin**
**for** $k$ ← 1 **to** *sparsity* **do** *moresparse*(*text, k*)
**end**

After executing the call *makesparse*(*text*, log $m$ − 1) each (log $m$ − 1)-block
contains only one non-zero entry $j$ with *WIT1*[$j$] = 0. The above process
takes a total of O($n$) = ($n$ + $n/2$ + $n/4$ + ⋯) operations and has depth log $m$.
Using Brent's theorem this can be converted into O(log $m$) time with
O($n$/log $m$) processors on a P-RAM.

After determining 'suspicious' positions (with a zero value of *WIT*, in our
example the positions 1, 6, 11, 16) we check for each such position $j$ in parallel
whether the pattern occurs at $j$. Each can be checked using $m$/log $m$ processors
in O(log $m$) time on a P-RAM. The standard technique using a balanced binary
tree for the computation of an associative function can be used. The number of
suspicious positions is O($n/m$) and hence we have the following lemma.

### Lemma 6.1
In the aperiodic case and assuming that the table *WIT* is already computed for
the pattern, string matching can be done in O(log $m$) time using $n$/log $m$
processors on a P-RAM.

### 6.1.2 THE PERIODIC CASE

Let the string *period*($w$) denote the shortest period of $w$. We also define
*periodsize*($w$) to be |*period*($w$)|. The string $w$ is said to be periodic if and only if
|$w$| ⩾ 2*periodsize*($w$). A basic property of periods is expressed by the so-
called periodicity lemma.

### Lemma 6.2 (the periodicity lemma)
If $w$ has two periods of size $p$ and $q$ and |$w$| ⩾ $p$ + $q$ then $w$ has also a period of
size gcd($p, q$). Here gcd is an abbreviation for 'greatest common divisor'.

*Proof*

Let $p > q$. We first observe that if the assumptions are satisfied then $w$ has also a period of size $p - q$. We see this as follows. Since $w$ has periods of sizes $p$ and $q$ then, for all $i$, we have that $w[i] = w[i + p]$ and $w[i] = w[i + q]$. Thus $w[i + p] = w[i + q]$. Then, for all $i'$ $(= i - q)$, $w[i'] = w[i' + (p - q)]$ and so $w$ has a period of size $p - q$. Such a reasoning is always possible because $|w| \geqslant p + q$.

Now consider a version of Euclid's method for computing $\gcd(p, q)$:

```
function gcd(p, q)
begin
p' ← p
q' ← q
while p' ≠ q' do {invariant}
    if p' > q' then p' ← p' - q' else q' ← q' - p'
gcd ← p'
end
```

The invariant of this algorithm is that $w$ has periods of sizes $p'$ and $q'$. The last values of $p'$ and $q'$ are equal to $\gcd(p, q)$. Hence $w$ has a period of size $\gcd(p, q)$. This completes the proof of the lemma. ☐

Assume that the string *pat* is periodic with *periodsize*(*pat*) $= P$ and consider the structure of its occurrences within *text*. The following lemma easily follows from the definitions and from the periodicity lemma.

*Lemma 6.3*

(a) If *pat* occurs at two distinct positions $i$ and $j$ then $|i - j| \geqslant P$.
(b) If *pat* occurs at $j$ and $j + D$, where $D \leqslant m - P$, then $D$ is a multiple of $P$.
(c) If *pat* occurs at $j$ and $j + D$, where $0 < D \leqslant m/2$, then *pat* occurs at $j + P$.

Let *period*(*pat*) $= u$ and *pat* $= u^s v$, where $|u| = P$ and $|v| \leqslant P$. Take *pat'* $= uv$. The new pattern *pat'* is aperiodic. We can find all its occurrences in O(log $m$) time using $n/\log m$ processors on a P-RAM assuming that the table *WIT* for *pat'* is already computed. This can be done using the algorithm from the previous section. ☐

Define $next(i) = i + P$ if the pattern *pat'* occurs at $i$, otherwise $next(i) = i$. For $next(i) \neq i$, let $largest(i) = \max\{k \mid next^k(i) \neq next^{k-1}(i)\}$. If $next(i) = i$ then we define $largest(i) = 0$. Provided that the table *largest* is computed, then all occurrences of *pat* can easily be determined using the fact that *pat* occurs at position $i$ if and only if $largest(i) \geqslant s$.

As an example consider $pat = ababab$ and $text = abababababbaabababa$. In this case $pat = (ab)^3$ and $pat' = ab$. After finding all the ocurrences of *pat'*, we have the string $10101010001010100 = match(pat')$. For our example $largest(1) = 4$, $largest(7) = 1$, $next(1) = 3$.

We show how to compute the function *largest* in $O(\log n)$ time using $n/\log n$ processors on a P-RAM if $match(pat')$ is given. We can decompose $match(pat')$ into $m$ subsequences (the $p$th sequence consists of positions $i$ with $((i-1) \bmod P) = p)$ for $p = 0, \ldots, P-1$. We take every $P$th symbol starting from a given position $1 \leqslant i_0 \leqslant P$. The sequence $10101010001010100$ from our example can be decomposed into $11110110$ and $00000000$. In this case $P = 2$. The first subsequence is the sublist of values for positions $1, 3, 5, 7, \ldots, 17$. The second corresponds to the sequence for positions $2, 4, 6, \ldots, 16$.

It is enough to compute in each such subsequence for each position containing 1 the number of consecutive 1s from this position to the right. The length of each subsequence is $n/P$, hence for a given sequence such a computation can be done in $O(\log(n/P))$ time using $(n/P)/\log(n/P)$ processors by recursive doubling. There are $P$ subsequences, hence the whole computation can be done in $O(\log(n/P))$ time using $n/\log(n/P)$ processors. It can be also done in $O(\log n)$ time using $n/\log n$ processors, because $\log n \geqslant \log(n/P)$ and we can group operations into 'bunches' of size $\log n/\log(n/P)$. This proves the following.

*Lemma 6.4*

If the pattern has been preprocessed and the table *WIT* computed, then for the periodic case string matching can be done in $O(\log n)$ time using $n/\log n$ processors.                                                                      □

We can use a more refined algorithm for the periodic case (this computes whether $largest(i) \geqslant s$ instead of computing its exact value) which makes it possible to perform the computation in $O(\log m)$ time with $n/\log m$ processors if the initialisation is free. This can be advantageous because $\log m$ may be much smaller than $\log n$. However, in the P-RAM model of computation, we assume that the initialisation of (assignments to) $n$ processors takes $\Omega(\log n)$ time.

### 6.1.3 COMBINED RESULTS FOR TEXT ANALYSIS

Here we bring together the results expressed in lemmas 6.1 and 6.4. Lemma 6.1

states that in the aperiodic case (and assuming that the table *WIT* is already available) string matching can be done in O(log *m*) time using *n*/log *m* processors on a P-RAM. Now log *n* ⩾ log *m* so that we can modify lemma 6.1, trading time for processors. We can always (for any parallel computation) reduce the number of processors at the expense of taking proportionally longer to perform the computation. In this case, reducing the number of processors by a factor of log *m*/log *n* brings lemma 6.1 into line with lemma 6.4 and we have the following theorem.

*Theorem 6.1*
If the pattern is preprocessed and the table *WIT* is computed then in all cases string matching can be done in O(log *n*) parallel time using *n*/log *n* processors on a P-RAM. □

## 6.2 Preprocessing the pattern

This is technically the harder part of parallel string matching. The main idea is to match the pattern against itself. In other words, the text is merely a copy of the pattern. The table *WIT* is now for the same string as the table *WIT1*. Hence we take *WIT* and *WIT1* to be the same. In section 6.2 *WIT* was only needed to be computed for the first half of the pattern, hence that is all we need calculate now. This means that *WIT* is to be computed for the segment $[1 . . 2^{\log m - 1}]$. Notice that the value of *WIT*(1) is not interesting since it is always zero.

We introduce the function *witness*($j, r$). This function is the same as *WIT*($j$) except for the fact that we consider only the initial part of the text of size $r$ instead of the whole text. Let *witness*($j, r$) = 0 if $pat[j . . r]$ is a prefix of *pat*. Otherwise *witness*($j, r$) = $k$, where $k$ is any integer $1 \leqslant k \leqslant r - j + 1$ such that $pat[k] \neq pat[j + k - 1]$. Figure 6.5 illustrates this.

It is easy to compute the function *witness*($j, r$) in O(log *r*) time using O(*r*/log *r*) processors on a P-RAM, or in constant time on a W-RAM using *r* processors (the binary tree method can be used with values at the leaves representing matches or mismatches between the symbols of the pattern and the text). We leave the details to the reader.

*Figure 6.5.* $pat[k] \neq pat[j + k - 1]$, hence *witness*($j, r$) = $k$

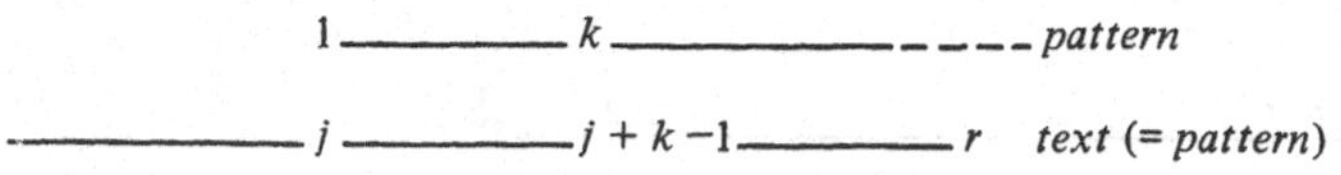

1——————— k ——————————————— _ _ _ _ _pattern

—————————— j ——————————— j + k −1——————— r    text (= pattern)

We shall assume that $m$ is a power of 2 but will drop this assumption at the end of the section. Informally, one stage of the preprocessing is as follows. We compute the table $WIT$ for a prefix of size $2^i$ of *pat*. Then using this we compute the table $WIT$ for the prefix of twice the length. If the computed part of $WIT$ for the segment $[2 .. 2^i]$ does not contain zero then $pat[1 .. 2^{i+1}]$ is aperiodic and we can compute $WIT$ for the segment $[2^i + 1 .. 2^{i+1}]$ using duels (utilising the procedure *makesparse* of subsection 6.1.1). After that only one position $j$ can survive ($WIT(j) = 0$) and we apply the function *witness* to this position. Otherwise if $WIT$ for the segment $[2 .. 2^i]$ does contain zero then $pat[1 .. 2^{i+1}]$ is periodic. We then compute the continuation of the period. If it continues to $2^c$ but not to $2^{c+1}$, then we compute $WIT$ for the segment $[2 .. 2^c]$ except perhaps for one surviving position $j$ (with $WIT(j) = 0$). In this case we shall satisfy sparsity using the periodicity of $pat[1 .. 2^c]$. The corresponding procedure is called *makesparseperiodic*.

Hence the general idea of the algorithm is to satisfy the notion of sparsity (as used in section 6.1) of $WIT$ for bigger and bigger lengths of the string. The next stage depends upon whether the currently processed part of the string is aperiodic. If it is aperiodic then *makesparse* is used, otherwise *makesparseperiodic* is used. Periodicity and aperiodicity are useful properties of strings. The algorithm makes efficient use of each as they arise.

A pattern is said to be *very aperiodic* if and only if, for $i = 1, 2, \ldots, \log m - 1$, every prefix of length $2^i$ is aperiodic (in the sense of section 6.1). We first consider the case of very aperiodic patterns. Notice that if $pat[1 .. 2^{i+1}]$ is aperiodic then $witness(j, 2^{i+1}) \neq 0$ for every $2 \leqslant j \leqslant 2^i$. If *pat* is very aperiodic and $m$ is a power of 2 then, using the above observation, algorithm 6.1 computes $WIT[k]$ for $k \leqslant m/2$. The *main invariant* for the correctness of the algorithm is

inv1($i$):  $WIT[k] = witness(k, 2^{i+2}) \neq 0$ for $k$ in $[2 .. 2^{i+1}]$ except perhaps one index $j$, $2^i < j \leqslant 2^{i+1}$

This is schematically illustrated in figure 6.6.

*Figure 6.6.* If inv1($i$) holds then $pat[1 .. 2^{i+1}]$ is aperiodic; however, $pat[1 .. 2^{i+2}]$ can be periodic with period $P = j - 1$. This has to be verified by computing $witness(j, 2^{i+2})$

1_____ $2^i$_____ $j$ ___$2^{i+1}$_____ $2^{i+2}$ .....

*Algorithm 6.1* $\{m \geqslant 4, m$ is a power of 2, the pattern is very aperiodic$\}$

**begin**
$WIT[1] \leftarrow 0$
$i \leftarrow 0$ {inv1(0)}
**while** $i < \log m - 2$ **do** {inv1(i)}
  **begin**
  let $j$ be the only candidate in $[2^i + 1 .. 2^{i+1}]$
  $WIT[j] \leftarrow witness(j, 2^{i+2})$ {now $WIT[j] \neq 0$}
  $makesparse\ (pat[2^{i+1} + 1 .. 2^{i+2}], i + 1)$
  $i \leftarrow i + 1$
  **end**
$\{i = \log m - 2,\ 2^{i+1} = m/2,\ WIT$ is correctly computed for the segment
  $[1 .. m/2]$ except perhaps for one index $j\}$
**if** there is an index $j$ in $[2 .. m/2]$ with $WIT[j] = 0$ **then**
                                 $WIT[j] \leftarrow witness(j, m)$
**end** of the algorithm {table $WIT$ is correctly computed for the first half of
  $pat$}

The depth of computing *makesparse* and *witness*, for a given $i$, is $O(\log m)$ and the total number of operations is $O(2^i)$. Hence the depth of the whole algorithm is $\log^2 m$ and total number of operations is $O(2^1 + 2^2 + \cdots) = O(m)$. Using Brent's theorem the algorithm can be implemented to run in $O(\log^2 m)$ time with $m/\log^2 m$ processors on a P-RAM.

As an example let $pat = abaabbabaabbabab$. This pattern is very aperiodic. At the start we set $WIT[1] = 0$ and $WIT[2] = 1$. We have inv1(0): $WIT = [0, 0, \ldots]$ with $j = 2$. We start the first iteration of the **while** statement. The value of $WIT[j] = WIT[2]$ is set to $witness(2, 4) = 1$. Next we perform *markesparse*$(pat[3 .. 4], 1)$. In the second 1-block $[3 .. 4]$ only position 4 survives. The value of $i$ is incremented. Now the situation is $i = 1$, $WIT = [0, 1, 2, 0, \ldots]$, $j = 4$; inv1(1) holds. We now compute $witness(4, 8) = 3$, hence $pat[1 .. 8]$ is aperiodic. Next we execute *makesparse*$(pat[5 .. 8], 3)$ and increment the value of $i$. We have the situation $i = \log m - 2 = 2$ and $WIT = [0, 1, 2, 3, 1, 1, 0, 1, 0, \ldots]$. The **while** instruction terminates and the first half of the table $WIT$ is computed except one position $j$. The only surviving candidate $j$ in $[5 .. 8]$ is 7. We compute $witness(7, 16) = 9$ and finally $WIT = [0, 1, 2, 3, 1, 1, 9, 1, 0, \ldots]$. Only positions 1 to 8 are needed.

Consider now the *general case* in which we assume that $m$ is a power of 2, but that the pattern need not be very aperiodic. The algorithm for the very aperiodic case can easily detect the situation when for some $0 \leqslant i \leqslant \log m - 2$

the subpattern $pat[1 .. 2^{i+2}]$ is periodic and the whole pattern is not very aperiodic. Such a situation happens when $witness(j, 2^{i+2}) = 0$ in algorithm 6.1. At that moment the following invariant holds.

> inv: $pat[1 .. 2^{i+2}]$ is periodic with period $P = j - 1$, $2^i \leqslant P < 2^{i+1}$
> $P$ is the smallest period of $pat[1 .. 2^{i+2}]$ (see figure 6.7)

The following subroutine computes the continuation $c$ of the period $P$, where $c$ is the maximal integer such that $P$ is the period of the first $c$-block.

> **function** *periodcont*$(j, currentcont)$
> **begin** $c \leftarrow currentcont$
> **while** $witness(j, 2^{c+1}) = 0$ **and** $c < \log m$ **do** $c \leftarrow c + 1$
> *periodcont* $\leftarrow c$
> **end**

In the periodic case we compute $c \leftarrow periodcont(j, i + 2)$. If $c = \log m$ then the computation is over. We have found a small period of the whole pattern and thus the whole pattern is not aperiodic. We stop preprocessing. We know the length $P = j - 1$ of the period and the table $WIT$ is computed for the segment $[1 .. P]$. This is all we need for the text analysis of sections 6.1 and 6.2. Otherwise the following invariant holds.

> inv2: $P = j - 1$ is the period of $pat[1 .. 2^c]$ and it is not the period of $pat[1 .. 2^{c+1}]$
>     $witness(j, 2^{c+1}) = w \neq 0$,   $2^i \leqslant P < 2^{i+1}$,   $c \geqslant i + 2$,   $0 \neq WIT[p] =$
>     $witness(p, 2^{i+2}) < 2^{i+2}$ for $2 \leqslant p < P$
>     inv1($i$) from the algorithm for the very aperiodic case also holds

Our aim is to increase the value of $i$ (perhaps by more than 1) and at the same time to preserve invariant inv1($i$). Using the invariants the value of $WIT(j + kP)$ can be set to $WIT(j) - kP$ for $j \leqslant j + kP \leqslant 2^c$, because of the periodicity of $pat[1 .. 2^c]$. We make the following definition: $p \bmod' P = $ **if** $p \bmod P \neq 0$ **then** $p \bmod P$ **else** $P$. For the same reason $WIT(p)$ can be set to $WIT[p \bmod' P]$ for every $P < p \leqslant 2^c - 2^{i+2}$ which is not of the form $j + kP$ ($p \bmod P \neq 1$). This is illustrated in figure 6.8.

*Figure 6.7.* Here $c$ is maximal such that the prefix of size $2^c$ has period of size $P = j - 1$

However, there is a problem with the last four $i$-blocks of $[1..2^c]$ for $c > i + 2$, because $WIT(p \bmod' P)$ can be close to $2^{i+2}$ (although it does not exceed $2^{i+2}$ because of $\mathrm{inv}1(i)$) and $p + WIT(p \bmod' P)$ can be outside the part of pattern scanned so far. However, we know that the first $i$-block is sparse, $0 \neq WIT[k] < 2^{i+2} \leqslant 2^c$ for $k$ in $[2..2^i]$. Using this fact we can apply *makesparse*$(block, i)$ for the last four $i$-blocks $B$ of $[1..2^c]$. Next we can compute, for each of four candidates obtained, $j' WIT[j'] = witness(j', 2^{c+1})$. Observe that from the periodicity lemma it follows that at most one of the candidates survives. Otherwise, assuming that candidates $p$ and $q$ survive, the subpattern $pat[1..2^{c+1}]$ would have a period $\gcd(p-1, q-1) \leqslant 2^{i+1}$. However at this moment $WIT[k] \neq 0$ for $k$ in $[2..2^{i+1}]$. Hence the invariant $\mathrm{inv}1$ still holds for the new value of $i = c - 1$. Notice that $c \geqslant i + 2$ (where $i$ is the old value). This is summarised in the following procedure.

> **procedure** *makesparseperiodic*$(i, j, c)$
> {$\mathrm{inv}2$ and $\mathrm{inv}1(i)$ hold, $P = j - 1$ is the size of period which continues to position $2^c$ but not to $2^{c+1}$, we compute the subsequent part of $WIT$ to satisfy $\mathrm{inv}1(c - 1)$}
> **begin**
> $WIT[j] \leftarrow witness(j, 2^{c+1})$
> $P \leftarrow j - 1$
> **for** all $b$, $P < p \leqslant 2^c$, $p - j \bmod' P = 0$, **in parallel do**
> $\qquad\qquad\qquad\qquad WIT[p] \leftarrow WIT[j] - (p - j)$
> **for** all $b$, $P < p \leqslant 2^c$   $2^{i+1}$, $p - j \bmod P \neq 0$, **in parallel do**
> $\qquad\qquad\qquad\qquad WIT[p] \leftarrow WIT[p \bmod' P]$
> **for** all of the last 4 $i$-blocks $B$ of $[1..2^c]$ **do**
> $\quad$**begin**
> $\quad$*makesparse*$(B, i)$
> $\quad$**for** the candidate $j'$ left in $B$ **do** $WIT[j'] \leftarrow witness(j', 2^{c+1})$
> $\quad$**end**
> {there is at most one candidate $j$ with $WIT[j] = 0$ in the interval $[2^{c-1}..2^c]$}
> {$\mathrm{inv}1(c - 1)$ holds}
> **end**

*Figure 6.8.* Let $k = WIT(p \bmod' P)$. Then $k < 2^{i+2}$. If $(p \bmod P) \neq 0$ and $p \leqslant 2^c - 2^{i+2}$ then $WIT(p) = k$ because $pat[1..2^c]$ is periodic with a period of size $P$

```
     1_____ k___          1_____ k_ _ _ _

1_____ p mod'P __*_____ p_____*_____ 2^c _ _ _
```

As an example consider $pat = abaabaabaa \ldots ab = (aba)^{10}ab$. Thus $m = 32 = 2^5$. The partition into 1-blocks is $|ab|aa|ba|ab|aa|ba|ab| \ldots |ab|$ and into 2-blocks is $|abaa|baab|aaba|abaa| \ldots |baab|$. Assume that $i = 1$ and inv(1) holds. We have the situation $WIT = [0, 1, 2, 0, 0, \ldots]$. Consider the only candidate $j = 4$ in $[2^i + 1 \ldots 2^{i+1}] = [3 \ldots 4]$. We compute $witness(j, 8) = 0$ and discover that the pattern is not very aperiodic. In fact $pat[1 \ldots 3]$ is the period of $pat[1 \ldots 8]$. The continuation of the period $P$ is computed. In our case $periodcont(j, 3) = 4$, since $witness(j, 16) = 0$ and $witness(j, 32) = 17 \neq 0$. We have $WIT = [0, 1, 2, 17, 0, 0, \ldots]$. Invariant inv2 holds with $P = 3, j = 4, c = 4$, $i = 1$. We execute $makesparseperiodic(1, 4, 4)$. The period $P = j - 1 = 3$, hence we can set $WIT[4 + 3] = 17 - 3$, $WIT[4 + 6] = 17 - 6$, $WIT[4 + 9] = 17 - 9$. We have $WIT = [0, 1, 2, 17, 0, 0, 14, 0, 0, 11, 0, 0, 8, 0, 0, \ldots]$. Then we set $WIT[5] = WIT[5(\text{mod}' 3)] = WIT[2] = 1$, $WIT[6] = WIT[6(\text{mod}' 3)] = WIT[3] = 2$, $WIT[8] = WIT[8(\text{mod} 3)] = WIT[2] = 1$. We have afterwards $WIT = [0, 1, 2, 17, 1, 2, 14, 1, 0, 11, 0, 0, 8, 0, 0, 0, \ldots]$. The suspicious blocks are the rightmost four $i$-blocks of the segment $[1 \ldots 16]$: $[15, 16]$, $[13, 14]$, $[11, 12]$ and $[9, 10]$. For each of these blocks we execute $makesparse(block, 1)$ and then we check surviving candidates $j'$ in each of these blocks (at most one per block). The operation $witness(j', 32)$ is performed four times. None of the candidates survives.

It is worth noting that if $c = i + 2$ then the last four $i$-blocks are also the first four $i$-blocks. This is rather a pathological situation and we could only execute *makesparse* for the last two $i$-blocks. However, we can ignore such a situation to make the algorithm shorter. The reader can check that correctness is not affected; the algorithm is just a little overworked in such a situation.

Using procedures *makesparseperiodic* and *periodcont* we can extend the algorithm in the case of a very aperiodic pattern to the general case.

*Algorithm 6.2 {$m \geqslant 4$, the pattern need not be very aperiodic, $m$ is a power of 2}*

**begin**
$WIT[1] \leftarrow 0$
$i \leftarrow 0$
**while** $i < \log m - 1$ **do** {inv($i$)}
  **begin**
  **if** there is no candidate $j$ in $[2^i + 1 \ldots 2^{i+1}]$ with $WIT[j] = 0$ **then**
                                               $i \leftarrow i + 1$ **else**
    **begin**
    let $j$ be the only candidate in $[2^i + 1 \ldots 2^{i+1}]$

$$WIT[j] \leftarrow witness(j, 2^{i+2})$$

if $WIT[j] \neq 0$ then {aperiodic case}

begin

  $makesparse(pat[2^{i+1} + 1 .. 2^{i+2}], i + 1)$

  $i \leftarrow i + 1$ {inv1(i)}

end else {periodic case, inv2 holds}

begin

  $c \leftarrow periodcont(j, i + 2)$

  if $c = \log m$ then return (pattern is periodic, $P = j - 1$)

  $makesparseperiodic(i, j, c)$

  $i \leftarrow c - 1$ {inv1(i)}

end

      end

   end

$\{i = \log m - 2, 2^{i+1} = m/2, WIT$ is correctly computed for the segment $[1 .. m/2]$ except perhaps for one index $j\}$

if there is an index $j$ in $[2 .. m/2]$ with $WIT[j] = 0$ then

$$WIT[j] \leftarrow witness(j, m)$$

return (pattern is aperiodic)

end of algorithm 6.2

We made an assumption that the length of the pattern is a power of 2. We now show how this can be dropped. If $m$ is not a power of 2, then instead of $m/2$ in the analysis of the text we can take the number $m\$2 = 2^{\log' m - 1}$, where $\log' m$ means the largest integer $k$ such that $2^k \leqslant m$. We redefine the periodic pattern to be a string without a period not exceeding $m\$2$ and essentially the same algorithm for text processing works, with the table $WIT$ computed only for $[1 .. m\$2]$. Hence we have only to show how to compute $WIT$ for indices in the range $[1 .. m\$2]$ and how to find the periodicity of $pat$. We do this as follows.

The algorithm is modified in such a way that it also reports the last values of $i$ and $j$. The algorithm is applied to $pat' = pat[1 .. \log' m]$. We have only to compute the table $WIT$ for the first $m\$2 = |pat'|/2$ positions of $pat'$ if $pat'$ is aperiodic. However, if $pat'$ is periodic with period $P$ which continues until position $2^{\log' m}$, then we have to check if this period continues to the end of the original pattern $pat$. If the algorithm reports that the pattern $pat'$ is aperiodic then the table $WIT$ is already computed for $[1 .. m\$2]$ and we stop ($WIT$ is computed for the first $m\$2$ positions and $pat'$ is aperiodic). Otherwise the algorithm reports that there is a period $P$ in $pat[1 .. 2^c]$, where $c = \log' m$. At this time the invariant $inv1(i)$ holds. We have that $2^i \leqslant P < 2^{i+1}$ and $WIT[2..2^i]$ contains no zeros and that $WIT[k] < 2^{i+2}$ for $k$ in $[2..2^i]$. We check whether $P$ is the period of the whole pattern *pat* (checking occurrence of $pat[1..m-P]$ starting at position $j = P + 1$. This can be done in $O(\log m)$ time with $m/\log m$ processors using a binary tree of processors). If $P$ is the period of the whole pattern *pat*, then we report that the period of *pat* is $P$ and the algorithm stops. Otherwise $P$ is the period of $pat[1..2^c]$, $c = \log' m$, and $P$ is not the period of $pat[1..m]$. We know the position of the mismatch and can set a non-zero value for $WIT[j]$. Now the first $2^{i+1}$ positions have the value of $WIT$ computed. If $i = \log' m - 2$ ($2^{i+1} = m\$2$) then the algorithm stops. Otherwise we execute $makesparseperiodic(i, j, \log' m)$. Observe that in this case $2^i \leqslant 2^{c-3}$ and the last four $i$-blocks in $[1..2^c]$ are now outside the prefix-interval $[1..m\$2]$. Hence, executing $makesparseperiodic(i, j, c)$, we can omit the part of the procedure which computes $WIT$ in these blocks (such a computation can cause some problems because it can be the case that there is not enough pattern to the right of these blocks to use duels between positions). Hence at this moment the table $WIT$ is computed for indices in the range $[1..m\$2]$, and it contains only one zero entry in the first position. The algorithm then stops.

### Theorem 6.2
Analysis of the pattern can be done in $O(\log^2 m)$ time using $m/\log^2 m$ processors on a P-RAM.

### Proof
The complexity analysis of the algorithm for the general case is similar to the corresponding analysis for the very aperiodic case. The depth is obviously $\log^2 n$. When we start the iteration for a given $i$ then the total number of operations before the value of $i$ changes is $O(2^i + 2^{i+1} + \cdots + 2^k)$, where $k$ is a next value of $i$, $k > i$. Notice that in the aperiodic case $k = i + 1$ and in the periodic case $k = c - 1$, however $c \geqslant i + 2$ (see inv2) and $k > i$.

The value of $i$ changes from 0 to $\log' m$. Hence the total number of operations is $O(m)$. We have here the algorithm with depth $\log^2 m$ and total number of operations $O(m)$. Applying Brent's theorem we obtain an algorithm working in $O(\log^2 m)$ time and using $m/\log^2 m$ processors. There is no problem with the scheduling of processors, the structure of the algorithm is a standard one ($\log m$ phases with the $i$th phase making $O(2^i)$ operations). This completes the proof. $\qquad\square$

The algorithm can be implemented to run in $O(\log m)$ time using $m/\log m$ processors on a CRCW-RAM (concurrent-read, concurrent-write parallel RAM). The CRCW-RAM is a parallel random machine in which concurrent reads and writes are allowed, many processors can simultaneously attempt to write into the same location, even if they try to write different data. One of them succeeds, though we do not know which one.

Computation of the function *witness* can be done on a CRCW-RAM in one step. Any of the processors which discovers a mismatch sets the value of *witness* to the position of mismatch. Many processors can try to set this to different values; only one of them succeeds. However, *makesparse* still requires logarithmic time. The algorithm can be changed in such a way that *makesparse* is computed in phases. Now we replace the instruction $makesparse(pat[2^{i+1} \ldots 2^{i+2}], i + 1)$ by $moresparse(pat[1 \ldots m\$2], i + 1)$ in the algorithm for the very aperiodic case. Observe that on the CRCW-RAM the last procedure can be executed in constant time using $m/2^i$ processors (one processor per block).

We invite the reader to check that in this case the algorithm works in $O(\log m)$ time on a CRCW-RAM and the total number of operations is still $O(m)$. The details can be found in [7]. Applying Brent's theorem one gets an algorithm working in $O(\log m)$ time using $m/\log m$ processors on a W-RAM and analysing the pattern in the very aperiodic case. Similar changes can be made to the algorithm for the general case. We refer the reader to [7].

## 6.3 Complexity of the whole pattern-matching algorithm

We bring together here the results expressed by theorems 6.1 and 6.2. In doing so we establish the complexity and processor requirements for the pattern-matching algorithm described in this chapter. Since $\log n \geqslant \log m$ we can state the main theorem of this chapter, which places the pattern-matching problem in *NC*, as follows.

*Theorem 6.3* (main theorem)
The pattern-matching problem can be solved on a P-RAM in $O(\log^2 n)$ time using $n/\log^2 n$ processors. $\qquad\square$

The following theorem which also follows directly from theorems 6.1 and 6.2 may place tighter bounds on the complexity and processor requirements for particular values of $m$ and $n$.

*Theorem 6.4*

The pattern-matching problem can be solved on a P-RAM in $O(\max(\log n, \log^2 m))$ time using $\max(n/\log n, m/\log^2 m)$ processors. □

In view of the remarks at the end of section 6.2 we can conclude that on a CRCW-RAM the string-matching problem can be solved in $O(\log n)$ time using $n/\log n$ processors. An interesting open problem is whether the same parameters can be achieved for the P-RAM. Another interesting problem would be to extend the algorithms to the two-dimensional case. It is known that two-dimensional string matching can be also done sequentially in linear time (here the size of the input is the size of the larger textual rectangle in which the rectangular pattern is to be found).

### Bibliographic notes

The linear-time (sequential) string-matching algorithm and its variations can be found in [5]. This was extended to the two-dimensional case by Baker.[1] An advanced time-space-optimal algorithm has been described by Galil and Seiferas.[4] Optimal parallel algorithms for string matching were provided by Galil[3] and Vishkin.[7] The presentation of this chapter follows Vishkin. Parallel algorithms for string matching in the presence of errors were given by Landau and Vishkin.[6] The problem is to compute, for each position $i$ of the text, how many errors there are in that position for an occurrence of *pattern*. This problem is rather more complicated than the one solved in this chapter. There is in fact probably no linear-time sequential algorithm for string matching with errors. It is easy to prove however that this problem is in *NC*.

### Bibliography

[1]  T. P. Baker. A technique for extending rapid exact-match string matching to arrays of more than one dimension. *SIAM Journal of Computing* 7, 4 (1978), 533–41.

[2]  R. S. Boyer and J. S. Moore. A fast string searching algorithm. *Communications of the ACM* 20 (1977), 762–72.

[3]  Z. Galil. Optimal parallel algorithms for string matching. *STOC 1984*, 240–8.

[4]  Z. Galil and J. Seiferas. Time-space-optimal string matching. *STOC 1979*, 13–26.

[5]  D. E. Knuth, J. H. Morris and V. R. Pratt. Fast pattern matching in strings. *SIAM Journal of Computing* 6 (1977), 322–50.

[6]  G. M. Landau and U. Vishkin. Efficient string matching in the presence of errors. *FCS 1985*.

[7]  U. Vishkin. Optimal parallel pattern matching in strings. *ICALP 1985*.

# CHAPTER 7

# *P*-COMPLETENESS: HARDLY PARALLELISABLE PROBLEMS

Using a computer with many processors might lead perhaps to the natural expectation of solving a given problem much more quickly than if only a single processor were used. From a practical point of view, the feasible number of processors available is bounded by a polynomial. We cannot expect to solve an exponential-sequential-time problem in polynomial parallel time using a polynomial number of processors. However, we would like to compute each sequential polynomial-time problem in polylogarithmic parallel time. By *P* we denote the class of problems which are solvable in polynomial sequential time and (as throughout the text) *NC* is the class of problems solvable in polylogarithmic parallel time using a polynomial number of processors. Probably the most important question about parallel computations is whether or not $P = NC$. There is a general belief, but not a proof, that $P \neq NC$ and hence that there are problems in $P - NC$.

*NC* is the class of well-parallelisable problems. The border between well-parallelisable and hardly parallelisable problems lies somewhere between *NC* and the class of so-called *P*-complete problems. A problem $L \in P$ is said (here) to be *P-complete* if every other problem in *P* can be transformed to *L* in polylogarithmic parallel time using a polynomial number of processors (such a transformation is said to be an *NC-reduction*). In other words *L* is a hardest problem in *P* from the point of view of finding efficient parallel computations. Clearly, if we could prove (an unlikely event) that $L \in NC$ then it would follow that $P = NC$. All previous chapters were about problems which are in *NC*. In contrast, this chapter is about problems which are unlikely to have efficient parallel solutions.

It is appropriate to mention here that the usual (classic) definition of *P-*

completeness is in terms of logarithmic space reducibility (see [12]). It can be proved that, if a problem $p_1$ can be transformed to the problem $p_2$ using very little space, then the transformation is also possible using an *NC* reduction. Such a correspondence between space and parallel time complexity is an extension of the parallel computation thesis. All reductions presented in this chapter work very locally. For example, if we reduce a circuit $G$ to some graph $G'$ then it is made on the basis of neighbourhoods of nodes. There are polynomially many 'local situations' and each of them can be computed in polylogarithmic parallel time as well as in sequential logarithmic space. In fact all our reductions can be done within logarithmic space. Whenever we prove that a problem is *P*-complete according to our notion of *NC*-reducibility then it is also complete in the stronger sense of space reducibility.[12] However, we omit the details of log-space reducibility because it is not strictly relevant to this text, and because it would require adding some new technical material.

In the next section we establish that a basic problem, called generability, is *P*-complete. This we do by showing that for every problem $L \in P$ there exists an *NC*-reduction to generability. This is the starting point for our proving that a selection of other problems are also *P*-complete. The subsequent section does this by demonstrating that, for each such problem, there exists an *NC*-reduction from one of the problems currently known to be *P*-complete.

## 7.1 A first *P*-complete problem

We start by defining our first *P*-complete problem. In doing so we introduce a standard format in which we shall conveniently describe problems; this is done as follows.

*Generability*

    *Instance*    A set $X$ and a binary operator $\cdot$. In addition a subset of (initial) elements $T \subseteq X$ and a goal element $x \in X$ are specified.

    *Question*    Does $x$ belong to the closure (with respect to $\cdot$) of $T$?

Given a set $S$ and a binary operator $\cdot$, the set $S \cdot S$ is defined by $S \cdot S = \{a \cdot b \mid a, b \in S\}$. Using this definition, the following procedure computes the closure (of $T$)

**function** *closure*(*T*)
**begin**

1. $T' \leftarrow T$
2. **while** $T' \neq T' \cup T' \cdot T'$ **do** $T' \leftarrow T' \cup T' \cdot T'$
3. $closure \leftarrow T'$
**end**

In the line labelled 2, the body of the **while** statement is iterated no more than $|X - T|$ times because each additional iteration adds at least one element to $T'$ and in addition we have that $|closure(T)| \leqslant |X|$. Thus computing the closure of $T$ is in $P$ as therefore is the problem called generability. If the operation $\cdot$ is associative then, as we shall show later, in this case generability is in $NC$. Without this restriction generability is $P$-complete as we shortly prove. For our proof we use an auxiliary problem which we call $gen'$: $gen'$ is defined in the same way as generability except that the binary operation $\cdot$ is replaced by a ternary operation $next(u, v, w)$. We first prove that $gen'$ is $P$-complete and then it is a small step to prove the same for generability. Obviously $gen'$ is also in $P$ by similar observations to those employed for generability. We want to show that for every problem $L \in P$ there exists an $NC$-reduction to $gen'$. From the technical point of view, the proof needs as simple a specification of (an arbitrary) $L$ as possible.

It is well known (see [1] for example) that every problem $L$ that is computable in polynomial time on a random-access machine can also be computed in polynomial time on a one-tape deterministic Turing machine. Without loss of generality (just as we concentrate on such problems in the theory of $NP$-completeness in sequential complexity theory) and for convenience we take $L$ to be a decision problem, the computation of which results in the value **true** or the value **false**. Let $L \in P$ be such a problem computable in polynomial time $P(n)$ on the Turing machine $M$. $M$ consists of an infinite tape of contiguous cells and a tape head (having a finite number of (internal) states) which can move from one cell to an adjacent cell in one step of the computation. During the computation, the tape head will therefore be constrained to scanning contiguous tape cells over a length of tape not exceeding $T(n)$ where $T(n) \leqslant P(n) + I(n)$ and $I(n)$ is the number of contiguous cells occupied on the initial tape configuration. We take $T(n)$ to be explicitly known.

In one step, depending upon the current state, $M$ moves the tape head to the right (or to the left) and, depending upon the symbol now under the tape head, changes the state and the symbol on that cell. If necessary, the reader is referred to [1] for a more detailed definition of Turing machines. To make our proof as transparent as possible we use an even simpler model than (but which is nevertheless an abstraction of) the Turing machine model. Our model, called a *tape model*, consists of a tape of contiguous cells on which local changes are performed. There are four points defining the model in more detail.

(1) The length of the tape is $T(n) + 2$ with tape cells numbered $0, 1, \ldots, T(n) + 1$ consecutively.

(2) The $p$th tape cell contains a symbol from a constant-size alphabet. For $p = 0$ and $p = T(n) + 1$ the (boundary) tape cells always contain the special symbol \$.

(3) For $1 \leqslant p \leqslant T(n)$ the content $c(p, t + 1)$ of the $p$th cell at time $t + 1$ is determined by $c(p - 1, t)$, $c(p, t)$ and $c(p + 1, t)$. This dependence is contained in the explicitly known function *trans*, where $c(p, t + 1) = trans(c(p - 1, t), c(p, t), c(p + 1, t))$. The two special boundary cells with $p = 0$ and $p = T(n) + 1$ guarantee that each non-boundary cell has left and right neighbours.

(4) The input is $c(p, 0)$ for all $p$, $1 \leqslant p \leqslant T(n)$, and the output is $c(1, T(n))$, where # encodes the value **true**.

If $M$ is a one-tape deterministic Turing machine working in polynomial time then it is easy to specify (by an *NC*-reduction) a tape model of the type described above which will simulate $M$. The function *trans* is then (for all $t$ and $p$) determined completely by the Turing machine program (the set of quintuples describing each possible step of the computation). At time $t$, the $p$th cell of the tape model can contain a pair (*char*, *state*). Here *char* is the symbol contained in the corresponding cell of $M$ at time $t$, and *state* = $q$ if at this time the tape head is in state $q$ and pointing at this cell, otherwise *state* = $\varnothing$. The value of $c(1, P(n))$ will correspond to the outcome of the computation on $M$. The computation on $M$ will be for a decision problem and the outcome will be the value **true** or the value **false**.

*Theorem 7.1*

  Problem  *gen'* is P-complete.

*Proof*

Let $L$ be a problem solved in deterministic polynomial time. We can assume that the problem is computed on the tape model described above. Let the triple $(t, p, sym)$ represent information concerning the $p$th cell of the tape at time $t$. Here *sym* is the current symbol in this cell. We construct an instance of the problem *gen'* from $L$. Here $X$, $T$ and $x$ will be as defined for the problem *gen'*. For the instance of *gen'* $X$ is the set of all triples of the type $(t, p, sym)$. The triple for the $p$th cell at time $t + 1$ is determined by the triples for cells $p - 1, p, p + 1$ at time $t$ as prescribed by the function *trans*. This is illustrated in figure 7.1. For $u, v, w, z \in X$ we define $next(u, v, w) = z$ if and only if $u$, $v$ and $w$ are triples associated with the cells $p - 1$, $p$, $p + 1$ at time $t$ and $z$ is the triple associated with the $p$th cell at time $t + 1$ as determined by the function *trans*. The function *next* is the ternary operator for our instance of *gen'*. The set $T$ of initial elements of $X$ is the set of all triples of the form $(0, p, sym)$ related to the initial contents of the tape.

The operation *next* has the following (easy to prove) property: $(t, p, sym)$ can be generated from $T$ if and only if $sym$ is in cell $p$ at time $t$. The tape model returns the value **true** if and only if the triple $(T(n), 1, \#)$ is contained in the closure of $T$. Hence the tape-model computation of $L \in P$ can be transformed to an instance of *gen'*. The transformation is an *NC*-reduction because the operation $next(u, v, w)$ can be computed in parallel for all $u, v, w$ in polylogarithmic time with a polynomial number of processors. The crucial point of the proof is that the size of *next* is bounded by a polynomial (because the number of tape cells, the number of values of $t$ and the number of tape symbols are all bounded by a known polynomial). $\square$

**Theorem 7.2**
Generability is *P*-complete.

*Proof*
Let the problem *gen'* be specified by the set of elements $X$, the set of initial elements $T$, the operation *next* and the goal element $s$. We construct an instance of generability from this instance of *gen'*. For the instance of generability we take the set $X'$ defined to be $X \cup X^2$, where $X^2$ is the cartesian product of the set $X$ with itself. We define $u \cdot v = (u, v)$ for each $u, v$ in $X$ and $(u, v) \cdot w = next(u, v, w)$. The operator $\cdot$ is the binary operator for our instance of

*Figure 7.1*

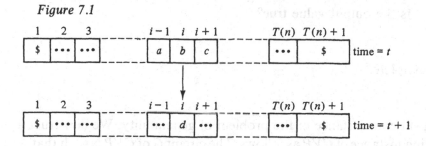

$next\,((\,t, i - 1, a), (t, i, b), (t, i + 1, c)\,) = (t + 1, i, d)$ where $d = trans\,(a, b, c)$

generability. This instance also has the same set of (initial) elements and the same goal element as *gen'*. It is easy to see that the goal element *s* is in the closure of *T* (with respect to the operator ·) for the instance of generability if and only if it is in the closure of *T* (with respect to the operator *next*) for the corresponding instance of *gen'*. This transformation from *gen'* to generability is easily achieved by an *NC*-reduction. $\qquad \square$

It is appropriate here to note that if the operation · is associative then generability is in *NC*. We can construct the graph with an edge $(x, y)$ if and only if $x \cdot z = y$ for some $z$ in $T$. If $s$ is in the closure of $T$, because · is associative $s$ can be generated as follows $((\ldots (a \cdot b) \cdot c) \cdot d) \cdot e) \cdot f \ldots)$, for certain $a, b, c, \ldots$ in $T$. Then constructing the graph as described will ensure that there is a path from $a$ to $s$. The determination of the existence of such a path is equivalent to determining whether $a$ and $s$ belong to the same component of the graph. For this we can use the polylogarithmic-time algorithm described in chapter 2.

## 7.2 A selection of *P*-complete problems

In this section we establish that a number of other problems are *P*-complete. Conceptually, we do this by constructing an out-tree whose nodes are these *P*-complete problems and whose directed edges are *NC*-reductions. At this stage we start at the root of this tree which contains the one problem, generability, which we know to be *P*-complete. The tree of *NC*-reductions we establish in the remainder of this chapter is shown in figure 7.14.

The next problem is a classic called the circuit-value problem (CVP); this is defined as follows.

*The circuit-value problem* (*CVP*)

  *Instance*  A boolean circuit with a specified set of input values.
  *Question*  Is the output value **true**?

*Theorem 7.3*
*CVP* is *P*-complete.

*Proof*
Let $(X, T, \cdot, s)$ be an instance of the problem of generability. We construct a corresponding instance of *CVP* as follows. The circuit $G$ of *CVP* is such that $X$ is a subset of the set of all nodes of $G$, $T$ is the set of input nodes (each having the

value **true**), and $s$ is the output node. For each element $x$ of $X - T$ we find all pairs of elements $(y_1, z_1), (y_2, z_2), \ldots, (y_k, z_k)$ such that $y_i \cdot z_i = x$ for all $i$, $1 \leqslant i \leqslant k$. Then that part of $G$ corresponding to $x$ (as illustrated in figure 7.2) is constructed to perform a computation $(y_1 \wedge z_1) \vee (y_2 \wedge z_2) \vee \cdots \vee (y_k \wedge z_k)$, where here we use the shorthand that $y_1$ (or $z_1$) is the value at the node $y_1$ (or $z_1$). The construction is illustrated in figure 7.2. There $(x_1, x_2), (x_2, x_3), (x_1, x_4)$, $(x_3, x_5)$ and $(x_5, x_6)$ are all pairs of elements $(y, z)$ such that $y \cdot x = x$ in the instance of generability. Thus this subcircuit associated with $x \in X - T$ will yield the value **true** if and only if there exists (at least) one pair of elements $y_i$ and $z_i$ such that $y_i \cdot z_i = x$, and $y_i$ and $z_i$ can be generated from $T$. The root of this subcircuit may play the role of an 'input' to other similar subcircuits in the construction as a whole. Thus the output of the total circuit (with root $s$) will be **true** if and only if the answer to the instance of generability is positive. The construction can be done for each $x$ in parallel and an $NC$-reduction is easily obtained from generality to $CVP$. This completes the proof. ☐

A monotone boolean circuit only uses the operations **or** and **and**; in particular the operation of negation (**not**) is not employed in such a circuit. $MCVP$ is the $CVP$ problem restricted to monotone circuits. In the $CVP$ problem if the nodes of the circuit $G$ are numbered $v_1, v_2, \ldots, v_n$ and such that predecessors of a given node have smaller subscripts than that node (thus smallest subscripts appear on input node and the output node is $v_n$) then the nodes are said to be *topologically ordered*. We have the following corollary.

*Corollary 7.1*
(a)  $MCVP$ is $P$-complete.
(b)  $MCVP$ restricted to circuits with topologically ordered nodes is $P$-complete.

*Figure 7.2*

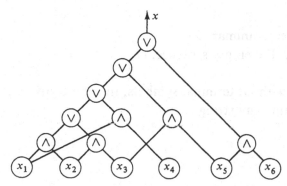

*Proof*

For (a) we just need to observe that the construction employed in the proof of theorem 7.3 did not use negation. For (b) we recall the proof of theorem 7.1. Within that proof we can assume that the elements of the set $X$ are numbered, the initial elements have lowest numbers and the element $s$ (the goal element) has the last number. Whenever $next(u, v, w) = z$ the number of $z$ is higher than that of $u, v$ and $w$. The numbers can correspond to the lexicographic ordering of the triples $(t, p, sym)$. Observe particularly that the time associated with the triple $z$ generated (using the function $next$) from $u, v$ and $w$ is always higher than the time associated with $u, v$ and $w$. This numbering of the elements of $X$ is easily contrived (via theorems 7.2 and 7.3) to yield a topological numbering of the nodes in an instance $MCVP$. The details are left to the reader.     □

It turns out that $CVP$ is also $P$-complete when the circuit $G$ is restricted to being planar. However, if there is no negation and simultaneously the circuit is planar then an $NC$ algorithm is possible.

*Remark*

If we treat boolean **and** as multiplication and boolean **or** as addition then every circuit computes a polynomial, and every circuit can be treated as a straight-line program. In chapter 3 we showed that if the degree of the polynomial is polynomially bounded then the problem is in $NC$. Unfortunately, many circuits produce polynomials which are of exponential degree. So the gap between $NC$ and $P$-complete problems can be viewed as a gap between polynomials of small degree and polynomials of high degree.

Now we consider the following problem.

*Context-free emptiness* (*CFE*)

    *Instance*   A given context-free grammar $G$.
    *Question*  Does $L(G)$ contain the empty sentence, $\varepsilon$?

If we consider any grammar $G$ without terminal symbols, then an equivalent problem is to ask if $L(G)$ contains any string.

*Theorem 7.4*
*CFE* is $P$-complete.

*Proof*

Let $(X, T, \cdot, s)$ be an instance of generability. We construct a context-free grammar $G$ with $X$ as the set of non-terminal symbols, $s$ the starting non-terminal symbol and productions $x \to yz$, whenever $y \cdot z = x$, or $x \to \varepsilon$ whenever $x$ is in $T$. In this way a non-terminal $x$ produces an empty string if and only if $x$ can be derived in the instance of generability. □

In the problem called $CFE$, the size of the input is the size of the grammar. In the chapter on context-free recognition we assumed that the grammar was fixed and that the size of the input was the length of the string to be parsed. We can prove that if there is no empty string in the productions of the grammar then the problem of context-free recognition is still in $NC$ whenever the size of the input is defined to be the sum of the size of the grammar and length of the string to be parsed. However, it becomes $P$-complete if the grammar uses the empty string. It is interesting to note how a very small change in a problem can dramatically affect its efficient parallelisability. If we consider the problem of generating any string then such a problem is still $P$-complete if the grammar does not use the empty string. Now for every $x$ in $T$ we add the production $x \to a$, where $a$ is any terminal symbol.

We now consider the following problem.

*Lexicographically first maximum clique (LFMC)*

  *Instance*  An undirected graph $G$ with vertex set $\{v_1, v_2, \ldots, v_n\}$.
  *Problem*  Find the lexicographically first (maximum) clique of $G$.

The following function returns the lexicographically first (maximum) clique.

**function** *clique*
**begin**
  1. *clique* $\leftarrow \varnothing$
  2. **for** $i \leftarrow 1$ **to** $n$ **do**
       **if** $v_i$ is adjacent to all nodes in *clique* **then** *clique* $\leftarrow$ *clique* $\cup \{v_i\}$
**end**

For example, if the graph of figure 7.3(a) is subjected to the algorithm we obtain the clique $\{v_1, v_2, v_5\}$.

  The following problem is closely related to *LFMC*. Algorithmically, instead of including (in the vertex set under construction) the node adjacent to all previously chosen nodes, we choose the node which is independent of (not adjacent to) all previously chosen nodes.

*Lexicographically first maximal independent set (LFMIS)*

 *Instance*  An undirected graph $G$ with vertex set $\{v_1, v_2, \ldots, v_n\}$.
 *Problem*  Find the lexicographically first maximal independent set.

Given a graph $G = (V, E)$, its complement is the graph $G' = (V', E')$ where $V = V'$ and, for any pair $u, v \in V$, $(u, v)$ is in exactly one of $E$ or $E'$. For example, the complement of the graph shown in figure 7.3(a) is shown in (b) and vice versa. If the vertex set $V''$ is a solution to *LFMC* for a graph $G$, then $V''$ is the solution to *LFMIS* for the complement of $G$. Thus $\{v_1, v_2, v_5\}$ is a solution to *LFMIS* for the graph of figure 7.3(b). Constructing the dual of a graph is an *NC*-reduction and so if *LFMC* is *P*-complete then so is *LFMIS* and vice versa.

*Theorem 7.5*
*LFMC* and *LFMIS* are *P*-complete.

*Proof*
We describe an *NC*-reduction from *MCVP* to *LFMIS*. Without loss of generality, we presume that in the instance of *MCVP* the set of nodes $V = \{v_1, \ldots, v_n\}$ is topologically sorted (corollary 7.1), the inputs are the nodes with smallest subscripts and the output is $v_n$. We construct an undirected graph $G' = (V', E')$, where $V' = \{v_1', v_1'', v_2', v_2'', \ldots, v_n', v_n''\}$. The nodes of $V'$ are numbered from 1 to $2n$ in the order shown, except that the order of $v_i', v_i''$ is reversed when $v_i$ is an **or** node in $G$ or when $v_i$ is an input node with the value **false**. We illustrate the construction for the circuit $G$ shown in figure 7.4. The nodes of $G'$ are ordered as shown from left to right in figure 7.5.

Next we construct the edges of $G'$ as follows.

(a)  For each node $v$ of $G$ there is an edge between $v'$ and $v''$ (this implies that only one of these nodes can be in the maximal independent set constructed for $G'$).

*Figure 7.3*

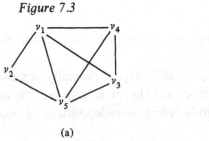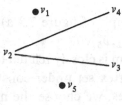

   (a)                                        (b)

(b) If $v$ is an **and** node and its sons in $G$ are $u$ and $w$ then $v'$ is adjacent to $u''$ and $w''$ (hence $v'$ is in the maximal independent set if and only if neither $u''$ nor $w''$ is).

(c) If $v$ is an **or** node and its sons in $G$ are $u$ and $w$, then $v'$ is only adjacent to $v''$ (which precedes it), also $v''$ is adjacent to both $u'$ and $w'$ (hence $v''$ is in the maximal independent set if neither $u'$ nor $w'$ is. Consequently $v'$ is in the maximal independent set if at least one of $u', w'$ is).

Using these rules we obtain the edges shown in figure 7.5 for $G'$ which corresponds to the circuit of figure 7.4. For example node 5 is an **and** node and its sons are 2 and 3. Therefore node $5'$ is adjacent to $2''$ and $3''$. Node 6 is an **or** node whose sons are 4 and 5. Therefore $6''$ precedes $5'$ and $6''$ is adjacent to $4'$ and $5'$.

It is easy to see that any node $v'$ is in the first lexicographically maximal independent set if and only if the value associated with $v$ in the circuit $G$ is **true**. The construction of $G'$ can be done for each node $v$ in parallel. □

The next problem concerns the parallelisation of the classical linear-time sequential algorithm for graph traversing known as depth-first search ($DFS$). The importance of this problem is that many highly efficient sequential algorithms on graphs use $DFS$ as a basic procedure. The reader can find a more detailed discussion in [1]. Here we briefly sketch the $DFS$ method. We only consider the case of directed graphs. The graph $G$ is represented by its adjacency lists. For each node $v$ we have a list $ADJ(v)$ of all nodes adjacent to $v$.

*Figure 7.4.* The circuit $G$

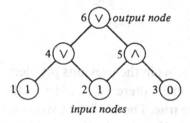

*Figure 7.5.* The graph $G'$ corresponding to the circuit $G$ of figure 7.4

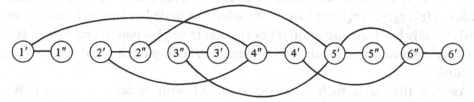

The depth-first search algorithm assigns a number to each vertex $v$, the number specifies the order in which $v$ is visited during the graph traversal. This number is called the depth-first index of $v$ and is denoted by $DFI(v)$. The procedure call $dfs(v_0)$ assigns depth-first indices to all nodes accessible from $v_0$ starting with $DFI(v_0) = 1$; counter is a global variable initially set to zero while the $DFI(v)$ for all $v$ are initially zero.

> **procedure** *dfs(v)*
> **begin**
> **if** $DFI(v) = 0$ {$v$ has not been visited before} **then**
>     **begin**
>     *counter* ← *counter* + 1
>     $DFI(v)$ ← *counter*
>     **for** all $u \in ADJ(v)$ in list order **do** *dfs(u)*
>     **end**
> **end**

Formally the *DFS* problem is described as follows.

*Depth-first search (DFS)*

   *Instance*   A directed (weakly) connected graph $G$ and a specified initial vertex $v_0$.
   *Problem*   Find the depth-first indices of the vertices of $G$ starting with $v_0 = 1$.

*Theorem 7.6*
*DFS* is *P*-complete.

*Proof*
We describe an *NC*-reduction from *CVP* to *DFS*. As in the previous problem, the main task is to represent within the target problem (here a *dfs* ordering) the fact that a given node $v$ of the circuit has the value **true**. There will be two nodes $s$ and $t$ associated with node $v$ and $val(v) =$ **true** if and only if $number(s) < number(t)$. We restrict ourselves to circuits whose nodes are topologically ordered $(v_1, v_2, \ldots, v_n)$ and such that each input node has the fixed value **true**, and the only boolean operation is $(x \cdot y) =$ **not** $(x$ **or** $y) = ($**not** $x)$ **and** $($**not** $y)$. It is an easy exercise to prove that *CVP* remains *P*-complete if restricted to such circuits.

Assume that $G$ is such a restricted circuit with nodes $(1, 2, \ldots, n)$. We construct the corresponding instance of *DFS*, namely the graph $G'$ whose structure is computed locally for each of the nodes of $G$. There is a subgraph $G_i$ corresponding to each node $i$ of $G$ and $G'$ is the union of these subgraphs. The subgraphs $G_i$ are edge-disjoint but they can have common nodes. The boolean value associated with node $i$ corresponds to a particular order of visiting nodes of $G_i$, and this affects the order of visiting nodes in components corresponding to nodes which are successors of $i$ in $G$. In other words the boolean operation · is simulated by a dependence of the order of visiting nodes in one component on the orders in two other (earlier) components. Special nodes $i \mathbin{\#} j$ (for each pair of nodes $i$ and $j$ such that $j$ is a successor of $i$ in $G$) play a key role in $G'$. Each such node $i \mathbin{\#} j$ $(i < j)$ is the only common vertex of the subgraphs $G_i$ and $G_j$.

Let $i > 1$ be a non-input node whose sons are $i_1$ and $i_2$, and let the successors of $i$ be $j_1, j_2, \ldots, j_k$. The subgraph $G_i$ has the following nodes: $i_1 \mathbin{\#} i, i_2 \mathbin{\#} i,$ $i \mathbin{\#} j_1, \ldots, i \mathbin{\#} j_k, \mathit{first}(i), \mathit{last}(i), s(i), t(i),$ and $k$ auxiliary nodes. Its structure is presented in figure 7.7 for the case $k = 3$. Here the auxiliary nodes are not labelled. If $i$ is an input node (which always has the value **true** in our restricted model) with successors $j_1, j_2, \ldots, j_k$ then the corresponding subgraph $G_i$ is shown in figure 7.6 for the case $k = 3$.

An important role is played by the order of edges in the adjacency lists for vertices of $G'$. The number labelling each edge $(i, j)$ in figures 7.6 and 7.7 indicates the position of this edge in the adjacency list for vertex $i$. If no number labels an edge $(i, j)$, then this edge is the first in the adjacency list for $i$.

*Figure 7.6.* The subgraph $G_i$ for an input node $i$ (there are no sons and $\mathit{val}(i) = $ **true**)

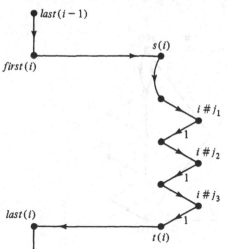

If we start at node $first(1)$ and visit $G_1$ then we enter $G_2$ through the edge $(last(1), first(2))$. Having visited $G_2$ we then visit (possibly parts only of) $G_3, \ldots, G_n$. We then arrive at node $last(n)$ and return to visit parts of $G'$ missed in this initial part of a depth-first traversal of the graph. For all $i$, we are essentially interested in which of the two nodes $s(i)$ and $t(i)$ are visited first. Both are visited in the active interval, and we can therefore assume that the traversing stops when $last(n)$ is reached, although some parts of the graph will not have been visited yet.

The main properties of the construction can be stated in the following lemma.

### Lemma 7.1

If $val(i) = \textbf{true}$ in $G$ then, in a depth-first traversal of $G'$ starting at $first(1)$, $s(i)$ is visited before $t(i)$ and all the nodes $i \# j_1, \ldots, i \# j_k$ are visited after visiting $first(i)$ and before visiting $last(i)$. On the other hand, if $val(i) = \textbf{false}$ then $s(i)$ is visited after $t(i)$ and not one of the nodes $i \# j_1, \ldots, i \# j_k$ is visited in the interval after visiting $first(i)$ and before visiting $last(i)$.

### Proof

The claim is trivially true for input nodes $i$. Assume that it is true for any node $j$, where $j < i$, and consider the traversing of the subgraph $G_i$. If $val(i) = \textbf{true}$ then

*Figure 7.7.* The neighbourhood of the circuit $G$ around the internal node $i$ and the corresponding subgraph $G_i$ in $G'$

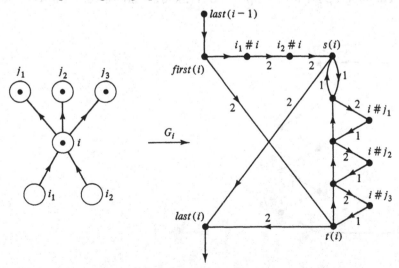

none of the sons of $i$ has the value **true**. Hence the nodes $i_i \neq i$ and $C$ were not visited before $first(i)$. Now the traversal (paying due attention to the order of edges in adjacency lists) of $G_i$ is as shown in figure 7.8 and the claim holds. Otherwise the traversal is as shown in figure 7.9 (In this figure, after passing from $last(i-1)$ to $first(i)$, it can be the case that $i_1 \neq i$ is visited before returning immediately to $first(i)$ and then the traversal continues as in the figure. This happens if $i_1 \neq i$ was not visited before $first(i)$, but in that case $i_1 \neq i$ must have been visited previously.) and the claim also holds in this case. That completes the proof of the lemma.                                                                    □

In view of the lemma the computation of the value of the output node $n$ of the circuit is reduced to checking whether $s(i)$ was visited before $t(i)$, and this is

**Figure 7.8.** The order of traversing $G_i$ for the first time (within the time interval of visiting $first(i)$ to visiting $last(i)$) when $val(i) =$ **true**

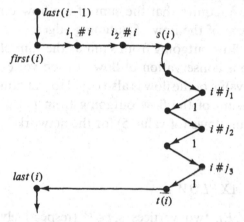

**Figure 7.9.** The order of traversing $G_i$ for the first time (within the time interval of visiting $first(i)$ to visiting $last(i)$) when $val(i) =$ **false**

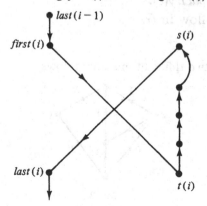

further reduced to the computation of the depth-first indices provided by a depth-first traversal. The transformation from the circuit $G$ to the graph $G'$ is trivially an $NC$-reduction. This completes the proof of theorem 7.6.  □

Although the last theorem is for directed graphs, the construction can be slightly modified and the same result holds in the case of undirected graphs (see [17]).

Our last $P$-complete problem is the maximum-flow problem in networks ($MAXFLOW$). A network is the directed graph $G$ with two distinguished nodes $s$ and $t$ (source and sink) and with a positive integer associated with each edge (called the capacity of the edge).

A network flow is an assignment of a non-negative integer to each edge (the flow for this edge) such that

(a)    $flow(e) \leqslant capacity(e)$ for each edge $e$,

(b)    for every node (except $s$ and $t$) we require that the sum of the flow on incoming edges is equal to the sum of the flow of outgoing edges.

The value of the flow is the sum of the flow outgoing from $s$ minus the sum of the flow incoming to $s$. Because there is conservation of flow at each vertex (except $s$ and $t$) it is easy to see that the value of the flow is also equal to the sum of the flow incoming to $t$ minus the sum of the flow outgoing from $t$. For example, $flow1$ and $flow2$ are maximum flows (of value 5) for the network in figure 7.10.

*Maximising the flow of a network ($MAXFLOW$)*

> *Instance*  A directed graph $G = (V, E)$, two vertices $s, t \in V$ (respectively called the source and the sink) and for each edge $e \in E$ a non-negative integer denoted by $capacity(e)$.
>
> *Problem*  Find the value of a maximum flow in $G$.

*Figure 7.10*. A network with capacities and two different maximum flows

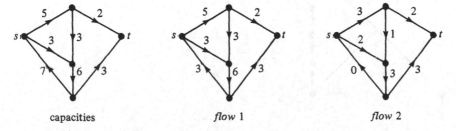

capacities                    flow 1                    flow 2

*Theorem 7.7*
*MAXFLOW* is P-complete.

*Proof*
It is well known that *MAXFLOW* can be solved by a polynomial-time algorithm (see [11] for example) and thus $MAXFLOW \in P$. In proving that *MAXFLOW* is P-complete we shall in fact consider an even weaker version of the problem. This version is the problem of computing the parity of the maximum flow value. We shall see that even this weaker version, which we call *PMAXFLOW*, is P-complete.

We shall describe an *NC*-reduction from *CVP* to *PMAXFLOW*. We restrict ourselves to monotone circuits such that the out-degree of each input node is 1 and the out-degree of any other node is at most 2. Moreover the output node is an **or** node. We leave it to the reader to prove that *CVP* remains P-complete in this case (the proof is straightforward, for example if the final node is an **and** node then we can make the output from the circuit be one input to an additional **or** node the other input of which is permanently set to the value **false**). Let $G$ be such a circuit with the vertex set $V = \{0, 1, 2, \ldots, n\}$. We can assume that $V$ is in reverse topological order, node 0 is the output **or** node. The number of a successor is lower than the number of its predecessor. Given $G$ we construct, for our instance of *PMAXFLOW*, the network $G'$ with a set of nodes $V \cup \{s, t\}$, where $s$ and $t$ are the source and sink nodes. We construct the maximum flow $f$ which simulates the circuit as follows. For each edge $(i, j)$, with $j$ in $V$, if $val(i) = \textbf{true}$ then $flow(i, j) = 2^i$ else $flow(i, j) = 0$. To this end we define the capacity of each edge $(i, j)$ in $G'$, with $i$ and $j$ in $V$, to be $2^i$. Let $d(i)$ be the out-degree of node $i$ in $G$ (with the exception $d(0) = 1$) and, for an internal node $i$ with predecessors $j$ and $k$, we define $surplus(i) = 2^k + 2^j - d(i)2^i$. In other words, if we assume that $flow(e) = capacity(e)$ for each edge $e$, $surplus(i)$ is the value by which condition (b) in the definition of a network is violated in that part of the network (except for node 0) defined up to now. This part of the network is illustrated in figure 7.11(b) where, for example, $surplus(3) = 80$.

We now define the capacities of edges with one endpoint in $\{s, t\}$ as follows.

(a)   For each input node $i$, $capacity(s, i) = 2^i$ if $val(i) = \textbf{true}$ in $G$, otherwise $capacity(s, i) = 0$.

(b)   For each **and** node $i$, $capacity(i, t) = surplus(i)$.

(c)   For each **or** node $i$, $capacity(i, s) = surplus(i)$.

(d)   $capacity(0, t) = 1$.

There are no other edges in $G'$. The complete network constructed in the prescribed manner for the circuit of figure 7.11(a) is presented in figure 7.12(a).

There are possibly many maximum flows. We construct one which simulates the circuit. In fact we are really interested in the value of the flow and there is therefore a lot of freedom to choose the most natural flow. Construction of the simulating flow is as follows.

(1)    For each input node $i$ with successor $j$ let $flow(i, j) = flow(s, i)$.

(2)    For each edge $(i, j)$ where $i, j$ are in $V$ let $flow(i, j) = capacity(i, j) = 2^i$ if $val(i) = $ **true** in $G$, otherwise $flow(i, j) = 0$. Moreover let $flow(0, t) = 1$ if

*Figure* 7.11. The circuit $G$ and the part of the network $G'$ consisting only of edges from $G$

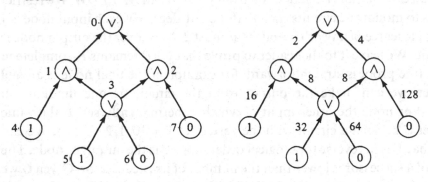

(a)    The circuit $G$ with the numbering of nodes

(b)    The part of $G'$ with capacities of edges determined by $G$

*Figure 7.12.* The network $G'$ with edge capacities shown in (a) while (b) presents the maximum flow simulating the circuit

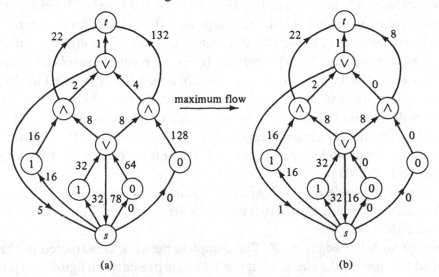

(a)                                    maximum flow $\longrightarrow$                                    (b)

*val*(0) = **true**, otherwise *flow*(0, *t*) = 0. Let *overflow*(*i*) denote the difference between the incoming and outgoing flow from the node *i* at this stage.

(3)    For each **and** node *i* let *flow*(*i*, *t*) = *overflow*(*i*).

(4)    For each **or** node *i* let *flow*(*i*, *s*) = *overflow*(*i*).

The constructed maximal flow for our example network is illustrated in figure 7.12(b). We leave to the reader to verify that it is a flow (in other words, that it satisfies conditions (a) and (b) of the flow definition). We need however to explain why this flow is maximal.

The main idea behind the construction is that we send as much flow from each node upwards as possible, with the edges leading directly to the sink having highest priority in this respect. We first send as much flow as possible through these edges. Anything sent directly to the sink increases the value of the flow. On the other hand the edges leading to the source have lowest priority; we send flow through these edges only to satisfy condition (b) of the network flow definition.

*Lemma 7.2*

The constructed flow has maximum value.

*Proof*

We define an augmenting path to be a sequence of distinct nodes beginning with *s* and ending with *t* such that if *i*, *j* are successive nodes in this sequence then

(a)    if (*i*, *j*) is an edge in *G'* then *flow*(*i*, *j*) < *capacity*(*i*, *j*) {(*i*, *j*) is called a *forward* edge},

(b)    if (*j*, *i*) is an edge of *G'* then *flow*(*j*, *i*) > 0 {(*i*, *j*) is called in this case a *back* edge}.

It is well known (see [11] for example) that the flow is a maximum if and only if there is no augmenting path. We prove that there is no augmenting path for our simulating flow. Suppose to the contrary that there is such a path *P*. It should start with a back edge (because each forward edge from *s* has its flow equal to its capacity) and it should end with the forward edge (because there are no edges out of *t*). Hence there should be three successive nodes *j*, *i* and *k* on *P*, *j* ≠ *t* and *k* ≠ *s*, where (*j*, *i*) is a back edge and (*i*, *k*) is a forward edge. This means that (*i*, *j*), (*i*, *k*) are edges of *G'*, with *flow*(*i*, *j*) > 0 and *flow*(*i*, *k*) < *capacity*(*i*, *k*). This is illustrated in figure 7.13. However, node *i* cannot be an input node because one of its (outgoing) edges *e* has *flow*(*e*) = *capacity*(*e*) whilst the other has zero flow. Moreover *i* also cannot be an **and** node because *j* ≠ *t*, and *flow*(*i*, *j*) > 0 implies that all edges out of *i* are full. Also it cannot be an **or** node because $k \neq s$ and $flow(i, k) < capacity(i, k)$ implies that all outgoing edges of $i$ have zero flow (see the definition of simulating flow). Hence our flow is a maximum and this completes the proof of the lemma. ☐

The value of the simulating flow is odd if and only if $flow(0, t) = 1$ (which is equivalent to $val(0) = $ **true**), since all other flows have even value. Hence the output value of the circuit $G$ is **true** if and only if the maximum value has an odd value. In this way we have reduced the restricted problem $CVP$ to the problem $PMAXFLOW$. This completes the proof of theorem 7.7. ☐

Figure 7.4 shows the tree of $NC$-reductions we have developed through the theorems of this chapter which, along with the proof that the problem *gen'* is *P*-complete, establishes some members of the class of *P*-complete problems.

### Bibliographic notes

A collection of basic *P*-complete problems can be found in Jones and Laaser.[17] Probably the most representative *P*-complete problem is the circuit-value problem.[18] Goldschlager proved that this problem is *P*-complete also for monotone and for planar circuits.[13] The path-systems problem is a generalisation of the generability problem; instead of a binary operation we have a

*Figure 7.13*

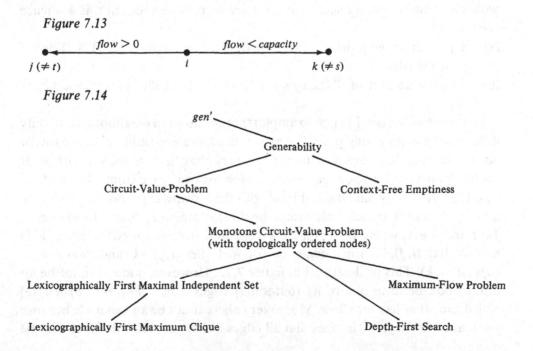

*Figure 7.14*

binary relation for generating new elements.[4] This problem is also very representative for polynomial-time computations.

The proof that the maximum-flow problem is *P*-complete was taken from [14]. The depth-first search problem was presented in [21] and the problems concerning greedy algorithms for maximal clique and maximal independent set were considered by Cook.[5]

There are many other *P*-complete problems. Dwork *et al.*[8] have described such a problem in logic related to unification. Avenhaus and Madlener[3] showed that some problems about free groups are *P*-complete, for example the problem of deciding whether a given element can be generated from a given finite subset of a free group. Spirakis[22] proved that the general deadlock detection problem is *P*-complete. The maximal-path problem is a simplified version of the depth-first search problem. One has to find a simple path (all the vertices are distinct) which starts from a given vertex and which cannot be extended. Anderson and Mayr[2] have proved that the lexicographically-first-maximal-path problem is *P*-complete, even if the graph is planar. Surprisingly, as they also describe, the problem of finding any maximal path (with a given starting node) for planar graphs is in *NC*. This shows that greedy algorithms are inherently sequential. It is hard to simulate such algorithms in parallel. We cannot extend known sequential algorithms based on this approach to obtain good parallel ones. New strategies have to be developed. The same situation exists for the maximal-(with respect to inclusion)-independent-set problem. The lexicographically-first-maximal-independent-set problem (the simulation of a greedy algorithm) is *P*-complete,[5] whilst the problem of finding any maximal independent set is in *NC* (see [19]), Several other interesting *P*-complete problems were recently presented in [20].

## Bibliography

[1] J. Aho, J. Hopcroft and J. Ullman. *The Design and Analysis of Computer Algorithms.* Addison-Wesley (1974).

[2] R. Anderson and E. W. Mayr. Parallelism and the maximal path problem. *Information Processing Letters* **24** (1978), 121–6.

[3] J. Avenhaus and K. Madlener. *P*-complete problems in free groups. Interner Bericht 32/80, Fachbereich Informatik, Universität Kaiserslautern (1980).

[4] S. Cook. Path systems and language recognition. *STOC 1971*, 151–8.

[5] S. Cook. The classification of problems which have fast parallel algorithms. *Foundations of Computation Theory.* Lecture Notes in Computer Science 158. Springer-Verlag (1983).

[6] D. Dobkin, R. Lipton and S. Reiss. Linear programming is log space hard for *P*. *Information Processing Letters* **8** (1979), 96–7.

[7] D. Dobkin and S. Reiss. The complexity of linear programming. *Theoretical Computer Science* **11** (1980), 1–18.

[8] C. Dwork, P. Kanellakis and J. Mitchell. On the sequential nature of unification. *Journal of Logic Programming* **1** (1984), 35–50.

[9] Z. Galil. Hierarchies of complete problems. *Acta Informatica* **6** (1976), 77–88.

[10] M. Garey and D. Johnson. *Computers and Intractability.* W. H. Freeman (1979).

[11] A. M. Gibbons. *Algorithmic Graph Theory.* Cambridge University Press (1985).

[12] L. Goldschlager. The monotone and planar circuit value problems are log space complete for *P*. *SIGACT News* **9**, 2 (Summer 1977), 25–9.

[13] L. Goldschlager. *e*-productions in context free grammars. *Acta Informatica* **16** (1981), 303–8.

[14] L. Goldschlager, L. Shaw and J. Staples. The maximum flow problem is log space complete for *P*. *Theoretical Computer Science* **21** (1982), 105–11.

[15] J. Hopcroft and J. Ullman. *Introduction to Automata Theory, Languages and Computations*. Addison-Wesley (1979).

[16] D. Johnson. The *NP*-completeness column: an ongoing guide (7th). *Journal of Algorithms* **4** (1983), 189–203.

[17] N. Jones and W. Laaser. Complete problems for deterministic polynomial time. *Theoretical Computer Science* **3** (1976), 105–17.

[18] R. Ladner. The circuit value problem is log space complete for *P*. *SIGACT News* **7**, 1 (1975), 18–20.

[19] M. Luby. A simple parallel algorithm for the maximal independent set problem. *STOC 1985*, 1–10.

[20] S. Miyano. The lexicographically first maximal subgraph problems: *P*-completeness and *NC* algorithms. *ICALP 1987*.

[21] J. Reif. Depth first search is inherently sequential. *Information Processing Letters* **20**, 5 (1985), 229–34.

[22] P. Spirakis. The parallel complexity of the deadlock detection problem. *Proceedings of the 12th Symposium on Mathematical Foundations of Computer Science* (1986). Lecture Notes in Computer Science 233 (eds. J. Grunska, B. Rovan and J. Wiedermann). Springer-Verlag.

# INDEX OF DEFINITIONS, TECHNIQUES
# AND ALGORITHMS

Printed in the United States
By Bookmasters